The **National Computing Centre** develops techniques, provides services, offers aids and supplies information to encourage the more effective use of Information Technology. The Centre co-operates with members and other organisations, including government bodies, to develop the use of computers and communications facilities. It provides advice, training and consultancy; evaluates software methods and tools; promotes standards and codes of practice; and publishes books.

Any interested company, organisation or individual can benefit from the work of the Centre – by exploring its products and services; or in particular by subscribing as a member. Throughout the country, members can participate in working parties, study groups and discussions; and can influence NCC policy.

For more information, contact the Centre at Oxford Road, Manchester M1 7ED (061-228 6333), or at one of the regional offices: London (01-353 4875), Bristol (0272-277 077), Birmingham (021-236 6283), Glasgow (041-204 1101) or Belfast (0232-665 997).

Do You Want to Write?

Could you write a book on an aspect of Information Technology? Have you already prepared a typescript? Why not send us your ideas, your 'embryo' text or your completed work? We are a prestigious publishing house with an international reputation. We have the funds and the expertise to support your writing ambitions in the most effective way.

Contact: Geoff Simons, Publications Division, The National Computing Centre Ltd, Oxford Road, Manchester M1 7ED.

Evolution
of the
Intelligent Machine

A Popular History of AI

Geoff Simons

PUBLISHED BY NCC PUBLICATIONS

British Library Cataloguing in Publication Data

Evolution of the intelligent machine: A
popular history of AI
1. Artificial intelligence
006.3

ISBN 0-85012-720-3

First published in 1988 by:
NCC Publications, The National Computing Centre Limited, Oxford
Road, Manchester M1 7ED, England.
Typeset in 11pt Times Roman by Bookworm Typesetting, Manchester;
and printed by Hobbs the Printers of Southampton.

ISBN 0-85012-720-3

Acknowledgements

Gratitude is due to various organisations and individuals for supplying useful information.

I am grateful to Tim Johnson (of Ovum Ltd, 7 Rathbone Street, London WIP 1AF) for making available his excellent report, *Natural Language Computing: the Commercial Applications;* and for giving permission to use material from that publication (my Figures 10.1, 10.2 and 10.3 are taken from the report).

Thanks are also due to I Kato Laboratory, Waseda University, Japan for supplying a photograph of the remarkable WABOT–2 robot, and for giving permission for it to be used on the cover and as Figure 13.2.

I would also thank Valerie Wells and Gill Gleeson (then both of the NCC Information Department) for making journals available for research.

Finally I am particularly grateful to Wilf Thompson, Divisional Manager, Operations Group, for his unfailing encouragement during the writing of this book. This has represented welcome support during a difficult transitional period.

Geoff Simons

Introduction

This is an overview look aimed at a wide cross-section of readers – students, intelligent laity, and IT professionals who want a heavily researched profile of AI. It has four main purposes:

1) to acquaint readers with the rich historical tradition, spanning millenia, that bears on the AI theme (the concept of artificial intelligence, far from being newly hatched in the computer age, has its origins in pre-Christian thought);

2) to acquaint readers (via Chapters 8 to 16) with the many topics that are of interest to modern AI researchers (there is a wide and growing range of disciplines and studies that bear on artificial intelligence);

3) to emphasise that the inspiration behind AI is multidisciplinary – drawing on biology, psychology, linguistics, philosophy, electronics, electrical engineering, mathematics, information theory, etc (this multicoloured picture is rarely painted in either general or technical books on artificial intelligence);

4) to offer a comprehensive bibliography of references to more detailed information (the reader can extend his/her study of all the principal AI topics by following up the citations given in this volume).

A central theme is that the mainstream evolution of electronics and computers is directly relevant to the development of artificial intelligence. It is convenient for various purposes to separate out 'obvious' AI tasks such as robotic vision and semantic processing from other computer applications such as company payroll and investment computation. Nonetheless a *biological* system – man or beast – able to calculate complex payroll adjustments would be deemed intelligent; and this highlights the arbitrary character of many efforts to define this or that computer application as a manifestation of intelligence. This suggests that first-generation glass-valve computers are as much in the AI tradition as are any fancy LISP processors of the late-1980s – and the book has been written with this in mind.

It is inevitable that, in a book that spans millenia and many multifaceted disciplines, there are many omissions and shortcomings (I myself, at a different time and in a different mood, may have preferred a different focus, a different selection of topics and emphasis). The overall objective is to convey the flavour of AI-linked ideas and interests through the ages, with particular emphasis on the explosion of AI activity in the modern age.

AI fascinates people because it touches upon many matters of intimate human concern – creativity (see Appendix 1), autonomy, choice, adaptation in a changing world. In its evident capacity to totally reshape our environment and our self-image, artificial intelligence has a dramatic significance for human society.

Contents

PART 7   1990 to . . .

PART 1
BC to AD

1   Myth and Machine

INTRODUCTION

No new technology springs forth spontaneously in a cultural vacuum: there are no beginnings that are not shaped by earlier circumstances. Instead we see a progressive evolution of trends and developments, a complex process that generates theoretical insights and practical innovations. And, with the nice logic of hindsight, we can describe how this or that technology came into existence. It is easier to scrutinise the past than to chronicle the future.

There is a teleological stimulus behind every technology, ie practical techniques are conceived, introduced and improved to achieve specific objectives; and the technology, once effective, can suggest new objectives. There is thus, at least in technologically developed societies, a fruitful dielectic between theory and practice, each feeding off the other to stimulate the evolutionary process. But, in all societies, theory easily outstrips practice: we can all imagine more than we can accomplish. And this is particularly evident in early, relatively primitive, cultures where 'theory' was more usually rooted in mythological imaginings than in scientific insights. Thus one account of human progress might be to chart how concept formation of one sort (yielding myth, legend, allegory, etc) evolved into concept formation of another (yielding well-formed empirical hypotheses, abstract formal systems, all the paraphernalia of scientific method). But it should not be thought that there are no myths in modern society: there are *countless* myths that variously serve as poetic allusions, entertainment strategems and comforting falsehoods.

Today fiction (in, for example, novel or feature film) can serve as did myth in ancient cultures. In the best fiction we encounter an imaginary framework that can engage our sympathies, hint at fresh possibilities, and deepen our understanding. Such matters, when they have a particular focus (as in science fiction), are clearly relevant to the emergence of new technologies. Ancient myth-makers were often no more than story-tellers whose fictions became fact in the modern age. So Icarus, relying on inadequate theory, tried to fly; and in the *True History,* written in the second century AD, Lucian of Samosata describes how waterspouts and winds could be harnessed to carry a Greek ship to the moon.

In such circumstances we are not surprised to find that many modern technologies are prefigured in ancient myth and legend, albeit crudely and with gross inaccuracies. It is interesting for our purposes that artificial intelligence (AI), often thought to be newly hatched in the modern age, can be found in the tales and mythologies of the Ancient World. AI, both as a concept and as hinted at by simple automata, is older than Christianity.

ANCIENT AI

We may regard ancient AI as illustrated (or suggested) by two classes of cultural phenomena:

 – myths, tales, fables, etc;

 – mechanical automata.

There are myths and tales that describe intelligent artefacts, fabricated devices that can act with wisdom and purpose. The actual contrivances, the mechanical automata, were far from intelligent: at best, in processing energy and information without human intervention, they were the precursors of the autonomous electronic systems that were to emerge in the modern age.

RELIGION AND MYTH

Creation myths, common in many religions, afford one type of example of ancient AI. It is interesting to reflect that when this or that god, according to this or that legend, decided to create *Homo sapiens* men and women were effective artefacts, artificial systems designed to serve a particular divine plan. Smart (1959) was one of the first to suggest that Adam and Eve were robots made by God and given their programs in the form of genes. And this idea can be compared with the suggestion by Richard Dawkins (1982) that human beings are 'gigantic lumbering robots' that serve as the survival machines for genes. It seems that the various species of divine creators had a common interest in artificial intelligence!

The myths tell of gods of various kinds taking earth, clay, dust or blood, etc and using it to construct men and women. Sometimes, as befits the sexism of most early (and later) cultures, the male is fashioned first and then, as a secondary creature, the woman. According to Assyro-Babylonian tradition, as revealed in tablets held in the library of Ashurbanipal in Ninevah, the great god Marduk used the blood of a defected divinity to mould the body of the first man. Similarly, the Judeo-Christian tradition holds that the male was created, out of the dust of the earth, before the female. According to the Talmud, dust was collected and then formed into a shapeless mass (golem), before the limbs were shaped and the soul infused. And it was said, long before the tale of Frankenstein, that rabbis had the power to fabricate golems as servants in the household or community. For example, in a tale by Yudl Rosenberg, the Rabbi Loew of Prague built a golem to protect the Jewish community from pogrom (this golem begins to run out of control until Loew succeeds in plucking the magic formula from the golem's brow and so converting the creature back to harmless clay).

In Sumerian legend the gods created deputies (the first industrial robots?) to perform unwelcome chores. Here, around 2500 BC, the goddess Nammu is said to have shaped clay into the form of a creature and then infused it with life. Similarly, in the Babylonian Epic of Gilgamesh, creatures shaped from lifeless substance are animated by blood. In later Egyptian myth, a man is made from clay by the god Khnum and then magically animated by the goddess Hather. Such tales illustrate what seems to be a general principle: it is one thing to shape a creature, quite another for it to achieve animation.

Swahili gods speak secret words to animate clay models, blood flowing through the artefacts to make the muscles ripple and the eyelids move. According to Maori Lore, the breath of a god is sufficient to animate a human figure built out of sand; and in Melanesia it was supposed that the first people were made like wooden puppets and brought to life by drum beats. Indians in North America reckoned that gods breathed life into models made out of earth and water. In Hopi legend, for example, it is the saliva of the Spider Woman that proved effective in animating the first man and woman.

In the prodigious Sanskrit epic, the *Mahabharata,* which includes the sacred *Bhagavad Gita,* we encounter Visvakarman, god of the mechanical arts, who is requested to produce an artificial woman. He produces Iilottama whose beauty drives the gods to distraction. And in the celebrated Asian poem, the *Epic of Gesar of Ling,* a young smith presents the king with metal humanoids constructed out of gold, silver, copper, iron and bronze. Here the creator is a human craftsman, magnificently skilled but lacking the magic of the divinities. The smith produces a vast population of humanoids (a lama and a thousand monks, 700 officials and courtiers, 10,000 soldiers, one hundred singing girls and a king) but – we are encouraged to believe – without relying on divine powers. This clearly represents an important departure from much creation legend. It is normally gods, not talented human craftsmen, that generate the animated artefacts. Perhaps in the *Epic of Gesar of Ling,* with talk of 'magic dolls' and 'metal dolls', we are witnessing the first movement towards a naturalistic robotics technology, an important departure from the assumption of occult powers.

Similarly in the eleventh century *Brihatkathasaritsagara,* another Asiatic work, we again encounter mechanical humanoids capable of speech and movement. These creations are similar to the golden maidens – filled with wisdom, and able to speak and walk – constructed by the crippled Greek god Hephaestus, divinity of mechanical arts and crafts. He also produced twenty tripods which 'run by themselves to a meeting of the gods and amaze the company by running home again' (*Iliad,* Book XVIII); and built the giant Talus out of brass – to guard Crete by crushing enemies to death against his heated body. And some myths describe how Hephaestus used clay to create Pandora, the first woman on earth. In a similar vein, Daedulus is said to have created a bronze warrior to confront the Argonauts.

In ancient China some men were thought to possess the skill of *khwai shuh*, the ability to bring statues to life. This is of course reminiscent of the Greek myth of Pygmalion, King of Cyprus, who produces the beautiful statue of Galatea. He prays to Aphrodite to bring Galatea to life and the goddess hears his prayers. In due course, Pygmalion and Galatea become man and wife. This in fact is a familiar theme in myth and fiction. The seventheenth-century *Pentamerone* (by Giambattista Basile), for example, includes a section where the heroine constructs a lover out of precious stones, scented water, sugar and other items. An obliging divinity animates the statue and the young woman consummates her passion. Similarly, a Chinese tale tells how the wife of the Emperor Ta Chou falls in love with a mechanical humanoid built by the court engineer: the emperor is jealous enough to order the destruction of the machine.

These few examples illustrate the multifaceted AI-linked tradition in religion and mythology, a complex arena in which artefacts (machines and human beings) are shaped out of clay or blood and then given life by men or gods with special powers. In all this we see the first halting steps towards a distant robotics technology, the building of autonomous machines made in man's image. It is obvious that early thoughts of artificial intelligence focused on the creation of whole beings, creatures with bodies and minds. In this sense, at least in the imagination, early AI was fully anthropomorphic. It was not until the modern age (see Part 6) that particular mental attributes could be simulated (or duplicated) in artificial systems that bore no physical resemblance to human beings. The mythical humanoid evolved into the functional robot of the twentieth century (with myth itself sustained in fiction, fantasy and feature film*), but today there is much in AI besides robots. The early authors of tales and myths were as much inspired by religious speculation, the pressing need to explain origins, as by contemporary technology; but with the development of modern science and technology the picture changed. Today the old creator gods have been evicted, and the generation of artificial anatomies and artificial minds owes nothing to occult powers.

Blade Runner, Saturn 3, Alien, The Terminator, etc

At the same time we should remember the early efforts to develop a naturalistic technology of automata. Not *all* the ancient dreams of artificial intelligence focused on fanciful tales and creation myths. It is obvious that the earliest engineers considered how to construct humanoid artefacts (and machines that resembled animals) that could function, to a degree, without human intervention. The functional automata of the Ancient World represented a further step towards the practical AI technologies of the modern age.

EARLY AUTOMATA

The earliest automata were necessarily very simple devices, of very limited functional capability. For example, a statue of Memnon, King of Ethiopia, could do no more than emit sounds when struck by the rays of the sun. Nonetheless this construction, dating to the 15th century BC, appears to have included a functional mechanism. Figure 1.1a shows a depiction (in Athanasias Kircher's *Oedipus Aegyptiacus,* 1652) of the statue; Figure 1.1b shows Kircher's portrayal of an ancient bird automaton, able to sing and move.

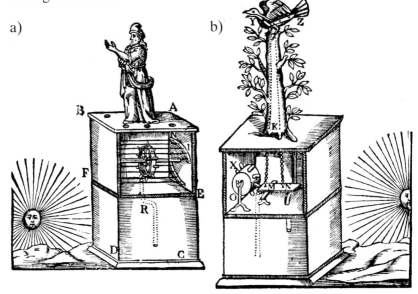

Figure 1.1   Automata depicted by Kircher, 1652

In ancient China there were many attempts to construct
working automata in the image of human beings or other animals.
For example, King Shu Jse, who dates to around 500 BC, is
credited with the construction of a moving/singing magpie built
out of bamboo, and of a wooden horse operated by springs. The
first Han emperor, two centuries BC, is said to have discovered a
mechanical orchestra of puppets in the treasury of Chhin Shih
Huang Ti. The artificial musicians held musical instruments –
lutes, guitars and mouth organs – and were connected to bronze
tubes one of which carried a rope. One person was required to
blow into the empty tube and another to pull the rope,
whereupon the orchestra performed. Other Chinese records
describe a mechanical monk, able to reach out its hands, cry
'Alms! Alms!' and put preferred coins into a bag. A wooden
otter, associated with the name of Wang Chu and dating to
around 790 AD, was said to catch fish; just as a wooden cat (made
by Han Chih-Ho, 890 AD) was supposed to catch rats and
dancing tiger-flies.

Prince Kaya, son of the Japanese Emperor Kanmu (794–871),
is credited with the construction of a humanoid figure with a big
bowl for functional use in his rice paddy. Once the bowl was full
of rain water, the figure would tip the bowl over its own face. The
simple folk of Kyoto were so amused by this performance that
they kept filling the bowl to make the figure perform – and so the
rice paddy was well watered.

In Byzantium, Philon, active two centuries BC, explored ways
of designing automata to exploit the animating power of water
and steam. Figure 1.2 shows how a Philon water automaton was
expected to work. And Vitruvius wrote that Ctesibius (exploiting
pneumatic power nearly three centuries BC) ' . . . discovered the
natural pressure of the air and pneumatic principles . . . devised
methods of raising water, automatic contrivances and amusing
things of many kinds . . . blackbirds singing by means of
waterworks and figures that drink and move, and other things
that have been found to be pleasing to the eye and the ear.'

Fragments of Philon's writings are preserved in Arabic, and
here he acknowledges the debt that Alexandrian pneumatics
owed to the Egyptians. It is clear that the science and technology
of Alexandria did not emerge spontaneously but drew crucially

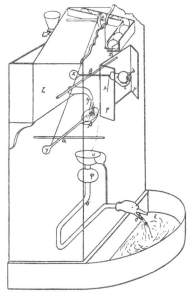

Figure 1.2
Philon Automaton

on prior accomplishments else-where. Philon was one of the most celebrated Alexandrian en-gineers. Hero was another.

Hero of Alexandria, working in the first century AD, wrote a copious range of engineering works (*Mechanics, Pneumatics, Siegecraft, Automaton-Making, Surveyor's Transit,* etc) and other treaties on such topics as geometry *(Measurement)* and optics *(Mirrors)*. A number of the works have disappeared in the original Greek but are avail-able in Latin or Arabic transla-tions. For our purposes his *Pneumatics* and *Automaton-Making* are perhaps the most significant.

These texts exploit a range of scientific principles to indicate how effective machines, including automata, can be designed and built. One device is an automaton theatre in which humanoid figures change positions before the eyes of the audience; and there are singing birds, animals that drink, and other moving specimens. Celsus, in the first century AD, declared himself sceptical of animals 'not really living but having the appearance of life'.

Some of the devices described by Hero were developed by other inventors and engineers (Philon, Vitruvius, Ktesibios and others draw attention to functional artefacts that were prevalent in the Ancient World). What is interesting for our purposes is how natural phenomena – water pressure, air pressure, the heat of the sun, the weight of coins, etc – are exploited to 'animate' mechanical devices. Such primitive automata prefigure the more sophisticated machines of the modern age, where electrical and electronic phenomena can be exploited to grant artefacts a degree of autonomy, the rudiments of intelligence.

SUMMARY

This chapter has indicated some of the speculations, imaginings and practical accomplishments that, in the Ancient World, prefigured the development of artificial intelligence in the modern age. The point to emphasise is the continuity of vision, the continuous speculative thread that runs through the rich tapestry of all human culture.

Here we have focused briefly on myths and machines, the simple tales and simple automata that suggest how artefacts might be imbued with intelligence and purpose. This theme is developed further: more automata are profiled in Chapter 3 where we also encounter the first mechanical calculators, unambiguous heralds of the modern computer. First we need to glance at the theoretical roots, the emergence of structured formal systems in ancient cultures. Modern computation – and so artificial intelligence – is partly about mathematics and logic. Here too there were significant accomplishments before the onset of the Christian epoch.

2　The Theoretical Roots

INTRODUCTION

We have seen that it is possible to identify more ancient AI-linked abstractions in myth and primitive engineering. In such areas we can detect the seeds of the later theorising that would yield all the conceptual fabric of the computer age. But there is much more to early thought than story telling, myth making and the building of simple machines. There is also a body of detailed analytical work that predated the formal structures developed by such thinkers as Boole and De Morgan in the nineteenth century and Russell and Turing in the twentieth. There was in fact a systematic logic in the Ancient World, a prodigious intellectual accomplishment which, partly as a result of clerical influence, became a brake on later thought.

Early logic is mainly associated with the name of Aristotle, though there were many early contributors to the tradition. Here some indication in given of activity before Aristotle and contemporary with him, and of his own work; and there is mention also of logical thought in ancient India (too often it seems to be assumed that only the early Greeks were interested in logical matters). Later (in Chapter 4), more recent logical developments, important to the development of modern computers, are briefly profiled.

BEFORE ARISTOTLE

There can be no doubt that people *practised* logic before the time of Aristotle: disputants would argue, criticising each other's inferences, striving to expose invalid reasoning. This is not to say that there was any conscious effort to *articulate the principles* of valid reasoning. But without such an attempt there is no science of logic: a person can reason skilfully without being a logician. In fact there are clues in Plato and Aristotle to suggest that earlier Greeks had begun to consider the principles of valid inference. It is likely that Aristotle, in producing the *Organon* (see below), was building on the work of predecessors and contemporaries.

Greek logic was concerned mainly with *demonstration,* in one form or another (ie drawing valid inferences from true and necessary premises). In *dialectical* arguments the premises need not be true; and so the conclusions, though validly inferred, may be false. It is likely that geometric demonstrations were the first explicit examples of Greek logic.

Many ancient cultures exhibited an empirical competence in geometry – as shown in contemporary agriculture, architecture and military technology. The Egyptians discovered a practical formula for calculating the volume of a pyramid, but failed to develop an abstract geometry with premises, inferences and conclusions. One ancient writer, Proclus (author of *In Primum Euclidis Elementorum Librum Commentarii*), states that Thales (640–546 BC) was the first person to prove a theorem in geometry, though there is evidence that the Pythagorean school was more influential in this field. Euclid is reckoned to have presented, in his *Elements,* a number of theorems that were known to Pythagoras (born in the sixth century BC) and his followers. Items in the works of various Greek writers (Plato, Aristotle, Proclus, etc) suggest that deductive treatises had been produced before the time of Euclid.

Early geometric reasoning contained features that were to characterise, albeit in a different context, the logic of Aristotle. There was, for example, emphasis on general propositions; on the concept of necessary truth; on the importance of definitions; and on how specific varieties could be subsumed under general rules. Other elements in early Greek logic were *dialectic* (already mentioned), often interpreted as a means of reaching new truths by the conflict of incompatible premises (Euclides of Megara was a celebrated dialectician); *eristics* (concerned with the logic of practical controversy); and *sophistry* (involved in such matters as paradoxical reasoning and legal advocacy).

Another item that indicates a pre-Aristotolian preoccupation with logic is the *Dissoi Logoi,* a fragment discussed in Diels (1956). This signals a treatise written in the fifth century BC to discuss such matters as falsehood and contradiction. Here it is proposed that incompatible theses can be simultaneously rendered plausible – a manifest theory of antinomy that predates Immanuel Kant by more than two thousand years.

INDIAN LOGIC

It is conventional for Western writers interested in the history of logic and philosophy to focus almost exclusively on the tradition rooted in the Greek contribution. There are good reasons for this preoccupation. In logic, for example, there is no formal treatise in Hindu or Chinese to compare with Aristotle's *Prior* and *Posterior Analytics,* elements in the *Organon.* At the same time there are various non-Greek contributions to ancient logical thought that should not be ignored. One of these concerns the framing of the *syllogism,* the method of arguing from premises to conclusions that is almost exclusively associated with the work of Aristotle (see below). It is interesing to note that at least one school of ancient Indian philosophy is interested in syllogistic theory.

The Nyaya school of philosophy, founded by Gotama before the time of Aristotle, has many interests. It is in part an existentialist doctrine, urging – through 'right knowledge' – a reduction of human suffering; but for our purposes we can emphasise the logic of Nyaya. In fact the word 'Nyaya' means argumentation, implying that the doctrine is concerned with such topics as truth, disputation and valid inference.

In Nyaya various types of knowledge are recognised: for example, perception is defined by Gotama as 'non-erroneous cognition which is produced by the intercourse of the sense-organs with the objects, which is not associated with a name and which is well-defined'. The second type of knowledge, *anuma,* is concerned with inference, the stuff of logic. There is a useful account of the Nyaya syllogism in Sharma (1960).

There are five elements ('members' – *avayavas*) in the Indian syllogism. Sharma cites the following as a typical form:

1 This hill has fire.
2 Because it has smoke.
3 Whatever has smoke has fire, eg an oven.
4 This hill has smoke which is invariably associated with fire.
5 Therefore this hill has fire.

There is close similarity between this syllogism and the Aristotelian form known as Barbara (see below), but it is clear that two of the terms in the Indian version are formally redundant (and if we wish to exclude redundant terms there are various options). We can, for example, convert the five-term form to the typical Aristotelian syllogism:

1 All things which have smoke have fire.
2 This hill has smoke.
3 Therefore this hill has fire.

At the same time it should not be assumed that Nyaya is aiming only at formal rigour. In a sense it is more ambitious, aiming to carry on inductive (as well as a deductive) significance and to accommodate psychological concerns. Inference is regarded as having two aspects: *svartha* (for oneself) and *parartha* (for others). The former is supposed to have psychological signi-ficance, perhaps hinting at a subjective route to truth; the latter, more akin to Greek logic, is concerned with formal demonstra-tion.

It has been suggested that Indian logic, from its inception, was influenced by Greek thought; and that, in consequence, the Nyaya syllogism is a derivative formalism ('But it is absolutely false' – Sharma). In fact it is likely that the science of logic had an independent birth in different cultures, and that when the different logical cultures made contact they were individually well established.

THE PLATONIC APPROACH

Plato seems to have been less interested in logic as a formal abstraction than in its use as a practical tool to expose falsehood and uncover truth. Plato's Academy in Athens had Aristotle as a pupil, and Plato who sufficiently impressed with him to call Aristotle 'the mind of the school'. It is likely that Plato's systematic approach to philosophy influenced his brilliant pupil.

Despite his apparent neglect of abstract logic, Plato did address important questions relating to truth and falsehood, valid inference and the nature of definition (the relevant works in this context are the *Theaetetus* and the *Sophist*). In the *Theaetetus* Plato tries to define knowledge, inviting an enquiry into what constitutes true and false opinion; and the enquiry continues in the Sophist by focusing on, in particular, the question 'how can there be falsity?'. In all this there is an interest in the relationship between verbal patterns on the one hand and psychological processes on the other; with valid inference seen as either a 'necessary connection' between sentences or between thoughts. Here we do not need to explore the options (see, for example, the discussion in Kneale and Kneale, 1962): it is enough to convey the flavour of logical enquiry in Plato.

He often suggests, for example, that correct thinking (eg valid inference) consists in following the necessary connections between 'forms' or 'ideals'. His model is geometric demonstration (there is a geometric demonstration given in the *Meno*), and Plato clearly aspires to the rigour that was to characterise the later abstract formalisms. And Plato also settled a number of ancient logic dilemmas that would otherwise have constrained the development of logical theory. There were traditional Greek problems over such matters as negation and falsehood: in removing such difficulties – by suggesting, for example, that an assertion is only significant if its denial is also significant – Plato helped to prepare the ground for the logical work of Aristotle.

ARISTOTLE

General

Of all ancient thinkers it is perhaps most difficult to convey an realistic impression of Aristotle (384–322 BC) in a short commentary. His intellectual range was vast, encompassing wide empirical research, metaphysical speculation and the construction of detailed formal systems. One biographer (Barnes, 1982) suggests that his works would amount to more than fifty

substantial volumes (printed in the modern style). He deals, for
example, with logic, ethics, law, history, psychology, mathematics, epistemology, biology, chemistry, physics and astronomy.
Above all, he was motivated by the desire for knowledge, in
every imaginable subject (an ancient biographer wrote of
Aristotle's 'excellence in every field'). A fifth of his works
survive, including his will; and his influence was profound,
particularly on later Christian philosophy.

It was inevitable, in such a prodigious output, that Aristotle
should have made many mistakes. His observational methods
were inadequate, and there are errors in his zoology and botany.
His interpretation of the structure of human knowledge is largely
sound but it is strange, to the modern mind, to see logic depicted
as a subclass of theology. There are formal errors in his logic, and
these made further progress difficult once Aristotle had been
enshrined as an unassailable authority. Bertrand Russell, writing
in 1946, emphasised that modern progress in logic, as in other
areas, 'has had to be made in the teeth of opposition from
Aristotle's disciples'.

Aristotle's contribution was to emphasise the possibility of
systematic work in one discipline after another, to show that
information could be accumulated to establish a corpus of
knowledge for every subject, and to demonstrate that abstract
speculation could generate formal systems to enlarge the power
of intellectual enquiry. It is unfortunate that Aristotle's work
became 'set in concrete' for so many centuries, but this is a
circumstance for which he can hardly be held responsible. His
accomplishments, over a period of about forty years, remain a
remarkable tribute to the power of the human mind.

The Organon

After Aristotle's death his pupils collected together his writings
on reasoning to form a corpus which in the sixth century AD
became known as the *Organon*. This body of work came to define
the field of logic (the word 'logic' was first used in the modern
sense by Alexander of Aphrodisias around 200 AD).

There are five works in the *Organon* (ie instrument of science).
The first two, the *Categories* and *De Interpretatione,* are usually

regarded as preliminary and aim to study the term and the proposition respectively. The metaphysical flavour of the *Categories* is perhaps as significant as its logical content, and the metaphysics came to have an impact on medieval philosophy. *De Interpretatione* (this is the work's post-Renaissance Latin name; it was first called *Peri Hermeneias*) is mainly concerned with what pairs of statements are opposed and what forms these various oppositions take. This enquiry provides ground-work for the investigation of dialectical reasoning in the *Topics* (with its appendix *Sophistici Elenchi*, another element in the *Organon*).

The two remaining works in the *Organon* are the *Prior Analytics* and the *Posterior Analytics*. These, written around 350 BC, represent the pinnacle of Aristotle's logical thought. It is in the *Prior Analytics* that Aristotle attempts to establish the syllogism as the basis of all reasoning, and it is this attempt that has become identified with his main logical contribution and which is often taken as synonymous with Greek logical enquiry.

At the beginning of the *Prior Analytics* Aristotle states what the enquiry is about. The subject matter 'is demonstration, ie demonstrative science' – by which he means deriving conclusions from premises. Definitions, necessary to an exploration of reasoning are then offered. Attention is given to such matters as singular and general terms, negation and propositions; and this prepares the ground for an investigation of the syllogism.

The Syllogism

Aristotle, (wrongly) assuming that all valid argument relied upon the deployment of true or false subject-predicate propositions, framed the doctrine of the syllogism. A syllogism is an argument defined by a major premise, a minor premise and a conclusion. There are many different kinds of syllogism, the most familiar type (called 'Barbara') having the following form:

All men are mortal (Major premise).
Socrates is a man (Minor Premise)
Socrates is mortal (Conclusion).

To avoid reliance on particular matters of empirical fact (eg whether or not all men are mortal) and to expose the purely formal nature of the syllogism, it is conventional to use letters to denote any possible subjects, predicates, quantifications, etc. This approach yields the following types of propositions (with S denoting the subject, P the predicate, and the vowel the quantification of the subject):

All S is P (SaP).
No S is P (SeP).
Some S is P (SiP).
Some S is not P (SoP).

In order that a valid inference can take place, a particular entity (a middle term, denoted by M) must be present in the two premises. In the example above, Socrates is S, the class of mortal beings is P, and the class of all men is the middle term M. It can be seen that the major premise involves P and M, and that the minor premise involves S and M. With this approach it became possible to identify all the valid forms of the syllogism. In fact no less than 256 types of syllogism can be written down, though most are invalid. We can see how the various forms can be constructed by observing how S, P, M and the various quantifiers (denoted by a, e, i and o) can be distributed. What are said to be the four 'figures' of the syllogism are represented as follows:

1	2	3	4
MP	PM	MP	PM
SM	SM	MS	MS
SP	SP	SP	SP

However, this representation, lacking the quantifiers, is obviously incomplete. The vowels can be inserted, as appropriate, to give all the possible forms of the syllogism. For example, a simple 'first-figure' syllogism is yielded when the quantifier (sometimes called a 'connective') is a in every case:

MaP
SaM
SaP

Hence 'Barbara' (with its repeated vowel) is a suitable mnemonic for one 'mood' of the syllogism in the first figure. The mnemonic, devised by medieval schoolmen, extends to all the syllogistic moods. It is enough here to quote the mnemonic for the first-figure moods:

Barbara, Celarent, Darii, Ferioque, *priors*

This is enough to convey the flavour of the Aristotelian syllogism (a detailed account can be found in Kneale and Kneale, 1962). It is of interest for our purposes not least because there is a similarity between the propositions of the syllogism and the 'production rules' of the modern expert system (Chapter 14). At the same time we should remember that formal defects have been found in syllogistic theory, that there are other forms of deductive reasoning apart from the syllogism, and that there are other forms of reasoning apart from deduction.

AFTER ARISTOTLE

After Aristotle there was little development in logic before the nineteenth century. In the Ancient World and throughout the Middle Ages Aristotle was the recognised authority, but Aristotle was followed by (according to Russell) 'over two thousand years of stagnation'. The medieval schoolmen enshrined Aristotle's logic and, after the thirteenth century, his metaphysics. Thus to question Aristotle, even in logical matters, became an impiety: there were medieval logicians but little of worth was added to the canon.

In the nineteenth century – as, for example, in the work of Boole – logic broke away from the weight of the Aristotelian tradition and new formalisms developed that were to prove important to the design of electronic computer systems. (Boolean algebra in briefly profiled in Chapter 4.)

SUMMARY

This chapter has briefly described some of the early work in logical theory. It is emphasised that, at least in the West, the logic of antiquity is identified largely with the work of Aristotle. At the same time it is suggested that Aristotle himself was influenced by predecessors and contemporaries, and that there is evidence of logical treatises already in existence when Aristotle came to write the works of the *Organon* (in particular, the *Prior Analytics* and the *Posterior Analytics*). And attention has also been drawn to the Indian logic of the Nyaya school, suggesting an origin of logical theory independent of the Greek tradition.

Ancient efforts in the science of logic have been highlighted for two main reasons:

1 Such efforts demonstrated the possibility of abstract formal systems and, to this extent, began the tradition that includes the modern formalisms that are essential to computer science (including artificial intelligence).

2 The ancient thinkers, in developing their formalisms, were also interested in defining such elements as knowledge, perception and consistency. We will see that such concepts are of crucial importance in AI. (We have also indicated that there are resemblances between syllogistic propositions and the production rules of expert systems.)

It is worth also mentioning a philosophic matter that is beyond the scope of the present book. Many of the ancient thinkers – Pythagoras is the best example – were aware of the importance of *number* to how the world worked. This awareness was evident in later thinkers (eg Descartes and Leibniz) and underlines modern computational theory (the mathematics of science, computational linguistics, etc). Again we can trace a continuity between antiquity and the high technology of the modern age.

PART 2
1000 to 1900

3 Automata to Calculators

INTRODUCTION

The incidence of automata in the Ancient World has already been highlighted (Chapter 1), and it is worth continuing the chronicle for more modern times. We have seen that the earliest automata were simple contrivances designed to mimic the movement or sound of lifeforms when some natural force (pneumatic pressure, heat, etc) was applied. Such devices were able, in some primitive way, to mimic the behaviour of human beings and other animals; and in this fashion served as the simple heralds of the complex AI systems of the electronic age.

The early automata has little or no capacity for computation; and it was to be via computation that efforts would be made, in artefacts, to mimic (or simulate) the *mental* capacities of living systems. Thus, to realise the age-old dream of artificial intelligence, it was necessary for the automata tradition to yield calculators, devices able to perform tasks normally associated with the human mind. We trace therefore a chronology from simple mechanical automata (with no computational ability) to the early mechanical calculators that would come to be recognised as the rudimentary ancestors of the modern electronic computer.

Through this period the purely fanciful aspect of artificial intelligence continues to be evident. There are fresh tales of magical humanoid inventions, designed largely to ease the lot of man. Again we can cite the *golem,* generated by rabbis with occult powers. Rabbi Loew's golem (in the Yudl Rosenberg tale) was created to wage war against the Blood Libel. There is no science here, but much magic. In 1580 the rabbi, his son-in-law and his best pupil marked out a man in the earth. Then the son-in-law circled the 'reclining golem' seven times and spoke a magic formula ('the golem turned as red as fire'). Then the pupil circled the golem and recited a different formular ('a vapour arose from the supine figure, which had grown nails and hair'). After more of the same, 'the golem opened his eyes and peered at us in amazement'. In such a fashion the Jewish community of Prague acquired a protector.

By the time of the nineteenth century the concept of artefacts being able to acquire mental attributes was gaining some currency. Samuel Butler (in *Erewhon*, 1872) had argued that even mechanical devices would in due course evolve consciousness; and Charles Dickens – a largely unscientific, though astute, observer – could muse (in *The Uncommercial Traveller*) on whether a motionless child was perhaps an 'automaton'.

Here we continue the brief profile of simple automata and introduce the earliest mechanical calculators that led to the work of Charles Babbage (see below) – the necessary prelude to the working robots and computer intelligence of the modern age.

AUTOMATA

In India the scholar Prince Bhoja (1018–60) wrote the celebrated *Samarangana-sutradhara* that dealt with the building of machines (or 'yantras'), some of which were automata in the traditional sense. Bhoja identifies various features of a good machine, including verisimilitude in the representation of animals. In China the ancient skills of producing animated dragons, humanoid figures, etc continued; though, following the Ming ascendancy in the fourteenth century, many automata – clocks, tail-wagging dragons, moving figures, etc – were destroyed as useless extravagances.

A further famous text, *A Book of the Knowledge of Mechanical Contrivances* (1206), was written by Al-Jazari at Amid on the Upper Jigris to describe such hydraulic devices as clepsydras and fountains. An 'automata' device for washing the hands, the 'Peacock Fountain', is another early Muslim achievement. When there is enough water in the basin, a humanoid figure emerges with a bowl of perfumed water, to be soon followed by a second figure offering a towel. In a similar vein the notebook of the craftsman Villard d'Honnecourt (around 1230) comprises thirty-three sheets of parchment covered with descriptions of mechanical devices such as a catapult, a water-powered sawmill, a clock escapement, a mechanical angel and various human and animal figures (the angel was intended to rotate on a cathedral spire to follow the path of the sun). A mechanical cockerel, active at Strasbourg cathedral in 1352, continued to operate until 1789: with every chime of the clock the bird appeared, flapped its wings, raised its head and crowed three times. An artificial eagle, constructed by Johannes Muller (1436–76), is supposed to have flown to meet the Emperor Maximilian when he entered Nuremberg in 1470.

Many of the tales of automata have been embellished in the telling. For example, Albertus Magnus (1204–72) was supposed to have built a fully operational robot servant that was virtually indistinguishable from a human being. The device was said to talk and move in a convincing fashion, opening the door for visitors and greeting them. It is also said to have spoken to Thomas Aquinas in the street, whereupon the pious saint set about destroying the robot, thinking it to be the work of the devil. Roger Bacon (1214–94) was reputed to have spent seven years constructing a talking head; and René Descartes is said to have manufactured a female automaton, 'ma fille Francine', around 1640 (only for the robot to be thrown overboard by a superstitious sea captain).

Humanoid figures were used in the Takeda theatre of automata that opened in 1662 in Osaka, Japan. Christiaan Huygens (1629–95) described figures of artisans able to mimic the characteristic movements of various trades, and other automata were described in a wide range of seventeenth- and eighteenth-century texts: for example, the Japanese treatise, *Karakuri-Kimon-Kaganigusa* (1730), described contemporary automata; and Maillard (around 1732) produced various automata designs (an artificial horse, an artificial swan, etc) for L'Academie des Sciences. A famous artificial duck was made out of gilded copper by Jacques de Vaucanson (1709–82), and it was said that the contrivance 'drinks, eats, quacks, splashes about on the water, and digests his food like a living duck'. A diagram of the duck shows internal cogs, levers, tubes, etc (including a coiled alimentary tract to enable the bird to 'eat' grain, 'digest' and 'excrete'. The reputation of Vaucanson is attested by the fact that he is referred to by writers as disparate as Voltaire, La Mettrie and Karl Marx.

Various automatic writing machines, talking machines and animated dolls were devised by Friedrich von Knauss (1724–89); one of the writing machines was supposed to be able to respond to dictation. And Baron Wolfgang von Kempelen (1734–1804) also produced a talking machine. Goethe observed that the device 'is not very loquacious but it pronounces certain childish words very nicely'.

By the nineteenth century a number of craftsmen in Europe and elsewhere were constructing mechanical automata able to mimic many characteristically human activities. For example, Swiss craftsmen were constructing humanoid figures that could variously speak, write, draw pictures and play musical instruments. Pierre (1721–90) and Henri-Louis Jaquet-Droz (1752–91) were perhaps the best known of such craftsmen. Their Scribe (sometimes called 'The Writer'), built in 1770, was an artificial child – with rosy cheeks, a fine head of hair and beautifully clad – who could dip a quill pen in ink, shake off the excess, and then write *cogito ergo sum* ('I think therefore I am' – Descartes) in copperplate handwriting. Clockwork was used to drive a complex array of precision cams.

The Draughtsman, like the Scribe, was intended to depict a boy aged about three; and this device, built in 1772, could draw various pictures with seeming skill, including a portrait of Louis XV. By contrast, the Musician was constructed to resemble a girl of about sixteen. Again the construction is highly complex, with clever use made of drums, levers, rods, cams, etc. The fingers, controlled by wires and rods, are articulated so that they can perform convincingly on an organ keyboard. One mechanism causes the girl's chest to rise and fall, to simulate breathing. She turns her head and moves her eyes as she plays, and at the end of a performance offers a graceful bow. Compare this with the

eighteenth-century Japanese tea doll, attributed to Hanzo Hoso-
kawa and described in the *Illustrated Book of Mechanisms* (1796),
in which cogs, springs and whale's whiskers are used to facilitate
walking, turning and other movements.

Other automata include the Pan-Harmonikon, an orchestra of
forty-two separate automata, built by Johann Nepomuk Maelzel
(1776–1855); the life-size trumpeter built in 1810 by Johann-
Gottfried and Friedrich Kaufmann; the Philadelphia doll, devised
by Les Maillardet in the early nineteenth century, able to draw
pictures and perform other tasks; the writing doll of Robert
Houdin (1805–71), equipped to sign Houdin's name; and George
Moore's steam-driven walking man, shown in engravings in *The
Picture Magazine* of 1893 (this humanoid specimen, resembling a
knight in armour, was powered by a 0.5 horsepower gas-fired
boiler, walked at 9 mph, and vented steam through its cigar).

This brief catalogue of automata depicts a number of modes of
activity that are central to artificial intelligence. Attention has
been drawn to such elements as artificial speech, response to
environmental conditions, creative competence, task performance and robot locomotion. Underlying many of the aspects of
automata performance are the rudiments of effective programming, whether accomplished by drums, precision cams, levers,
etc. The rich field of mechanical automata, extending from
antiquity to the modern age, has suggested in countless ways how
realistic artificial intelligence might be accomplished via human
technology. We will glance at the chronology of mechanical
calculators before profiling aspects of nineteenth century logic
(Chapter 4) and moving into the electronic age.

CALCULATORS

Pre-Babbage

We do not encounter many mechanical calculators in antiquity,
though many methods of calculation were devised. Babylonian
clay tablets carry details about how numbers can be manipulated,
as do the later papyri of the ancient Egyptians and Greeks (see,
for example, the account in Smith and Ginsburg, 1956). The
Senkereb Tablet, found near the site of ancient Babylon and
about four thousand years old, carries cuneiform numbers laid

out in rows and columns as an aid to computation. This number system used the base 60 – in contrast to the familiar decimal of much modern calculation and the binary of electronic digital computers. The Babylonians also developed a base-2 numbering system (they counted arms as well as fingers); and the Mayans, counting toes and fingers, used a base-20 ('vigesimal') system. One writer, Reid (1985) has proposed that since ET has eight fingers he is sure to use octal notation.

Early numbering systems were developed for a host of practical tasks; for example, calendar compilation, military logistics, agriculture and stock control. The Babylonians were among the first to use a positional strategy to aid calculation, but did not thereby always manage to avoid ambiguity. The Table Texts, as with the Senkereb Tablet, were used to facilitate calculation of various sorts: the Babylonians used the Table Texts for multiplication and division, for squares and cubes, and for geometrical functions. The Babylonians are also credited with the invention of zero.

Further computational advances were made by the Egyptians, the Chinese, the Greeks, etc; and these influenced later cultures. Various mathematical innovations are indicated in the Egyptians Ahmes Mathematical Papyrus, around four thousand years old and now part of the Rhind collection in the British Museum. Egyptian mathematicians, without a positional strategy, used extra symbols for large numbers, a clumsy convention. The Chinese developed computational methods in isolation from other cultures, but the golden age of Chinese mathematics was relatively late, considering the great antiquity of Chinese culture. Hindu mathematical achievements are recorded in the Sulva sutras, the oldest dating to around 400 BC; and the Arabs were developing their own rich mathematical tradition (we owe the words 'algebra' and 'algorithm' to them).

Perhaps the earliest mechanical calculators were bones and sticks carrying scratched linear patterns. Carefully positioned rocks, as with Stonehenge, were used to signal the rising the setting points of the sun, the moon and the observable planets. The ancient Chinese invented the *abacus,* an immensely successful mechanical calculator still in wide use in the modern world.

Various types of abacus have been invented (for example, the Chinese saucepan, designed with an intermediate cross-bar). The Romans and Greeks used the abacus and began the difficult task of building more complex mechanical calculators. The *hodometers* of the ancient Greco-Roman world, working on a similar principle to mechanical milometers, were a simple type of calculator that came to influence future computational systems. And it is worth mentioning also the *Antikythera* machine, an astronomical 'computer' that was built centuries before the birth of Christ (one such mechanism was retrieved in 1900 by a crew of Greek sponge divers). The device included hinged plates, gearing, graduated scales, dials, cogs, movable slip rings, etc (a description is given in Sprague de Camp, 1977). Al-Biruni, an Iranian traveller in India described a similar machine around 1000 AD. And *clocks,* particularly the mechanical devices that were invented in the tenth century AD, have been depicted as computing systems that calculate time by counting events.

The Spanish Franciscan thinker Ramon Lull (1232–1315) is said to have used a mechanical device ('a kind of primitive logic machine' – Gardner, 1958) to facilitate the operation of a logic system. It is said that in 1274 Lull climbed Mount Randa on Majorca in order to seek spiritual illumination, after which he retired to a monastery to compose his *Ars magna,* the 'Great Art' supposedly revealed to him by God. This work, comprising about forty texts, is said to be the earliest attempt in the history of formal logic to use geometrical diagrams to reveal nonmathematical truths.

Lull's influence was considerable. The automatic 'book generator' in Swift's *Gulliver's Travels* (Part III, Chapter 5) is thought to have been inspired by Lull's method. And Giordano Bruno, the celebrated Renaissance martyr, regarded Lull as 'omniscient and almost divine'. Perhaps the most significant Lullian impact was on Leibniz who, aged nineteen, wrote his *Dissertio de arte combinatoria* in 1666. In this work Leibniz claims to detect in Lull's writings the rudiments of a universal algebra able, by purely deductive methods, to uncover a host of moral and metaphysical truths. In fact it is Lull's approach to logic that is his most important contribution to thirteenth– and fourteenth-century thought.

We are not surprised to find that Lull's logical work is, at least in part, a response to Aristotle (there were discernible efforts in thirteenth-century universities to expand on the accomplishments of the *Organon*); nor are we surprised that Lull, as a theologian, was mainly interested in deploying logical techniques to bolster the received 'truths' of Christianity.

He began by identifying what he took to be the *absolute* predicates (eg goodness) that together could define the nature of God. Then he explored the *relative* predicates (difference, equality, etc) that described the relationships between creatures. In such a way, Lull established the basic concepts upon which his logic could be based and from which the necessary truths could be derived. An important innovation was to use symbolism, letters standing for concepts. Once the fabric of the logic had been established, the ambitious aim could be attempted – nothing less than a demonstration of the fundamental principles of metaphysics and all the sciences. Most importantly, for our purposes, Lull describes *mechanical computing devices,* using concentric and rotating circles or disks, able to demonstrate the various possible combinations of the basic concepts.

Today there is little in the Lullian method that influences modern thinkers but the questions raised are obviously relevant to many modern disciplines, including artificial intelligence. What is the nature of knowledge? What is the relationship between knowledge and inference? Can new knowledge to obtained by purely deductive techniques? Is creativity nothing more than fresh combinations of familiar elements? Such questions occur in many branches of AI, not least in the design of expert systems (Chapter 14) intended to solve problems and to aid human decision making in science, management and other areas.

In the fifteenth century, bankers and money-lenders used the squares of a tablecloth (resembling a chequerboard) to carry out financial calculations (hence the term 'cheque' – just as abacus beads, *calculi,* give us the word 'calculate'). At the same time, Leonardo Da Vinci was considering how a mechanical calculator might be built, a preoccupation that was to become increasingly important in the centuries that followed.

One of the first mechanical calculators was built by Wilhelm Schickard (1592–1635), a thinker with wide interests in logic and mathematics (see, for example, the account in Flatt, 1963). This was one device in what was to be a growing family of contrivances intended to aid arithmetic and related tasks. In one listing (Mills, 1983), machines for the performance of calculation can be divided into five groups (reference to Mehmke's *Encyclopädie der mathematischen Wissenschaften*):

- simple addition devices, such as the 'Pascaline' (invented by Blaise Pascal in 1642);

- simple addition devices with modifications to allow for multiplication (multiplication being repeated addition), such as the Leibniz calculator invented in 1671;

- other multiplication devices (eg the Léon Bollés device, 1888);

- difference machines (eg Johann Helfrich von Müller, 1786; and Charles Babbage, 1822);

- analytical devices (1834 and after).

Pascal (1623–62) offered his calculating machine with the words: 'I submit to the public a small machine of my own invention by means of which alone you may, without effort, perform all the operations of arithmetic, and may be relieved of the work which has often times fatigued your spirit.' In fact the Pascaline was a modest device: it measured 36 x 13 x 9cm, and could only be used for addition and subtraction. It included eight dials and a metal stylus. The French monetary unit of the day, the livre, was divided into 12 deniers, each comprising 20 sols; and dials were allocated for sols, deniers and up to 999,999 livres. A decimal transfer provision was incorporated, by arranging for a toothed wheel to move on one unit (a tenth of a revolution on each wheel except those designated for deniers and sols). When a wheel was moved from 9 to 0, a lever, lifted by pins and fastened to a pawl, fell downwards, causing the next wheel to move one step forward. Numbers set on drums could be seen in windows on the front of the machine.

   The Pascaline was a relatively simple device, though ambitious for the times. Pascal himself appears to have been impressed by the potential of the machine: his sister is supposed to have observed that his 'mind had somehow been taken over by the machine' – a familiar enough theme to those readers acquainted with the literature on technophobia, computer addiction, etc. Perrier (1963) gives an account of Pascal's work and records his sister's evident anxiety. In 1666, Sir Samuel Morland produced a machine similar to the Pascaline (Samuel Pepys commented: 'Very pretty but not very useful').

The calculator invented by Wilhelm Gottfried von Leibniz (1646–1716), shown in Figure 3.1, is similar in appearance to the Pascaline (they both resemble shoe-boxes). It was however a more ambitious instrument, able to add, multiply, divide and extract square roots. Here too there is decimal transmission, but achieved by means of stepped rolls rather than toothed wheels. Other components included a cog-wheel, a square shaft, setting devices and a scale. When a crank was turned, a number could be read in the windows of the product register.

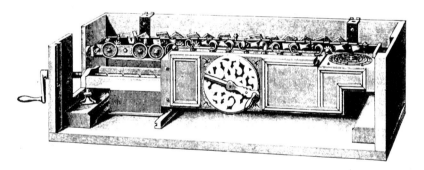

Figure 3.1 The Leibniz Calculator

The seventeenth century also saw the invention of logarithms by John Napiet, a Scottish mathematician. He also invented a set of rotatable wooden 'bones' that could be used to aid computation. The slide rule, still much in use well into the twentieth century, was invented at about the same time.

Later mechanical calculators are associated with the names of Odhner (in the eighteenth century) and Jewna Jacobson, a Minsk clockmaker who invented a calculator machine, in 1770, that could handle numbers up to five digits. There was now growing interest in the possibility of automatic computation, and new technological developments were expanding the range of options that could be attempted. One significant development of this sort was the automatic drawloom invented in 1801 by Joseph Marie Jacquard (1752–1834). Here use was made of a train of punched cards to control the lifting of thread and the consequent generation of the fabric pattern. The Jacquard loom is now seen as, in effect, a programmed computer, the first device to use punched cards to store a program and control a machine. (Jacquard himself declared himself to be 'obsessed' with his research. When it yielded practical successes he was thrown in the river Rhone by unemployed weavers. Even in the early days, automated systems were a perceived threat to jobs!)

The technological scene had now accumulated a number of practical innovations and theoretical concepts that would facilitate the emergence of more ambitious computational projects. By the early nineteenth century, engineers could supply a host of components for mechanical systems: cogs, levers, toothed wheels, ratchets, drums, spined cylinders, etc were commonplace. And there was a parallel evolution of number theory and new insights into the logical relations that would prove essential to the computing innovations of the twentieth century. The scene was set for new advances in practical computing. In fact what emerged was disappointing in practical terms but nonetheless laid the basis for the general computer architectures of the modern age. This accomplishment is associated with the name of Charles Babbage.

BABBAGE

Charles Babbage was born on 26 December 1791 (though the baptismal register carries the date 6 January 1792) and died on 18 October 1871. He is often represented as the 'father of modern computing', and as such he is also the progenitur of artificial intelligence, though this is rarely said. With J F W Herschel and George Peacock he formed the Analytical Society to discuss original work, largely of a mathematical nature. By 1821 he had written five books and nearly twenty papers and other items. With Herschel he also founded the Royal Astronomical Society and was obliged to compile reference tables. When Babbage remarked 'I wish to God these calculations had been executed by steam!', Herschel is said to have replied that it should be possible.

At this time he also wrote to Sir Humphrey Davy, president of the Royal Society, proposing that a machine could be developed to replace 'one of the lowest occupations of the human intellect'.

Babbage's first mechanical calculator was presented to the Royal Astronomical Society. Using a technique based on calculating the differences between numbers it was called the Difference Engine. A main purpose was to calculate and check mathematical tables. In a simple version the machine worked to six decimal places, but production problems proved too difficult for a larger, more complicated machine. It was in 1832 that Babbage instructed his skilled mechanic Joseph Clement to construct a portion of the Engine, the device that can today be seen in the London Science Museum. In 1859 a version of the Engine was constructed to build life tables for insurance companies wanting to calculate premiums. (In 1926, L J Crombie at the British Nautical Almanac began work to automate the calculation of the positions of the sun and stars, the original task for which Babbage had wanted mechanical assistance. In 1882 Burroughs invented an adding machine. Crombie realised that a particular Burroughs calculator could be used without modification as a Difference Engine.)

By the early-1830s, Babbage realised the limitations of the machine, and so embarked on the creation of a difference type of calculating system. He was not optimistic that he would receive the support of his compatriots. In 1835 he wrote to an American: 'You will be able to appreciate the influence of such an engine on the future progress of science – I live in a country which is incapable of estimating it' (quoted by Hyman, 1982). Now Babbage was embarked on the design of a general-purpose computing machine, the Analytical Engine. In developing the device, he appears to have provided no single coherent description of the machine (he was evidently poor on documentation!). The best account we have is largely due to Ada Lovelace, Babbage's co-worker for many years.

It has been suggested that in 1834 Babbage saw 'a vision of a computer, and remained enthralled for the rest of his days' (Hyman). For many years he was to work on the development of a mechanical computing system that would prove to be disappointing in practical terms, but that would lay the basis for the theory of computer architecture. Babbage realised, before the middle of the nineteenth century (more than a hundred years before the invention of the transistor), that computers would have to include five key elements or facilities:

- *input*, to allow numbers to be fed into the machine. Babbage used the punched cards originally developed by Jacquard for the automatic control of looms. Cards were still used for computer input well into the 1970s;

- *store*, to be used as a memory for the numbers used in calculations and for the program instructions. For this purpose, Babbage considered using punched cards and metal disks on spindles;

- *arithmetic unit*, to perform the actual calculations. Babbage called this the *mill* ('mill time' is still used, though not commonly, to denote the time spent by a program in processing activities);

- *control unit*, to control task performance under the direction of the stored program. Today the arithmetic unit and the control unit are usually combined to form the central processing unit (CPU);

- *output*, to communicate to users the results of processing. Babbage considered using punched cards and setting up type automatically to give printed output.

These elements characterised the various designs of the Analytical Engine, an 'architectural precursor' of modern electronic digital computers. One account of the emerging new machine was written in 1842 by L F Menabrea, a young Italian military engineer who attended a Babbage lecture in Turin. Ada Lovelace translated the paper (from French) into English, whereupon Babbage encouraged her to write many detailed additions of her own. These included programs that she had discussed with Babbage and that, with one exception, she had originated. She also discovered 'a grave mistake' in Babbage's proposal for calculating Bernoulli numbers – perhaps the first recorded example of a program bug! The Menabrea paper was expanded by Lovelace to three times its original length, and the

impressive potential power of the Analytical Engine was demonstrated. (Lovelace commented: 'We may say most aptly that the
Analytical Engine weaves algebraic patterns just as the Jacquard
loom weaves flowers and leaves.')

The machine used the Jacquard punched-card approach, a
convenient way of representing instructions to a mechanism.
(Other French engineers – Falcon and Vaucanson – had also
proposed using cards to control machines.) Babbage introduced
punched cards in 1836 and it was possible to discern the various
architectural units that still typify computers: input/output, store,
mill and control (the term 'mill' was a direct analogy with cotton
mills – items were held in store until they were needed for
processing).

About three hundred drawings were produced to describe the
specification and operation of the Analytical Engine (Jarvis,
Babbage's principal draftsman, had also worked on the Difference Engine). It soon became clear that the manufacture of a
fully-fledged Analytical Engine was a task of immense difficulty,
though Babbage pursued the goal for nearly four decades.
Imaginative ideas were introduced at almost every stage. Toothed wheels constituted the store of the Engine; the punched cards
were used in three main ways – as *number* cards (to introduce
constants), as *variable* cards (to define the axis which was to carry
the number), and as *operation* cards (to control the working of
the mill); and the fixed store decoded the instructions, feeding
appropriate information to the various parts of the system. Nor
should it be thought that the Analytic Engine was a discrete
isolated concept. Babbage was also thinking of a family of such
systems and other devices of different types. Hyman (1982) refers
to ideas for Algebra Engines and an array processor, concepts
that became functionally realistic with the development of
electronics in the second half of the twentieth century.

Charles Babbage, with immense industry and uncommon
engineering and mathematical imagination, explored computational matters in an unprecedented fashion. He achieved vital
insights into the requirements of computer architecture and left
an indelible mark on the electronic systems that were to emerge
three-quarters of a century after his death. When Babbage died in

1871, his youngest son Henry struggled to cope with the formidable legacy of the mechanical computational 'engines'. In 1879 a committee was formed in an effort to stimulate further work, but little was achieved. Henry Babbage managed to build a processor that made tables of multiples of *pi* (the machine, now in the London Science Museum, kept breaking down), and published various accumulated documents (as *Babbage's Calculating Engines*) which influenced future workers.

The US statistician Herman Hollerith (1860–1929), in tabulating the 1890 US census for a sixty-five million population, followed Jacquard and Babbage in using punched cards. In the early-1900s the Spanish cybernetician Leonardo Torres y Quevedo (1852–1936) worked on mechanical automata that owed much to Babbage. Hyman (1982) suggests that Alan Turing, in developing the theory of the highly influential 'Turing machine', was also heavily influenced by Charles Babbage. It is clear that Babbage, his co-workers (in particular, Ada Lovelace, Clement and Jarvis) and his followers set the scene for the emergence of electronic computers in the modern age.

SUMMARY

This chapter has profiled some of the mechanical systems (simple automata, early calculators, the Babbage engines) that served as effective heralds of the computer age. We have seen now simple automata prefigured effective AI in the modern world and how simple mechanical calculators gave clues for the architecture of modern digital computers.

There have also been brief references to advances in computation theory in various ancient cultures, following the profile (Chapter 2) of the (mainly) Aristotelian logic of the Ancient World. We also cited Ramon Lull, partly because he envisaged mechanical means of computation and partly because he conceived the notion of symbolic formal systems. Before we begin (in Part 3) to approach electronic computers and the explosion of interest in practical AI, we need to glance at the logic theory that was being developed in parallel with the work of Babbage and his contemporaries.

4   Boole et al

INTRODUCTION

The nineteenth century saw not only the development of mechanical calculators that established many of the architectural principles of today's electronic computers; it also witnessed a rapid development of the logical theory that would come to assist the design of computer circuits. Thus by the twentieth century, important enabling theories – in system architecture, sequential programming, symbolic logic, etc – were in place, awaiting further developments in the theory of machine computation and in the emerging technology of electronics.

Thus the modern digital computer, like all complex systems, is a nicely organised synthesis of elements deriving from a wide range of disparate theories and concepts in different disciplines. We have already considered practical achievements – in simple automata, mechanical calculators, computation engines, etc – that prefigured the computer age in general and artificial intelligence in particular. Here we glance at some of the logical developments that later were to enhance the computational capacities of artefacts. First it is necessary to bridge, albeit quickly, the lengthy gap between Aristotle and the nineteenth century.

MEDIEVAL STAGNATION

The title of this section is mildly contentious. Most writers suggest that logic developed very little between the time of the *Organon* and the modern age. Thus Kilmister (1967) declares that 'Logic developed hardly at all after it left the hands of Aristotle until the 19th century'; and, in a similar vein, Russell (1946) represents the Aristotelian logic as 'a dead end, followed by over two thousand years of stagnation'. Other writers, perhaps with a particular vested interest, prefer an alternative interpretation. The Jesuit FC Copleston, writing in 1972, remarks that 'it was a common enough idea that no logical developments of any value had taken place in the Middle Ages . . .' but, he adds, 'Nowadays we have a better understanding of the continuity between ancient, medieval, Renaissance and modern philosophy.' In fact, in Copleston's *The History of Medieval Philosophy* the idex entry under *logic* is, together with the entries for *propositions* and *faith and reason*, one of the largest. At the same time it is hard to represent the medieval logicians as in any way as significant as Aristotle in the history of logic: there is no medieval equivalent to the *Prior Analytics*.

We have already mentioned Lull (1232–1315), largely because of his interest in the possibility of mechanical devices able to perform computation. Few other medieval thinkers had this sort of engineering focus, but many wrote about logic, usually seeing it as a powerful tool for securing religious truths revealed in other ways. Lull himself had a particular interest in both developing logical methods and spreading Christian propaganda in Moslem Africa.

Boethius (c. 480–524), another significant medieval thinker, held office under the Ostrogoth king Theodoric and is best known for his work *De consolatione philosophiae (On the Consolations of Philosophy)*. He translated much of the *Organon* into Latin, so helping to generate a Latin vocabulary of logical terms. His contribution was largely to give other medieval thinkers access to the Aristotelian canon; and, like many of his contemporaries and successors, he saw theology as a principal philosophic concern. St Anselm (1033–1109), for example, believed that logic should be deployed to support what were assumed to be religious truths. Abelard (1079–1142) wrote commentaries on Aristotle and spent time on the so-called 'old logic', the contribution of Boethius. And at the same time various philosophers and logicians were active outside the Christian tradition. Abu Ibn-Sina (980–1037), known in the Christian world as Avicenna, regarded logic as essential to philosophy and proposed a grand structural division of knowledge that was reminiscent of Aristotle. Avicenna developed Aristotle's interpretation of necessity and investigated conditional propositions. Again there was the discernible preoccupation with theology, though in relation to Islam rather than Christianity. Similarly, the Spanish rabbi Hasdai Crescas (c. 1340–1410) believed that logic should be used to support religious beliefs (this time, Judaism) and wrote a *Refutation of the Principal Dogmas of the Christian Religion.*

Other medieval works, today not thought to be particularly important, focused exclusively on logic. William of Sherwood (born early in the thirteenth century, died c. 1270) wrotes *Introductiones in Logicam (Introductions to Logic)* in six parts, and the thirteenth-century Peter of Spain (died 1277) produced a *Summulae Logicales,* arguing that since logic has to be conducted through language, any study of logic must begin with an investigation of terms and their functions. And William of Ockham (c. 1285–1349), remembered mainly for his celebrated 'Razor' ('do not multiply entities beyond necessity', ie choose the simplest hypothesis that fits the facts), wrote various logical works including an ambitious *Summa totius logicae (Summary of the Whole of Logic).* Copleston (1972) suggests that Ockham anticipated logical laws usually attributed to the nineteenth-century logician Augustus De Morgan (such a law is that concerning the negation of conjunctions and disjunctions).

What we see is a continuity, through medieval times, of interest in logical theory. The interest is maintained, though – despite the recognised importance of logic – there are only significant insights, rather than 'revolutionary' innovations, over the period. It may be that theology laid an effectively 'dead hand' on most medieval speculation, insisting on the protection of imagined absolutes rather than on progressive evolution to new knowledge and fresh modes of enquiry. Despite some efforts to transcend Aristotle and Ockham's anticipation* of some elements of nineteenth-century logic, the whole medieval period did little to advance the science of reasoning.

---

*Ockham writes (*Summa totius logicae,* II, Chapter 32): 'the contradictory opposite of a copulative proposition is a disjunctive proposition composed of the contradictory opposites of the parts of the copulative proposition.' This is a statement for which De Morgan is credited.

BOOLE ET AL

Background

We have seen how enthusiasm for Aristotelian logic was maintained up to modern times, and how few advances on the *Organon* were achieved until the nineteenth century. In his *Nouveaux Essais* Leibniz (1646–1716) describes Aristotle's logical doctrine as 'one of the most beautiful discoveries of the human spirit', declaring it 'an art of infallibility' which can be developed into 'a sort of universal mathematics'. At the same time, Leibniz believed that there was more to reasoning than syllogistic form.

The idea that proofs could be *formally* achieved was one of the key concepts that Leibniz derived from his study of Aristotle. To the modern ear this sounds an obvious enough doctrine, but in fact proofs are often psychologically sustained rather than rigorously secure in a formal sense. For example, what passes as commonsense argument would seldom survive formal scrutiny. Leibniz recognised that *psychological,* rather than *logical,* reasons were at the root of much philosophic thought (hence his criticisms of Locke and Descartes). His insistence on the importance of formal demonstration in logical argument came to be a clear assumption in the logical work of the nineteenth and twentieth centuries.

Leibniz was influenced by Lull's *Ars Magna* and Hobbes' *Computatio sive Logica* (the *De Corpora* of 1655) into considering the possibility of a universal symbolic system, drawing both on aspects of mathematics and on traditional logic. With this in mind, he aimed to present logic as a calculus, though not to subsume it under the broad head of mathematics (despite dubbing the new science 'universal mathematics'). The aim was to provide a general theory (described in his *Doctrina Formarum continet Logicam et Combinatoriam*) that would facilitate new discoveries. But though he devoted several years to the project it was not successful: for instance, it was not developed sufficiently to cope with the whole theory of the syllogism, much less to bring fresh insights into logic, mathematics and science. A principal contribution was to extend current attitudes on what could be attempted in the construction of formal symbolic systems (the symbolism is explored in Kneale and Kneale, 1962).

Among other thinkers who considered logical matters we can mention the Italian Jesuit Gerolamo Saccheri who wrote *Logica Demonstrativa* in 1697. This text, modelled on the form of the *Organon*, is devoted to the requirements of geometrical proof. Another mathematician Johann Heinrich Lambert (died 1777) highlighted various similarities between logic and ordinary algebra; and Leonhard Euler, publishing influencial *Lettres* in 1768, followed Leibniz's approach of illustrating logical connections by means of geometrical analogies. Other eighteenth- and nineteenth-century thinkers with an interest in logic include Kant, Hamilton, Bolzano and Mill, though their purely formal contributions were relatively slight. For example, a compilation of Kant's lecture notes was published as *Logik* in 1800, but here he seems largely satisfied with the durable Aristotelian corpus. The most significant nineteenth-century contributions to logic were to be made by Augustus De Morgan and George Boole.

Boole and De Morgan

Leibniz, influenced by earlier thinkers, had tried to develop a comprehensive calculus to underpin scientific and mathematic work. He failed, but extended the frontiers of the logical imagination. He had appreciated that there was a resemblance between such logical notions as disjunction and conjunction on the one hand and the familiar arithmetical operations of addition and multiplication on the other. George Boole (1815–64) managed to achieve a formal statement of this resemblance: it appears in his *Mathematical Analysis of Logic* (first published in 1847).

Boole, born in East Anglia, was still in his teens when he became intrigued by the idea that algebraic formula might be used to express logical relations; he mused on the possibility while working as an usher in a private school in Lincoln. His main achievement was to introduce a special algebra that could quickly demonstrate the theory of the syllogism; and moreover expose errors in Aristotle that had remained undetected by logicians for more than two thousand years. Logic was on the move again.

Boole's interest in logic was further stimulated by a published dispute between Sir William Hamilton and Augustus De Morgan. Boole contacted De Morgan who was at the time working on a logical tract, and they agreed they should both publish before discussing together their work. De Morgan's *Formal Logic* thus appeared at the same time as Boole's *Mathematical Analysis of Logic* (Boole's status had already been established by an 1844 essay, *A General Method in Analysis,* in which he deployed the 'separation of symbols' to develop generalised algebraic reasoning). In 1848 Boole published an account of his innovative 'Calculus of Logic' in the *Cambridge and Dublin Mathematical Journal.*

A year later, Boole was appointed to the mathematics chair at Queen's College, Cork (his parents were Irish) and in 1854 he published the book that most observers regard as his most important work: it labours under the title *An Investigation of the Laws of Thought on which are founded The Mathematical Theories of Logic and Probabilities.* Boole later declared himself dissatisfied with what, using Ockham's Razor (!), came to be known as his *Laws of Thought.* (He was not of course dealing with the 'laws of thought' in any psychological sense but in the sense of laws that should govern valid reasoning – the nice distinction emphasised by Leibniz.)

Today Boolean algebra, the logical system upon which modern computer circuits are largely based, has been expanded far beyond Boole's original formulation. Various workers (for example, Schröder in the United States) have developed aspects of Boolean algebra for particular purposes; and parallel developments in mathematics have enlarged the scope of formal systems.

The Algebra of Logic

Boolean algebra rests on a number of insights and innovations. In particular, symbols such as x and y can be used to denote the *classes** that are inherent in the traditional Aristotelian logic. Using this approach it was possible to develop sets of expressions to denote all the required logical relations. The following conventions, subject to the ordinary rules of algebra but with

---

* Thus 'all men are mortal' (a typical Aristotelian major premise) means that the class of all men is a subclass of the class of all mortals.

special interpretations, were central to the new scheme:

1. xy is used to denote the class (set) of members of x which are also members of y.

2. Where x and y have no members in common, x + y denotes the class of objects belonging to either x or y.

3. All the objects not belonging to x are collectively denoted by 1 − x.

4. A class x with no members is denoted by x = 0.

5. Where x and y have common members, x + y (said by Boole to be 'uninterpreted') can occur in the working but not in the final answer.

The similarity between Boole's symbolic representation of class features and the traditional symbolism for standard multiplication led to the intersection of classes being termed their *logical product*. But the evident similarity should not be allowed to disguise the difference. Where x is a class, its intersection with itself is denote by xx = x, which appears arithmetically odd. Similarly, where x, y and z are classes it does not follow from xy = yz that x = y (though at the same time we should remember that we cannot argue from the fact that 4 x 0 = 5 x 0 to the equation 4 = 5).

Using the established Boolean conventions (1 to 5, above) the following relations can be derived:

$$x + y = y + x$$
$$x\,y = y\,x$$
$$x + (y + z) = (x + y) + z$$
$$x\,2 = x\,x = x$$
$$etc$$

Now it is possible to convert the standard Aristotelian propositions (see Chapter 2) into the new Boolean symbology (where s and p are the Boolean equivalent of the Aristotelian classes):

All S is P (SaP) gives $s\,(1 - p) = 0$

No S is P (SeP) gives $s\,p = 0$

Some S is P (SiP) gives s p 0

Some S is not P (SoP) gives s (1 – p) 0

With this approach, Boole greatly simplified the Aristotelian scheme (at the same time exposing undetected errors) (for a detailed discussion of Boolean logic, see Kneale and Kneale, 1962, VI, 3).

AFTER BOOLE

The work of Boole stimulated developments in various directions. It was followed by (for example):

- Frege's use of truth tables (in his *Begriffsschrift*, 1879) for representation of Boolean relations;

- Venn's use of topological models (overlapping regions, 'Venn diagrams') to indicate class relationships and propositional truth values (in his *Symbolic Logic*, 1881);

- Jevons' tabulations of permissible combinations of general terms and discussion of their relevance for logical calculations (in his *Elementary Lessons in Logic*, 1870);

- Lewis Carroll's development of a scheme for determining the validity of syllogisms (in his *Symbolic Logic*, 1896).

For our purposes it is of particular interest that the neat formalisations introduced by Boole invited further developments in the mechanisation of computation. Jevons was one of the first to appreciate that Boole's methods could be encapsulated in physical systems. In 1869 he built a logical machine which was demonstrated the following year to the Royal Society (an account of the machine's operation is given in Jevons, 1870). The device included keys, much like the later cash registers, and today is preserved in the Museum of the History of Science at Oxford.

Thus before the onset of the twentieth century it was clear to some observers that Boolean algebra, enjoying enhancements at the hands of various researchers, would stimulate new modes of automatic computation. It was less clear that the greatest successes in this area would be achieved via the emerging technology of electronics. Before automatic computation became

electronic, it needed to evolve through a procession of mechanical, electromechanical and electrical options. The most
rudimentary electronic digital computers did not appear until
nearly eight decades after the death of George Boole.

SUMMARY

This chapter has profiled some of the logical developments – from
the Middle Ages to the nineteenth century – out of which much of
the theory of modern computer science has evolved. It is
interesting to reflect that Aristotle's work on the syllogism in the
fourth century BC led through the medieval logicians and
nineteenth-century formalisms to all the paraphernalia of electronic computation in the twentieth century.

The aim has been to give a flavour of logical thought at various
times. Often the published works have had an *interest,* a concern
to demonstrate (usually religious or metaphysical) beliefs held on
other grounds. It is one of the significant accomplishments of
modern logicians, inspired by Aristotle, that they have been able
to develop symbolic systems that are effectively purged of
psychological special pleading. And the development of such
formalisms has also influenced the framing of computer programs.

It is inevitable, within the scope of this book, that only a few
aspects of logical theory have been sketched. Nothing has been
said about, for example, Cantor's set theory, the Russell/
Whitehead *Principia Mathematica,* Kurt Gödel and Turing
machines. There is an abundant literature in all these areas. We
will have occasion to consider Alan Turing in what follows, but at
the same time we should remember that modern computer
technology, itself a rich tapestry, is rooted in the practical and
theoretical efforts of many seemingly disparate researchers.

PART 3
1900 to 1940

5   Towards Electronic Computers

INTRODUCTION

The late-nineteenth and early-twentieth centuries saw developments in both logic and electronics that would facilitate the emergence of the first electronic digital computers. The first computers of this sort, which with hindsight became known as 'first-generation' (Chapter 6), evolved from practical technologies designed originally to serve other purposes. In early electronics, for example, there was no assumption that the innovative components would one day be incorporated in systems capable of rapid computation. There was no imagined connection between an enhanced Boolean algebra and the thermionic glass valve developed by the early electronics pioneers.

This chapter sketches the evolution of electronics that was to provide the practical fabric of the first-generation computers of the 1940s. And brief attention is also paid to the theoretical work of Alan Turing who, with a singular commitment to the potential power of automatic computers, was one of the leading heralds of the AI age. Claude Shannon, in the 1930s, was demonstrating how electrical circuits could switch in an on/off fashion to simulate the necessary operations in Boolean logic; Vannevar Bush had developed the first analogue computer, the differential analyser, for solving differential equations; and Turing had developed the powerful theory of the 'Turing machine' to determine the computational scope of automatic systems.

There were also various attempts in the pre-war years to built working systems that could demonstrate artificial intelligence.

Many experiments had been carried out to investigate the learning abilities of animals. Mice, for example, had been required to find their way out of mazes – repeatedly, until the exact route was learned; and it occured to some researchers that a mobile machine, an artificial mouse, might be constructed to perform in the same way. In 1938 the American researcher Thomas Ross built a mouse that, by trial and error and travelling on toy-train tracks, could learn to find its way to a correct goal.

It is clear that by the onset of the Second World War, all the elements were in place for the 'quantum leap' emergence of the electronic computer age. We can highlight the elements that together would help to define the character of the first 'thinking machines':

- the understanding, originally articulated by Babbage, of the architectural requirements that had to be met by computational systems intended to operate with a degree of autonomy;

- Boolean logic, indicating a tidy formalism that could specify, in a quite general way, how valid inference could be achieved; developments in Boolean algebra showed how arithmetic computation could be accomplished using such standard Boolean operators as *and, or* and *not*;

- the demonstration by Claude Shannon, a research assistant at the Massachusetts Institute of Technology that components with two possible states (ie binary devices) could embody Boolean logic (later, Shannon was a key figure in developing information theory);

- the development of devices – first, such things as electromechanical relays and then thermionic valves – that could operate in binary fashion to realise in a practical way the logical and computational options of Boolean logic;

- the development by Alan Turing of a theory of automatic computation that illuminated the scope of artificial systems (his celebrated 1937 paper, 'On computable numbers', is frequently quoted as a seminal work);

- an intellectual climate that was increasingly sympathetic to
the concept of artificial autonomous systems (simple electromechanical devices were variously performing day-to-day
computations, learning to escape from mazes and generally
demonstrating the capacity to embody 'intentional' modes;
and the age-old tradition of mythical AI was continued by
such key works as Karel Capek's 1920 play *Rossum's
Universal Robots* and the 1926 film *Metropolis*).

To these key elements that together enabled the emergence of
electronic digital computers must be added the pressures of the
Second World War. There is nothing like war (or the thought of
war) to stimulate the technological enthusiasm of governments.
The electronic computer was born in such a climate and
subsequent developments owed (and continue to owe) much to
military interest.

EVOLUTION OF ELECTRONICS

From the point of view of computer technology, there are a few
practical innovations that have been of particular importance:
one thinks immediately of the glass valve and the solid-state
circuits (transistors, integrated systems, etc) that are based on
semiconductor materials (usually silicon). First-generation computers are based on glass (thermionic) valves, with all the later
functional computer generations based on semiconductors.* It is
interesting to reflect that glass-valve electronics and semiconductors have had a *parallel* development (we are sometimes tempted
to think, because of the chronology of computer generations, that
semiconductors technology only began in the post-war world).

A thermionic valve is essentially an evacuated glass bulb in
which metal electrodes are set: voltages are applied across the
electrodes to control currents flowing in the vacuum. When an
electrode is heated, electrons are emitted and, in the appropriate
circumstances, a current flows. The phenomenon of thermionic

---

* It has been suggested that sixth- and later-generation systems may in
the future be based on optical components or organic materials (see
Chapter 16).

emission was observed for the first time in 1883 in the Menlo Park laboratory of Thomas Edison – and so it was dubbed the 'Edison Effect'. The researchers at Menlo Park did not understand the phenomenon but Edison, thinking that it might come in useful, filed a patent. When there was no immediate application, he seems to have lost interest ('Well, I'm not a scientist. I measure everything I do by the size of the silver dollar. If it don't come up to that standard then I know it's no good' – this commercial pragmatism has a familiar ring in the modern climate).

Much research at Menlo Park focused on the (unsuccessful) attempt to build a storage battery and prodigious efforts – involving experiments with aluminium, tree bark, cat gut, human hair, etc – to develop a filament for the incandescent light. A metal plate was placed in the glass canopy in an attempt to prevent the bulb becoming black. This did not achieve the desired effect but current was detected in the plate. Moreover when the filament current was increased there was a proportionate increase in the current flowing in the plate. The only explanation was that current was flowing from filament to plate, across the vacuum.

Further research – notably by John Fleming, employed by Edison in the British subsidiary – revealed that even with *alternating* current in the filament, the current in the metal plate was still *direct*: thus in 1884/5 it was demonstrated that the Edison-Effect lamps had the ability to convert alternating current to direct current. The filament came to be called a 'cathode', and the elongated glass tube used in later work a 'cathode ray tube' (to become ubiquitous in twentieth-century television receivers). In 1897 J J Thomson experimented with the cathode ray tube by placing magnets around it to deflect the ray (occasional collisions with non-evacuated ions would produce ions that glowed).

In a parallel development Robert von Lieben (1878–1914), working in Vienna, added a third electrode between what were now widely called the cathode and anode; and the new preforated electrode helped to define the nature of the new thermionic 'triode' (having three electrodes). The impulse behind this work was to improve the methods of communication. The third electrode was fed with the sound impulses coming from the telephone transmitter, and used to control them and amplify them as required. The American researcher Lee de Forest (1873–1961) modified the Fleming valve (to produce the 'audion') to facilitate radio communications. It was appreciated at this time that the thermionic valve could act as an effective switching device.

At the same time it was known that semiconductors had interesting electronic features. Early rectifiers used to convert the transmitted alternating current into the direct current that echoed the 'intelligent' shape of the original signal employed semiconductor crystals. Fleming, working on the problem of rectification, had quickly appreciated the value of the thermionic valve's switching potential; in particular, the relevance of this to effective communication. It was the characteristic features of the glass valve (which itself was nothing more than a glorified light bulb) – ie such capabilities as amplification, rectification and switching – that for a time enabled it to eclipse semiconductor technology and serve in the first generation of electronic computers. (More is said about semiconductors in Chapter 7.)

TURING

Two phrases, above all, are associated with the name of Alan Turing: 'Turing machines' and the 'Turing Test'. We encounter the first below, the second in Chapter 8.

He was born in London in 1912; though he showed little promise at school he later achieved a PhD at Cambridge and became one of the acknowledged giants of computer thought. One biographer observes that he was a 'friendly, pleasant person' but, since he was an avowed atheist and (sometimes) undisguised homosexual, others may have disagreed. His particular talent was in mathematics; his particular enthusiasm for the prospect of intelligent thinking machines.

There were various significant influences in Turing's early life. One was a book entitled *National Wonders Every Child Should Know,* written by Edwin Tenney Brewster and published in 1912. Turing was excited to find that the human body could be regarded as a *machine*: 'It is a vastly complex machine, many, many times more complicated than any machine ever made with hands; but still after all a machine.' (This of course is a familiar theme in philosophy. In 1747 Julien Offray de La Mettrie explored the idea in *L'Homme Machine*, as did Samuel Butler, more briefly in *Erewhon*, first published in 1872. In *The Summing-Up*, 1938, Somerset Maughan remarked of the great many medical books that 'told me that man was a machine subject to mechanical laws; and when the machine ran down that was the end of him' – when he saw men die in hospital 'my startled sensibilities confirmed what my books had taught me'. I tried to bring the man-machine concept up-to-date in *Is Man a Robot?*, published in 1986.) The notion that a human being can be defined *in toto* by identifiable physical constituents organised in particular complex ways is important for the history of AI; for such a notion immediately suggests that if the human mechanism is adequately understood then analogous *artificial* mechanisms can be built – to mimic or duplicate aspects of human performance (including mental acts).

Another early influence on Turing was Alfred Beuttell, a pioneer in the science of illumination who aimed to reduce 'the physiology of vision to a scientific and mathematical basis'. Beuttell leanings to Theosophy did not impress Turing but a common interest in how the brain worked resulted in many discussions. For instance, they explored the idea that the brain operated on electrical principles, with particular moods being determined by electrical potentials. Today we would give greater emphasis to the role of biochemistry but the important point, from Turing's point of view, was that it was possible to discuss mental phenomena in the context of organised physical systems. It was this approach that was to uniform much of his later theorising about artificial intelligence (see Chapter 8), an approach that is common today but that much less common four decades ago.

Turing was to be further influenced by the work of the mathematician D Hilbert who, at the beginning of the twentieth century, posed seventeen unsolved questions to the mathematical world. Working on these problems, Turing soon became fascinated by the possibility of designing a machine that could perform any computation, provided that adequate instructions were provided. It was through this preoccupation that the theoretical notion of the *'Turing machine'* was born.

As a boy, Turing had been intrigued by machines, how simple organised components could yield complex modes of behaviour. The familiar typewriter held a special interest. He realised that there was a sense in which the typewriter was *programmed* by its structure, and that its current *configuration* (eg operating in upper or lower case) determined its response. Other features (eg the variable position on the printing line) were also recognised as crucial. At the same time the typewriter, in the context of Turing's purposes, was too limited a device. It fulfilled the requirements of being able to handle symbols, but it lacked even the rudiments of autonomy: it relied totally on a human operator to select the required symbols and to determine the particular configuration. Turing was keen to develop (theoretical) machines that were much more competent. So (in the words of his biographer Andrew Hodges, 1983), 'he imagined machines which were, in effect, super-typewriters'. In fact because of the method of operation, it would have been impossible to build an actual 'Turing machine': the theory was sound but it would have yielded an impossibly large device.

The concept resulted in a 'machine' that was, in effect, an evolved typewriter. The paper became a tape marked off into unit squares that could each carry a symbol: so only one line of writing was to be used, enabling such details as margins and line control to be ignored and allowing the tape to progress indefinitely from right to left or from left to right. The machine would be equipped to scan the symbols, and also to print new ones, and to respond accordingly. The tape would proceed one unit square at a time, allowing the system to function as an automatic machine without human intervention.*

The machine would behave according to its current configuration and the symbol scanned: these factors would cause the machine

 – to respond to the scanned unit square (writing a symbol in a blank, retaining the existing symbol, or leaving a blank);

---

* Much of the computational theory intended to govern the working of the Turing machine is implied by the celebrated paper, Turing (1937), already cited.

- to retain the configuration or move to another;
- to move the tape to right or left, or to return it in the same position.

A 'table of behaviour' could be written out to specify any particular Turing machine, and an infinite number of such tables (and so machines) are theoretically possible. In such a way it became possible to define a mechanical process to achieve a wide range of computational results: a vital step had been taken to lay the theoretical basis for the electronic computers that were soon to emerge. (It is beyond the scope of this book to provide a detailed description of the working of a Turing machine. Excellent accounts are given in Kilmister, 1967, Chapter 10; and in Hodges, 1983, pp 96–110.)

Again we can emphasise a key element in Turing's approach. A central aim was to provide autonomous machine operation, computation carried out – once the system had been configured and programmed – without human involvement. The Cambridge mathematician G H Hardy had already speculated on the idea of a 'miraculous machine', a mechanical system that could solve the problems posed by Hilbert. Turing, in fact, did not believe that such a machine, able to solve all mathematic problems, could be built; but he was convinced that a *universal* machine could be designed to take over the work of any *particular* machine, *including the human brain*. This again was a key impulse behind Turing's thought on artificial intelligence. He assumed that a Turing machine of sufficient complexity would be able, by operating with the symbols on its tape, to duplicate the full range of human mental activity. Turing was one of the great creative heralds of artificial intelligence.

He is celebrated also for his war-time work at Bletchley Park on the Enigma codes (hence the title of the Hodges Biography, *The Enigma of Intelligence;* and the title of the long-running West End play, *Breaking the Code,* based on the life of Turing). This work further developed the theoretical basis for the imminent emergence of electronic computers. Turing himself was encouraged to design one of the earliest electronic stored-program digital computers, but for various bureaucratic and other reasons the efforts were unsuccessful. He was unappreciated as a visionary mathematical pioneer by officialdom – and moreover subject to persecution as a homosexual. Turing committed suicide in 1954.

COMPUTER SYSTEMS

We have noted the development of mechanical calculating systems in the nineteenth century, notably the 'engines' of Babbage (Chapter 3). It is also interesting that industrial robots are prefigured by various nineteenth-century inventions. For example, in 1892 a patent was taken out by Seward Babbitt of Pittsburgh for a rotary crane equipped with a motorised gripper for removing ingots from furnaces. Like the modern electronic computer, modern robots (Chapter 13) have many enabling antecedents. Willard Pollard, for instance, in 1938 developed a jointed mechanical arm for spray-painted, an ancestor of the sophisticated computer-controlled systems now commonplace throughout the world.

In the nineteenth-century there were few post-Babbage developments that helped to prepare the way for the electrical computing systems that were to emerge in the twentieth-century pre-war environment. Lord Kelvin developed a machine in the 1870s to predict tidal movements. As with Babbage the theory had to be realised in the technology of the day – so cogs, wheels and sets of gears (with continuously variable ratios) enabled mathematical integrations to be performed. In 1876 Lord Kelvin published a paper proposing the idea of a general-purpose analogue machine, the *difference analyser*. And, before the turn of the century, William S Burroughs had introduced the first commercially available adding machine. It included a keyboard for the input of numbers (this typewriter-style facility had already appeared in Dorr E Felt's Comptometer) and a compact printing device for recording numbers was added. Burroughs is today one of the largest computer manufacturers.

In the mid-1920s Vannevar Bush at the Massachusetts Institute of Technology (MIT) put Lord Kelvin's idea for a difference (or differential) analyser into practice using thermionic valves. (Claude Shannon, who saw the possibility of developing two-state electrical systems to embody Boolean functions, was one of the operators of the MIT differential analyser.) A number of similar analogue machines were developed in the 1920s and 1930s.

By 1937 IBM had decided to invest $1 million into the construction of the giant Automatic Sequence Controlled Calculator (ASCC), to be operated by US Navy personnel for the Bureau of Ordinance Computational Project at Harvard. A central aim was to provide solutions to problems in ballistics, and another purpose – not known to the early operators – was to perform calculations relating to the development of the atomic bomb. Los Alamos, the centre for atomic weapon development, was then using punched-card calculators (following Hollerith's nineteenth-century innovations) and plug-board programming methods. Bunches of cards had to be physically conveyed between machines to enable a computation to proceed. In such a fashion a typical equation could be solved in less than a month, with a staff of about twenty people working in shifts. The cumbersome ASCC was soon to give way to the glass-valve electronic computers of the first generation (see Chapter 6).

In summarising the computing devices of the 1930s one observer (Lavington, 1980) identifies three types:

- mechanical and electromechanical calculators able to add, subtract, multiply and divide (using mechanisms typically based on German, Swedish and American inventions);

- electromechanical punched-card machines (eg sorters and tabulators), based on the early work of Hollerith and James Powers, and used for scientific computations in the late– 1920s and after;

- the differential analyser, a highly specialised system for solving equations (a project at Iowa State College, between 1937 and 1941, for the binary electronic solution of equations was never completed).

These systems used electrical, mechanical and electromechanical methods to solve a wide range of computational problems – but often in a painstaking and laborious fashion. The speed of electronics was soon to change the face of computing, but already abundant theoretical insights had been gained by the development of non-electronic computing systems on the one hand and computational theory on the other.

In the 1930s, Konrad Zuse developed a series of electromechanical binary equation solvers in Berlin. The first (entirely mechanical) Zuse machine, the Z1, was built in 1935 from rods, metal sheets and mechanical switches (for the binary store). Input was via a keyboard, and output was signalled via flashing lights. This device, a typical mechanical monstrosity, was built in his parents' living room and was ambitiously designed to follow the algorithmic flow of a computation. The Z2 used electromechanical relays (secondhand telephone relays) instead of mechanical switches, and punched-paper tape for input.

The Z3 machine, a yet more ambitious version, was working in 1941. Numbers, but not yet instructions, were internally stored; and techniques of sequence-controlled calculation were employed. Zuse and his colleague Helmut Schreyer conceived of the idea of using thermionic valves instead of electromechanical relays, but he received little official support (otherwise the Nazis may have had a first-generation electronic computer). The Zuse computers – the Z3 and Z4, and the process-control S1 and S2 fixed-program machines – were used for the German war effect and some were damaged by Allied bombing. In 1948 Zuse again began building computing machines, before founding his own company Zuse KG in 1950. The firm was taken over by Siemens in 1969.

By the early-1940s many of the key requirements for electronic computation had been set in place. Researchers were familiar with, for example, stored-program concepts, the algorithmic computational flow, the computational significance of Boolean relations and the switching properties of the thermionic valve. In the United States and Britain many workers were striving to design and then build the first electronic digital computer.

SUMMARY

This chapter has surveyed the development of electronics and computer thought from the late-1880s to the onset of the Second World War. Again an attempt has been made to convey an impression of both theoretical insights (Lord Kelvin, Turing, Shannon, etc) on the one hand and practical innovation (Edison, Hollerith, Zuse, etc) on the other. As always, it is inevitable that progress in computing is achieved by mixing together theory and practice. And again it is worth emphasising that this book can do no more than sketch the various contributing elements.

By 1940 the scene was set for the emergence of electronic digital computers. Partly under the stimulus of war, governments in Europe and elsewhere were to see their interest in developing effective methods of automatic computation. At the same time (as with Turing and Zuse), politicians and officials were often slow to appreciate the gathering momentum of a technological revolution that would in a few decades reshape the world.

It is also important to remember that many technologies are running along in parallel, that there is not a one-dimensional chronology of innovation. So semiconductors were being investigated throughout the application history of the thermionic glass valve, and mechanical and electromechanical computing applications were simultaneously being made commercially available. This consideration has relevance to our brief profile of first-generation systems (Chapter 6) and of semiconductor developments (Chapter 7). While first-generation systems, dubbed 'electronic brains', were assisting specialists and mystifying the public, semiconductors were waiting in the wings. With the arrival of the semiconductor it was tempting to believe that there was only one route for computer system evolution. With hindsight we will probably find that the technologies of future computer generations (Chapter 16) had their roots in the twentieth century.

PART 4
1940 to 1950

6 Enter First Generation

INTRODUCTION

The emergence of electronic computation marked the end of one era, the start of another. We have already emphasised the characteristic technologies of pre-electronic system: simple mechanical switches or electromechanical relays were organised in logical arrangements that could perform effective computation. The ASCC (Automatic Sequence Controlled Calculator), already discussed, was one such electromechanical monstrosity. This machine, known as the Harvard Mark I (not to be confused with the Manchester Mark I – see below), was built at the IBM Laboratory at Endicott in 1943 and measured fifty feet in length and eighty feet in height. Like Zuse and Schreyer, Howard Aiken – Harvard mathematics professor who supervised the building of the Mark I – considered using thermionic valves to provide the system logic. The possibility was rejected because of the unreliability of glass valves. In the opinion of some writers, the Harvard Mark I was the first fully automatic computer: though not based on electronics, it could perform complex sequences of operations under program control.

Various companies achieved important advances in computing in the immediate pre-war years. Bell Telephone Laboratories, carrying out research that often overlapped that of IBM and other corporations, had started work on relay-based computer systems. Here R Stibitz was able, by 1939, to develop a computer to perform a wide range of calculations. And at the same time research was being conducted on the electronic configurations that would facilitate a quantum leap in the speed and scope of automatic computing systems.

EARLY TECHNOLOGY

The basic electronics technology of first-generation computers (spanning much of the 1940s and 1950s) was in place long before the Second World War. In fact it was in 1919 that W H Eccles and F W Jordan first demonstrated how a pair of triode valves could be linked to provide a circuit with two stable states. After that time, the 'Eccles-Jordan trigger', commonly known as a 'flip-flop' or 'bistable multivibrator', was recognised as a binary device capable of representing ones and noughts. By the turn of the century, researchers were also aware of Boolean relations and the requirements of computer architecture (in particular, the stored-program concept. It is interesting to reflect that another two decades passed before researchers showed enough imagination to link the three or four basic concepts that would stimulate the birth of the electronic computer age. War, as always, was an effective technological catalyst.

The basic switching concept, underlying all automatic computation, had been used for many decades. Electromagnets were used to pull relay contacts together to represent, say, a 1; a zero might be represented by an open circuit. However electromechanical relays were susceptible to dust and wear, and so were prone to failure. Moreover they were very slow compared to the speed of electronic devices. Thermionic valves, themselves prone to failure for characteristic reasons, nonetheless offered a massive increase in speed, allowing calculations to be achieved in a fraction the time necessary for electromechanical systems. This is the main reason why the bulk of first-generation computers used thermionic valves, mainly triodes, throughout most of the 1940s and much of the 1950s.

There were in fact various types of thermionic valves used for different purposes. Apart from the familiar diodes and triodes (with, respectively, two and three electrodes), there were five-electrode pentodes and the ten-state neon-based decatron (this latter used in counting operations). The disadvantages of thermionic valves, in computing applications, were soon obvious. Typical first-generation computers required thousands of valves in close proximity, so a vast amount of heat was generated which had to be removed in some way: the massive computers often needed mighty cooling systems. Thus energy was wasted and the systems were very expensive to run. Moreover the cathode heaters, essential to the generation of electrons inside the valve, tended to wear out, especially when the equipment was often turned on and off. System failure was one of the principal concerns of the early electronic computer engineers. This was a problem that would largely disappear with the emergence of semiconductor circuits (see Chapter 7), already been researched while thermionic glass valves were being deployed in their thousands in practical computer systems.

COLOSSUS

It was war that stimulated the British development of valve-based computing systems (though at the same time the Germans showed little interest in backing Zuse). A group of mathematicians, including Alan Turing, was established at Bletchley Park to design and build a machine able to crack German codes. Colossus I, comprising two thousand valves and regarded by some observers as the first electronic computer, went into operation in 1943. It was not intended to have the general-purpose character of most later computers but was specifically tailored for cryptographic analysis. Photoelectric readers were used to detect the absence or presence of holes in paper tape that carried the programs.

During the Second World War the Germans used various machines to encode signals prior to transmission. In particular, use was made of the Geheimschreiber system (called 'Fish' by the Bletchley Park team) and of the Enigma series. Messages were effectively 'scrambled' by means of a complex mechanism of rotors which made it very difficult to decipher the messages. A recipient *could* decipher the messages if he had an appropriate machine with appropriately set rotors. The Geheimschreiber devices, with ten rotors, were used for the most secret messages; the portable Enigma machines (with three or four rotors) were used for day-to-day military communications. Deciphering the Enigma codes was accomplished by means of electromechanical relay machines and hundreds of operators, with considerable mathematical input from Turing and his colleagues. But it was soon obvious that electromechanical systems were far too slow to decipher the Geheimschreiber codes. The answer was to develop Colossus, an all-electronic deciphering computer.

It was in January 1943 that a small team, led by T H Flowers and using mathematical input from M H A Newman, set about designing the Colossus computer. Flowers was one of a growing band of researchers who, acquainted with the use of thermionic valves, was convinced that they could carry out the switching tasks traditionally performed by relays. He had used valves in his Post Office work in the 1930s and gradually became aware of their potential for computing. (In 1984 he observed: 'It seems so obvious now but few people understood it then'.)

Colossus I, comprising 1500 thermionic valves, was designed and constructed between February and December 1943. No less than eleven Colossus machine were built: the first of the ten Mark II versions was in operation in June 1944. However, we should remember that the Colossus II did not contain an internal program store. The machines had been built for a particular purpose, and an internal program was not needed. At the same time it had been demonstrated that thermionic valves, despite all the difficulties, could perform reliable computations.

ENIAC

In 1943 J P Eckert and J W Mauchley at the Moore School of Electrical Engineering, University of Pennsylvania, proposed an all-electronic computer based on the Eccles-Jordan trigger ('flip-flop'). The aim was to build a device to be used by the US War Department for the generation of ballistic tables. This machine, ENIAC (Electronic Numerical Integrator and Calculator) took about two years to complete and was operational in February 1946. This machine, a significant advance, used programs on switchboard circuits and could add 5000 numbers per second. ENIAC was 30 metres in length and contained 18,000 valves; it used 100 kwatts of power and it was said that the start-up transient always blew at least three valves. The machine was finally taken out of operation in October 1955.

Like Colossus, ENIAC was a dedicated system, but not programmable in the modern sense (it did have a reprogramming capability but programs could only be changed with laborious and time-consuming effort). The system used decimal notation for calculation, employing twenty accumulators for storage, each able to hold a 10-digit decimal number and its sign. Basic addition and subtraction operations could be performed, with special units provided for division and square root operations. ENIAC performed the required ballistics calculations, solved partial differential equations and carried out various other operations (for example, it computed π to 2000 decimal places). This computer, though not easily reprogrammable, was an important step towards the realisation of stored-program first-generation systems.

EDVAC

One of the key mathematicians involved in the work on ENIAC was John von Neumann, though he joined the development team late as an 'advisor' in 1944. He and the other leading researchers, Eckert and Mauchley, began increased speculation about the possibility of designing a stored-program electronic computer. The result of such speculation was the now famous *Draft Report on the EDVAC*,* produced in April 1945. (and dated 30 June 1945). The EDVAC (Electronic Discrete Variable Calculator) design laid great stress on the availability of fast electronic memory. It not only advanced the concept of stored program, but also illuminated the developing idea of artificial intelligence.

The *Draft Report* emphasised the analogy between a computer and the human nervous system. For example, there was persistent use of the word 'memory'; and on comparison was implied between input and output mechanisms on the one hand and biological afferent and efferent nerves (respectively) on the other. And the proposal was also influenced by a paper written in 1943 by the Chicago neurologists W S McCulloch and W Pitts: here an effort was made to describe the behaviour of neurons in logical terms. It was becoming increasingly realistic to highlight the similarities between artificial and biological systems. Norbert Wiener was to emphasise such similarities, albeit in a slightly different way (see Chapter 8).

---

* The report is signed by von Neumann but it is clearly a joint enterprise.

The EDVAC proposal has been seen, with hindsight, as having beaten British researchers to publication (Hodges: 'British originality had been pipped at the post by an American publication'). However the American initiative gave impetus to Turing's plans. Von Neumann's motivation derived from the lure of the universal stored-program computer. Turing's aim was the same – to develop a general-purpose system free of the constraints of dedicated working.

ACE

Alan Turing was stimulated by von Neumann's *Draft Report* to write his own paper, *Proposed Electronic Calculator*. This came to be known as the 'ACE Report', though Turing does not use the acronym ACE (for Automatic Computing Engine) in the proposal. The ACE design was developed from 1946 to 1948. In his 1948 paper, 'Intelligent Machinery' (published in *Machine Intelligence*, eds, B Meltzer and D Michie, Edinburgh, 1969), Turing observes that it is not necessary to have 'an infinity of different machines doing different jobs'. Instead it is possible to 'program' the universal machine to do the required jobs. So the machine architecture is to remain unchanged, the specific program in operation determining what job is being performed.

Turing recommended that the Draft Report on the EDVAC be read in conjunction with his own proposal. Nonetheless it is inevitable that the Turing paper should be influenced by his own work on 'computable numbers' and in particular his theory of the universal machine. We may say that ACE was intended to be a realised Turing machine. He incorporated logical operations (absent in the EDVAC design) and indicated the advantage of binary representation; he also considered various storage options, deciding eventually on mercury delay lines because they were available. The Turing proposal was important for many reasons, not least because he stated its purpose of solving 'those problems which can be solved by human clerical labour, working to fixed rules, and without understanding' (a prescient observation about the likely de-skilling consequences of which computers would later be accused).

The practical realisation of the ACE design was never accomplished. The chronology of events – with its various technical, personality and 'political' aspects – is described in detail by Hodges (1983, Chapter 6) and succinctly by Lavington (1980, Chapter 5). There were many people who regarded the ACE project as a vitally important national venture (some called ACE the 'British National Computer'), but by 1947 it was clear that the project could not succeed. One factor was the climate of austerity in post-war England (Lavington: 'There were problems enough without the scientific oddity of a universal computer!'); and there were other factors.

MANCHESTER MARK I

In some judgements, the honour of being the first operational stored-program electronic computer goes to the Manchester Automatic Digital Machine (MADM), usually known as the Manchester University Mark I (Figure 6.1). After the Second World War, a group at the British Telecommunications Research Establishment under Dr Frederick C Williams were working on storage devices. In particular, efforts were made to develop a method of storage using conventional cathode ray tubes. The result came to be known as the Williams tube: bits of information were stored as small electrical charges on the CRT screen. Because the charges were apt to leak away, constant refreshment was necessary. The new storage methods, allowing *random*-access to word locations (as opposed to the *sequential* access in conventional delay-line stores), were soon taken up by researchers in the US and elsewhere.

A few days after Williams obtained the patent for the new storage device in late-1946, he was made Professor of Electrical Engineering at Manchester University. He arrived there with the researcher Tom Kilburn in December 1946, and within a year a successful prototype stored-program computer, based on Kilburn designs, was built. The Mark I ran its first program in June 1948 to become the first working stored-program digital computer.

The prototype system ran a 52-minute factoring program on the 21 June, and the way open for further system development. The research group expanded and efforts were made to expand the computer into a useful facility (a program to investigate Mersenne prime numbers was run in April 1949). Key features of the evolving machine were the provision of index registers and

Figure 6.1   Manchester University Mark I Computer

the combination of a small random-access store backed by a larger sequential store.

The University Mark I was used until 1950, when it was dismantled to make way for further developments. Nine production Mark I and Mark I Star computers were manufactured by Ferranti between 1951 and 1957, with the first Ferranti Mark I being delivered to Manchester University in February 1951 (this made the Mark I the first commercial computer system to be supplied. It was of course inevitable that the Ferranti Mark I, as well as being used for a range of industrial applications, should be involved also in the development of atomic weapons. (Dr Alec Glennie, doing military work at the government's Fort Halstead site, developed his 'autocode' in 1952, perhaps the world's first compiler.) In the early 1950s the Williams/Kilburn team developed MEG (the Megacycle engine), a successful Mark II system. It was more compact than the Mark I and much faster; its first program ran in May 1954. The system served as the prototype for the Ferranti Mercury computer.

EDSAC

In 1946, Maurice Wilkes and a team from Cambridge University attended lectures given by Eckert and Mauchley at the Moore School of Electrical Engineering, University of Pennslyvania. This encouraged Wilkes to develop ideas for an Electronic Delay Storage Automatic Computer (EDSAC): the construction of the system began in 1947 and it performed its first fully-automatic calculation in May 1949.

The main innovations of EDSAC were its software features. The hardware – storage comprising five-foot long (!) tubes of mercury – was not new; but efforts had been made to provide standard program subroutines to perform frequently-used calculations. There were also aids to help find errors in programs and EDSAC included the world's first *operating system* (software able to organise the system resources to meet the needs of other programs). Up to the time of EDSAC, programming was regarded as a relatively trivial clerical task – and so was often left to women! It soon became obvious that software was much more complex (David Wheeler, Stan Gill and Maurice Wilkes wrote the first book on programming* in 1951), and then the men took over.

EDSAC was able to offer a regular computing service from early-1950 until the computer was shut down in July 1958. This represented the first service of its type to be run on a proper stored-program machine. The computer used conventional glass values and paper tape, and incorporated various software innovations. Wilkes, in 1951, was the first to propose the principle of microprogram control as an element in machine design, a concept that was to influence the evolution of small and medium-size computers.

EDSAC continued to develop until the mid–1950s, with an EDSAC II becoming operational in 1957. A version of the EDSAC was constructed as LEO (Lyons Electronic Office), a system able to perform regular clerical jobs for J Lyons & Company by November 1951. And by 1954 LEO was able to offer a full business data processing service. The LEO Computers company was formed in November 1954.

RESEARCHERS

It is worth recalling some of the key figures who contributed during the crucial period of first-generation system design and construction. We have already such importance reseachers as Zuse, Schreyer, Aiken, Stibitz, Eccles, Jordan, Turing, Flowers, Eckert, Mauchley, von Neumann, Williams, Kilburn, Wilkes, Wheeler, Gill and Shannon. To this list we should add the names of John Backus who pioneered the high-level Formula Translation system (FORTRAN) in the 1950s; Bob Overton Evans who in 1951 was a key worker on IBM's first production computer, the 701 system; Jay Forrester who invented the magnetic core memory for use on MIT's Whirlwind computer, the fastest machine of the early-1950s; Grace Hopper who worked on the Harvard Mark and the Univac (the first commercial computer) and, with Charles Phillips, invented the Common Business-Orientated Language (COBOL); and Hideo Yamashita, who proposed a statistical calculation machine, using binary and relay

---

* *The Preparation of Programmes for an Electronic Computer*, 1951

circuits, in 1940 – and who helped lay the basis of the Japanese computer industry.

Many researchers, mathematicians and engineers, working in many different countries, helped to lay the basis for the electronic computer age. The early first-generation systems now seen absurdly slow, cumbersome and unreliable. What was needed was a new technology that could implement, in a more effective way, the evolving computer architectures. The ground was prepared for the emergence of the integrated circuit: research into semiconductors that had been proceeding for several decades was about to expand dramatically into many areas of electronics, including computing.

SUMMARY

This chapter has profiled the technology and systems of the first generation of electronic digital computers. Brief attention has been given to prevailing electronic and electromechanical components (thermionic valves, relays, delay-line stores, cathode ray tubes, etc) and to some of the components that were to be built out of such components (for example, Colossus, ENIAC, Harvard Mark I, EDVAC, EDSAC, ACE and the Manchester Mark I). Particular system features, often notable 'firsts', have been highlighted, though detailed descriptions should be sought elsewhere (references are given to sources of further information).

Mention is also made of leading researchers in Britain, Europe, Japan and the United States. It was already clear in the 1940s that the computer industry would evolve as a transnational phenomenon, drawing on the seminal contributions of mathematicians, engineers, programmers, system designers and entrepreneurs.

It was also emphasised that the first generation of electronic digital computers was a necessary stage in the evolution towards today's efficient high-speed systems. The technological breakthrough that was to end all first-generation options was the transistor, the first semiconductor integrated circuit that was to enlarge prodigiously the scope of automatic computation and reshape totally the burgeoning international computer industry.

PART 5
1950 to 1970

7 Semiconductors to Microprocessors

INTRODUCTION

Once the initial first-generation electronic computers had demonstrated their effectiveness, many other machines were assembled and put to use. Lavington (1980), for example, talks of the 'veritable flood' of stored-program computers that burst upon the American scene alone, including 'BINAC, CADAC, EDVAC, ERA 1101, MANIAC, ORDVAC, RAYDAC, SEAC, the IAS computer and the Eckert-Mauchley UNIVAC I' (these are described in more detail in his Appendix 3). The enthusiasm for investment and development showed little awareness that the increasingly ubiquitous glass valve was soon to be outflanked by electronic components of a completely different kind. Today investors are (supposedly) careful in acquiring systems that may soon be overtaken by technological progress – so investment in information technology often proceeds on the assumption that acquired systems can be upgraded and expanded rather than discarded. Such a principle was less evident in the days of first-generation systems, and perhaps investors and others were not to know that soon all systems based on glass valves would be regarded as nothing more than historical curiosities. The new components that were to fire this revolution were based on semiconductors.

We have already seen that research into semiconductors was being conducted before the advent of glass-valve computers. Often the research was desultory, promising few commercial or other rewards. The unsettled 1930s, however, gave a fresh stimulus to work on semiconductors; and the 1940s were to see dramatic innovations that were to involve a Nobel prize, to lead a total reshaping of the electronics industry, and give a new impetus to the development of truly intelligent machines.

The prospect of war suggested to some European nations that it might be helpful to focus on scientific and technological research that might enhance military preparedness. Researchers in England and Germany, for example, quickly perceived that it might be helpful to detect approaching planes – so work was undertaken to develop a means, using radio signals, of providing an early-warning system. The British scientists – having managed to develop their Radio Detection and Ranging (radar) system – won the race. In this system a radio beam was transmitted and then reflected back off incoming aircraft, enabling the plane's direction, position and speed to be quickly determined. However, the early radar equipment depended upon unreliable thermionic tubes, and a superior technology was an urgent requirement.

FOCUS ON SEMICONDUCTORS

One essential radar requirement was for a rectification capacity that could handle high-frequency signals, and again the thermionic-valve technology was inadequate. It was for these and related reasons that a fresh look was taken at the crystal rectifiers, based on semiconductors, that had been around for a long time but not enjoyed much technological development. The birth of the semiconductor age proper was imminent.

The development of semiconductor physics – owing much to such scientists as Bohr and Einstein – quickly showed immense practical promise with relevance to industry, commerce and military affairs. The science of semiconductors is rooted in the simple fact that some elements – for example, silicon and germanium – have electron-ring characteristics at the subatomic level that places such substances midway between conductors and insulators. Moreover when semiconductors are 'doped' with selected impurities (boron, for instance), their electrical characteristics can be altered in interesting and useful ways.

According to the type of doping, the silicon atoms can either receive a surplus of electrons (resulting in an overall negative charge) or electron gaps ('holes', resulting in an overall positive charge). Negatively-charged silicon, in this sense, is termed 'N-type'; positively-charged 'P-type'. Such seemingly unremarkable details led to the dramatic explosion of the semiconductor industry. This chapter profiles one of the first fruits of the freshly importance semiconductor science – the transistor – and traces how it led to the development of the microprocessor, the integrated circuit, and the plethora of intelligent machines in the modern world.

ENTER THE TRANSISTOR

On 29 December 1939, William Shockley – who was to become one of the three co-inventors of the transistor – wrote in his laboratory notebook: 'It has today occurred to me that an amplifier using semiconductors rather than vacuum is in principle possible.' Thus the germ of the technology that would come to enable the second generation of electronic computers was already in existence before the birth of the first generation.

The transistor was invented in 1947 by William Shockley, John Bardeen and Walter Brattain at the Bell Laboratories in the United States. In 1950 Shockley published his definitive text Electrons and Holes in Semiconductors, now universally regarded as one of the basic works on semiconductor physics. The transistor was soon dubed the 'discovery of the century', and the three researchers were awarded a Nobel prize in 1956. Shockley, a holder of more than ninety engineering patents, was later to run into controversy because of his views on race and intelligence. Bardeen, having first studied semiconductor physics under the Nobel Laureate Eugene Wigner, won a second Nobel prize in 1972 for his work on superconductors. Brattain, the practical experimentalist, was able to convert the theories of Shockley and Bardeen into working systems, though not always predictably – of the first transistor, an untidy concotion of germanium and wire, he wrote that it could be made to work 'if I wiggled it just right'.

Research had focused on the various attributes of the P-type and N-type semiconductors; and in particular on bipolar germanium, a semiconductor strip doped to be P-type at one end and N-type at the other. The point at which the different semiconductor types met, the P-N junction, was seen to be particularly important (acting as, for example, a diode rectifier). The work led to the production of a germanium triode, a 'solid-state' semiconductor device able to amplify a current one hundred times. It is interesting to reflect that whereas germanium was used for the world's first transistor, it was silicon that was to reap the semiconductor glory in the years that followed. It was on 23 December 1947 that the germanium based triode was first demonstrated at the Bell Laboratories. The transistor age had begun.

The functional success of the first cumbersome transistor led Shockley to develop the *junction* transistor that was to reshape the electronics industry. He wrote down the basic concept of the junction transistor on 23 January 1948. It included two back-to-back P-N functions and was able to amplify current flow in a controlled and useful way. The three sections of the solid-state configuration were closely analogous to the three electrodes of the vacuum triode; but now, instead of an unreliable glass valve, a compact semiconductor device was offered that was virtually indestructible and that needed very little power to operate. The new transistor was also immensely fast as a switching device, a characteristic that was to make possible a whole new generation of computer systems.

Many difficulties were encountered in manufacturing the first transistors, and they were not used commercially until 1952 (at that time they were first used in hearing aids. When the inventors of the transistor received their Nobel prize in 1956, no less than twenty companies were manufacturing transistors (see Hanson, 1982); one of the firms was Shockley Semiconductor Laboratory. Shockley engineers were to recommend a switch from research into four-layer diodes to research into silicon transistors, the advantages of which were already becoming apparent. When Shockley refused, the engineers obtained backing from Sherman Fairchild to launch Fairchild Semiconductor – the first company, following the important development work at Texas Instruments, to work exclusively with silicon-based products. Shockley's firm eventually closed down and he became a professor at Stanford (he also contributed to the 'Nobel Sperm Bank', The Repository for Germinal Choice in Escondido, California).

Semiconductor transistors were soon being used for applications in a host of industry sectors. Various technological innovations (for example, the planar process invented at Fairchild by Jean Hoerni to facilitate the diffusion of selected impurities) aided the growing trend towards volume production. In particular, for our purposes, the relevance of transistors to computer design and production was becoming increasingly obvious. Bell was quick to experiment with the use of transistors in computing circuits, and in the early 1950s there was growing military interest in the computational possibilities offered by the new technology. The US Air Force contracted Bell to produce the TRADIC special-purpose computer. It contained 700 germanium transistors and a plug-board programming facility; it worked for the first time in 1954.

During the same period, under Kilburn's direction at Manchester University, two versions of a transistorised computer were completed in 1953 and 1955 respectively (the first, operating in November, is reckoned to be the first transistorised computer to have successfully run a program*). Six Metropolitan-Vickers MV950 computers, based on the Manchester University research, were built (the first completed in 1956), mainly for internal company use. At the UK Atomic Energy Research Establishment, Harwell, the transistorised CADET computer ran a test program in February 1955. Using about 400 transistors, the machine was offering a regular service from August 1956.

Developments in transistor technology led to the use of surface barrier devices in the MIT Lincoln Laboratory's TX-O computer which began work in 1956, and the Philo Corporation TRANS-AC S-1000 computer (1957). At the same time, Kilburn and his team were working on MUSE (a 'microsecond engine', ie able to perform approaching a million instructions a second). In 1958 Ferranti decided to support the project and the computer was renamed Atlas (by 1962 considered to be the most powerful machine in existence).

---

* Some observers declare the National Cash Register NCR 304 to be the first transistorised computer.

We were now witnessing a growing family of transistor-based computers in Europe and the United States. Second-generation systems were well established, and were constantly serving to expand our concepts as to what could be accomplished with automatic computation. But second-generation computer systems were themselves about to be supplanted by further technological developments arising out of semiconductor research.

ENTER THE INTEGRATED CIRCUIT

Soon after the invention of the transistor, researchers were discussing the possibility of building a whole electrical circuit on the surface of a piece of semiconductor. The idea was that a number of transistors, together with the other necessary circuit elements, could be fabricated on the same crystal and then linked together on the semiconductor surface by aluminium or some other suitable conducting material. This suggested that the various electronic components could be connected together without the traditional external wiring.

The origin of the integrated circuit is associated with the names of Robert Noyce, Jean Hoerni and Jack Kilby (a legal dispute to establish who had invented the first solid-state circuit took place between Noyce and Kilby). For several years, Robert Noyce had been thinking about the problems of interconnecting components in a solid-state environment. He observed that transistors were being manufactured in a perfect array on a single wafer, after which 'we cut them apart into tiny pieces and had to hire thousands of women with tweezers to pick them up and try to wire them together'. This was seen as stupid, expensive and unreliable. There had to be a better way.

The answer – which became known as The Monolithic Idea – is associated with Hoerni development of a 'planar process' for transistor fabrication. It was seen that there were advantages in leaving a plane of oxide on top of the silicon; in particular, the oxide would hold in place wires passing through it. And then, most important of all, it was realised that the connecting strips could be printed on the oxide layer in one manufacturing process.

In such a fashion it became possible to link transistors and other components on a single layer of silicon. On 23 January 1959 Noyce wrote down not only a full description of an integrated circuit but also a description of a computer circuit, an adder, that could be achieved in an integrated form.

However, four months earlier Jack Kilby had successfully demonstrated an integrated circuit at Texas Instruments, though there was little immediate development of the idea. In 1961 the US Patent Office awarded the patent to Robert Noyce of Fairchild Semiconductor. Fairchild and Texas Instruments eventually agreed that both men should be regarded as co-inventors of the integrated circuit. (There is a good description of the Kilby/Noyce battle in Reid, 1985.)

There is now a massive gobal market in silicon chips. The annual electronics business, running at well over $100 billion, is totally dependent on diminutive integrated circuits. However today's ICs are far removed from the simple configurations achieved in the early Kilby/Noyce days. Today ICs can serve as complex-memories and sophisticated information-processing circuits. The microprocessor is one key information-processing configuration, relying on silicon chips, that dramatically expanded the scope of what was possible in a wide (and growing) range of automatic systems.

ENTER THE MICROPROCESSOR

The microprocessor is an advanced silicon chip, the equivalent of the central processing unit (CPU) in earlier computers (it serves as the effective CPU in microcomputers and is applied to processing information in countless other ways). By the Early-1970s, integrated circuits were manufactured with a complexity of around 1000 transistors. The first microprocessor, produced by Intel Corporation in 1971, was based on a single ¼-in-square silicon chip which carried the equivalent of 2250 transistors, all the necessary CPU circuitry for a tiny computer. By the mid-1970s, chips of this size using large-scale integration (LSI) could carry more than 20,000 components. In the decade after the arrival of the first micro, the Intel 4004, the processing power of a single chip increased several hundred times.

The invention of the microprocessor is attributed to Ted Hoff: his main inspiration – a logical leap in semiconductor technology – was to design all the CPU functions onto a single chip. One observer, Bylinsky (1981), has commented: 'Hoff now had in hand a rudimentary general-purpose computer that not only could run a complex calculator, but also could control an elevator or a set of traffic lights, and perform many other tasks, depending on its program.' In the late–1960s Noyce also had speculated on the possibility of a computer on a chip (when a critic remarked that he would not want to lose his computer through a crack in the floor, Noyce replied: 'You have it all wrong, because you'll have 100 more sitting on your desk, so it won't matter if you lose one' – quoted by Bylinsky).

In June 1969 a group of Busicom engineers arrived from Tokyo to talk with Hoff and his colleagues, and in October presented a design for an integrated calculator chip-set at Intel. Hoff ('I looked at the Busicom plans, and I wondered why the calculator should be so much more complex' – than the PDP–8 minicomputer with which he was working) then offered proposals for a microprocessor, and an Intel-Busicom contract was drawn up, giving exclusive rights to Busicom for the Intel micro. At the beginning of 1971, Hoff and his team had produced the first working microprocessor. The 4004 was the fourth custom chip produce by Intel (the 4000 signified that the custom device had been designed for Busicom). Gordon Moore, president of Intel, commented: 'Now we can make a single-microprocessor chip and sell it for several thousand different applications' (quoted by Bylinsky). Texas Instruments announced an eight-bit microprocessor four months after Intel has announced the 4004, and then – a month later – Intel announced its own eight-bit micro, the 8008.

It was soon realised that microprocessors could serve as the effective intelligence for microcomputers, and the microcomputer boom began with the launch of the Intel 8080 microprocessor in 1973. Microcomputer leaders at that time were Altair and Apple. Hoff himself resigned from Intel in 1983 and became vice-president of R & D at Atari (he has observed: 'If we had not made the 4004 in 1971, someone else would have invented the microprocessor in a year or two'). With the invention of the microprocessor, yet another dramatic phase opened in the accelerating saga of computer development.

EVOLUTION OF THE MICROPROCESSOR

After the Intel launches of the 4004, the 8008 and the 8080 (this latter the first *de facto* industry standard), various other companies were to invent microprocessor products that were to help shape the rapidly changing computer industry.

In 1974, Motorola introduced the 8-bit microprocessor. Compared with the 8080, the 6800 had a simplified power supply, simpler control circuitry, and instructions more compatible with larger computers. This microprocessor, with programmable input/output facilities, was to become the second *de facto* industry standard.

Intel and Motorola both announced 'true single-chip processors' in 1976, by which time many other companies were making important contributions. National Semiconductor had introduced the IMP-16 chip set in 1972, a bit-slice system that developed into the Pace microprocessor. 1975 and 1976 saw the emergence of a number of enhanced systems. The Zilog Z80 was an enhanced 8080, with more instructions and registers, a one-chip clock and other features.

The first 16-bit microprocessors also emerged at this time, with 4-bit and 8-bit devices continuing to evolve for particular purposes. The first widely-available 16-bit devices were the TMS9900 and TMS9980 from Texas Instruments. Such microprocessors could multiply and divide, unlike many of their 8-bit contemporaries.

The earliest microcomputers were slow and relatively inflexible. Their storage capacity was low and there were software problems. However, new technological developments added speed and storage capacity, and enhanced the applications flexibility. Today, in 1979, some *micro*computers are offering *mini*computer performance levels. 16-bit microprocessors such as the Intel 8086, the Motorola MC68000 and the Zilog Z8000 offer large address spaces, wide data paths, and speeds of more than 500,000 instructions per second. Since 1971, microprocessor complexity has doubled every two years.

Intel's relatively new 8086 has brought the 8080 family of microprocessors into the 16-bit world. The new device has enhanced capabilities and new peripheral support circuits (clock generator, bus controller, etc). It has been designed to meet the requirements of a broad class of new applications. Similarly, the Motorola MC68000 has been designed with greater capability and enhanced peripheral support. Its internal data paths, registers and processing sections are 32-bits wide. Support peripherals include a memory manager, a direct-memory-access controller, and a bus arbitration circuit. The Z8000 is accompanied by a whole new family of peripheral chips.

One of the most significant development areas in microprocessor technology is the provision of support chips. This was well shown at Wescon (1978) where a wide variety of new products were exhibited (American Microsystems S2811 signal processing peripheral, TRW high-speed multipliers, semicustom logic arrays from Fairchild and Motorola, etc). These and parallel developments indicate that microcomputers will continue to grow in capability, enlarging their applications potential, and offering alternatives to conventional minicomputer (and even mainframe) usage.

MICROPROCESSOR TECHNOLOGIES

General

The circuitry for computers (microcomputers, minis, mainframes) is built out of standard families of integrated circuits. The various integrated-circuit devices – counters, registers, adders, etc – are combined according to a theoretical design to perform the required functions. There are various *semiconductor technologies* upon which the families of integrated circuits are based.

Most computer circuits in use today are based on *transistor-transistor* logic (TTL). This technology is common, a virtual standard, in large computers, but considerably less popular in microcomputers. A very wide range of devices are available in TTL from many manufacturers. TTL has been the most popular logic family for more than a decade: it provides high speed, high immunity to noise, moderate power dissipation, and large 'fan-out' (ie TTL devices can drive a large number of other circuit components). Other integrated-circuit families are often judged according to how well their devices can interface with TTL. Non-TTL devices that use signal levels within the range of standard transistor-transistor logic are termed 'TTL-compatible'.

There are two variations on standard TTL: Schottky (54/74 S) and low-power Schottky (54/74 LS). The Schottky variant can provide higher speed than standard TTL. Lower power dissipation is possible with low-power Schottky. Both these variants are more expensive than standard devices.

Transistor-transistor logic was first produced by Sylvania in 1965, with Texas 7400 TTL becoming the effective industry standard logic in 1968. A year later, *metal-oxide semiconductor* (MOS) technology was first used in the manufacture of large-scale integrated (LSI) circuits. MOS technology (sometimes regarded as *metal-oxide silicon*) is the basis for most current memory chips and microprocessors. Some TTL LSI devices are available (eg the Ferranti F100-L microprocessor).

Devices based on MOS technology represent the second largest family of circuit elements. The *complementary metal-oxide semiconductor* (CMOS) process produces components that are more expensive and slower than ones based on TTL. At the same time they are more rugged and use less power, being suitable for a wide range of applications: industrial, military, portable equipment, domestic (eg watches), etc. They are useful in artificial satellites where low power dissipation is important. CMOS elements can be damaged by static charges.

Some high-speed (and high-cost) CMOS devices use an insulating sapphire substrate. This technique is termed *silicon-on-sapphire* (SOS), a technology which offers potential for very large-scale integration (VLSI) but which has failed in some production attempts (eg the now withdrawn GA processor manufactured by Rockwell). It is likely that cost savings will be achieved in SOS circuit manufacture using new techniques. RCA is developing a method of growing sapphire substrates for integrated circuits in ribbons instead of in cylindrical boules. This is expected to cut the cost of raw materials for silicon-on-sapphire CMOS by around 80%. This will allow CMOS circuits built on bulk silicon wafers to challenge NMOS devices (see below).

Hewlett-Packard, already using CMOS/SOS in a range of computer products, is also considering the effectiveness of ribbon-grown sapphire crystals.

Emitter-coupled logic (ECL) is the only other widely-used technology for computer circuits. It is used in mainframes, high-speed memories, precision instruments, and high-speed communications equipment. ECL is expensive and heavy on power consumption. It requires special circuit boards and carefully regulated supplies. ECL families are small and lack standardisation. It is difficult to mix ECL with either TTL or CMOS. ECL circuits have been enhanced with 'gate arrays' (or uncommitted logic arrays, ULA) uncommitted sets of LSI functions tailored by the final metalization to particular applications.

Microprocessors

Neither TTL nor CMOS techniques are ideally suited to meeting the requirements of cheap, single-chip microprocessors, though microprocessors in both these technologies are now available. Most microprocessors are based on either the P-channel or the N-channel metal oxide semiconductor technologies (PMOS and NMOS). In using single-chip microprocessors, it is often required to interface PMOS and NMOS devices to standard TTL and CMOS circuits.

P-channel metal oxide semiconductor (PMOS) technology was the first MOS technology for LSI purposes. It is used in calculator chips and in other applications that do not require high speed. PMOS, though allowing only slow operation, does provide the circuit density essential in large integrated memories and single-chip microprocessors. PMOS components are not strictly TTL-compatible, ie they do not operate at TTL voltages and they provide small output current. Thus additional circuits are necessary to allow PMOS microprocessors to be used with devices from the standard TTL families. Common PMOS microprocessors are the Intel 4004, 4040 and 8008; the National IMP, PACE and SC/MP; the Texas Instruments TMS 1000 NC; and the American Micro-Systems 9209.

N-channel metal oxide semiconductor (NMOS) technology has proved a more suitable basis than PMOS for microprocessor models. It allows higher speed and great density of integrated elements. With some extra circuitry, NMOS devices can operate with TTL components. Common NMOS microprocessors are the Intel 8080, and Motorola 6800, the Fairchild F-28 and the Texas Instruments 9900. NMOS is the most popular microprocessor technology. TTL and ECL microprocessor, relatively uncommon, are used where high-speed operation is required.

Integrated-injection logic (I^2L) is being developed as a relatively new microprocessor technology. It was conceived as allowing high speed and high integration density, at the same time having low power requirements. The future of I^2L technology is uncertain: there is only limited compatibility with other technologies. An example of an I^2L microprocessor is the Texas Instrument SBP 0400.

NMOS microprocessors, with fact access to associated memories and with fast cycle times, will continue to predominate. The problem of interfacing to circuits based on other technologies is likely to persist. There will be more special interface devices, more on-chip interfacing functions, and further efforts to combine technologies on a single substrate. Other technologies may become relevant (eg electron beam lithography).

USES OF ICs AND MICROS

Integrated circuits – used as memories and to process information – now form the hardware basis for all modern computer systems. Microprocessors are the effective 'brains' of all modern microcomputers, and serve to enhance the flexibility and performance of countless other artefacts. It is to integrated circuits that we owe the relative cheapness and power of today's smallest computers (the tiny Intel 4004 had the same processing power as the 30-ton ENIAC); and the vast processing abilities of the world's largest computing machines, the supercomputers applied to meteorological, military and other tasks.

It is thus integrated circuits – today predominantly silicon-based but with a growing family of products based on other technologies (eg gallium arsenide) – that provide the effective intelligence for modern AI systems. Increasingly it appears that the hydrocarbon substances out of which biological nervous systems are built have no permanent prerogative regarding intelligence. Intelligence, we are finding, can be structured into artificial systems based on silicon circuits. It is time to focus again on the theme of artificial intelligence that is central to the present book.

SUMMARY

This chapter has focused on the emergence of semiconductor technologies as the basis of modern computer systems. The early transistor, a discrete device, ushered in the second generation of computers. When it was found possible to link several transistors and other components on the same integrated circuit, the third generation was born. With more complex integrated circuits – for example, microprocessors able to incorporate all the traditional CPU functions – we moved into the fourth generation; and moreover were encouraged to imagine the further computer generations that would follow.

As with all evolutionary processes, the semiconductor developments that occurred from the late-1930s to the early 1970s proceeded in small (often seemingly obvious) steps. However the cumulative impact on computer technology has proved both dramatic and revolutionary. It is easy to represent this period as the one in which the intelligent machine was first perceived as a practical possibility. We need to trace, albeit briefly, the growing AI consciousness during this period.

8   AI in Focus

INTRODUCTION

We have seen that artificial intelligence has been a persistent concept in human thought over the centuries, though modern specialists usually prefer to place its practical origins in, say, the 1950s. This is partly a semantic matter. Define AI one way, and it is four thousand years old; define it another and it is only forty; and some sceptics would argue that it has not yet arrived. It is worth glancing at some definitions of artificial intelligence before profiling its character in the 1950s and 1960s.

There are in fact many difficulties in defining 'intelligence' – whether natural or artificial. We can ask whether it is concerned with thought or behaviour. Is it concerned essentially with effective symbol manipulation? Or with such activities as willing, choosing, remembering and feeling? We all agree that there are *types* of intelligence: the skilled musician may be hopeless at mathematics; the innovative mathematician may be a dullard in human relationships. Though at the same time it is tempting to regard intelligence as a *general* characteristic, somehow portable between different intellectual or practical demands. Pyle (1979) has suggested that 'intelligence' is a 'situation-specific' word, able to take on different meanings at different times and in different circumstances. We can indicate briefly how various researchers tended to view intelligence:

> Binet: to judge well, to comprehend well, to reason well.

> Spearman: general intelligence ... involves mainly the 'education of relations and correlates'.

Terman: the capacity to form concepts and to grasp their significance.

Vernon: 'all-round thinking capacity' or 'mental efficiency'.

Burt: innate, general, cognitive ability.

Heim: intelligent activity consists in grasping the essentials in a situation and responding appropriately to them.

Wechsler: the aggregate or global capacity of the individual to act purposefully, to think rationally and to deal effectively with the environment.

Piaget: adaptation to the physical and social environment.

Workers in AI are often no less troubled about the nature of intelligence, wanting to devise useful definitions to satisfy an often sceptical laity. Douglas Hofstadter, for example, an AI researcher at Indiana University, has indicated what he regards as the 'essential abilities for intelligence' – these include the ability to respond to situations flexibly, to exploit fortuitous circumstances, to make sense out of ambiguous or contradicting messages, to find similarities in situations separated by differences, and to generate new concepts and novel ideas. We can speculate on the extent to which computers can behave in such ways. Hofstadter (1979) has remarked that 'the strange flavour of AI work is that people try to put together long sets of rules in strict formalisms which tell inflexible machines how to be flexible'.

Feigenbaum and McCorduck (1983) suggest that 'if we can imagine an artifact that can collect, assemble, choose among, understand, perceive, and know, then we have an artificial intelligence'. Though, paradoxically enough, not all AI specialists see the study of artificial intelligence as throwing light on *machine* capabilities. Thus Boden (1977) reckons that AI is 'the use of computer programs and programming techniques to cast light on the principles of intelligence in general and human thought in particular'. And she is not much interested in hardware ('Computers are metallic machines of intrinsic interest to electronic engineers but not, as such, to many others'), though if machines are to behave intelligently in the world then appropriate hardware is essential. A computer program *per se* is only an arrangement of symbols: for manifest intelligence to exist, the program will have to run on a physical system.

The active character of AI is conveyed by Marvin Minsky in a much-quoted definition: 'Artificial intelligence is the science of making machines do things that would require intelligence if done by men.' But this clearly begs the question of intelligence: it assumes that we can recognise intelligence when we see it. A definition framed by Aaron Sloman (1978), an AI worker at Sussex University, combines some of the research requirements individually preferred by different specialists. Here AI is defined by identifying its three main aims:

- theoretical analysis of possible effective explanations of intelligent behaviour;
- explaining human abilities;
- construction of intelligent artefacts.

This approach has the merit of presenting a wide agenda, but again it makes no attempt to define intelligence.

The term 'artificial intelligence' is usually regarded as having been invented by John McCarthy in 1956, then an assistant professor of mathematics in Hanover, N.H. At that time he convened a conference at Dartmouth College that signalled to many observers the beginning of AI as a separate branch of computer science. A central aim was to bring together serious workers in the field and to establish communication between them. A number of those who attended – Allen Newell, Herbert Simon, Marvin Minsky and John McCarthy himself – are now universally regarded as leading AI pioneers.

There are other reasons also for regarding the 1950s as an important launchpad for what was to become, albeit in a somewhat disjointed fashion, one of the most important technological developments of the twentieth century (see Turing; and Wiener and Cybernetics, below). Patrick Winston, Professor of Computer Science at the MIT Artificial Intelligence Laboratory, has (in Winston and Prendergast, eds, 1984) depicted the pre-1960 years as the 'prehistory' of artificial intelligence, with 'dawn' breaking out in the late-1950s. We can see AI coming into focus in the 1950s and 1960s, ready for dramatic expansion in subsequent years. This chapter charts some of the early developments that prepared the ground for what was to follow.

(It is worth highlighting, in view of the rapid computer developments over the last four decades, the early notion that *all* computers were effective examples of artificial intelligence. For various practical, philosophical and psychological reasons, AI is today regarded as a subset of computer science. But a first-generation stored-program computer could do differential equations. A dog that could do as much would be regarded as highly intelligent.)

THE DEVELOPING ATMOSPHERE

The 1950s and 1960s were highly amenable to the development of artificial intelligence. The post-war optimism was allied to an enthusiastic search for new methods and techniques in industry, commerce and elsewhere. There was a certain exhilarating flexibility of thought and attitude. The atmosphere was right for a fresh look at what the new computer-based systems might achieve. But it was inevitable, in such an atmosphere, that imagination should outrun practical accomplishment. This led to a reaction against AI ambitions (AI workers were seen as long on promise, short on delivery) – until, in the late 1970s, the AI quest again achieved a high profile and began to deliver practical working systems.

In the immediate post-war world, observers – not always well-informed – were quick to draw analogies between computers and the human brain. Often the analogies were crude and unhelpful, but the idea that there is a discernible parity between certain types of natural and artificial systems is a central theme of the AI doctrine. Efforts to highlight the (real or imagined) similarities between biological nervous systems and the emerging families of computers were inspired in part by the pioneering work of such thinkers as Turing, von Neumann and Norbert Wiener (see below). Today it is often forgotten how much such early researchers were interested in biological, as well as electrical or electronic, phenomena.

It is worth indicating some 1960s publications that were typical
of the genre:

J Diebold and Associates (1963) developed an idea for 'an
organic computer'. This followed the first (1960) conference
on bionics (*bio*logical electro*nics*), a word coined by Hans
Oestreicher of the Wright-Patterson Air Force Base, Ohio,
to denote the design of artefacts based on biological
principles. In the early–1960s a programme of research at
Tulane University aimed to use bioelectronics to correlate
recorded brain activity with human behaviour.

B Kh Gurevich (1962) describes similarities between 'reasoning' automats and the brains of the higher mammals.
Attention is given to the automats designed by D M Mackay
and to his views. This report, distributed by the US
government is a translation of a Russian article.

A report in *Computer Digest* (*2*, 12, 1967) cites a Russian
cybernetics expert who believes that artificial intelligence
will be based on such biological elements as self-
preservation, the instinct for reproduction, and social behaviour. Von Neumann wrote a piece on self-reproducing
automata in 1966.

Various papers dealt with the concept of thinking machines
(eg Smith, 1963; Steel, 1966; Pfeiffer, 1962; Samuel, 1963;
Kernan, 1965). One author – Culbertson (1963) – aimed to
explain in detail how states of consciousness can be created
artificially. Others propose specific design features for AI
systems, often drawing on biological example (eg Carne,
1965; Burton, 1967; Hammond, 1965). One contemporary
publication on artificial intelligence (Lachenbruch et al,
1962) carried a bibliography of 1129 supplementary specific
references and 67 general sources.

H A Simon (1967) described how human emotions may be
construed as information-processing interrupts, and other
researchers wrote in a similar vein. Kilmer et al (1969)
described a biological command structure rooted in computational concepts.

We can see that there was a veritable explosion of interest in AI matters in the 1960s. This is well shown in the collections of papers edited by various specialists: see, for example *Computers and Thought* (Feigenbaum and Feldman, 1963) and *Semantic Information Processing* (Minsky, 1968). And it can be seen from such publications that various detailed research programmes were under way and influencing the climate of thought.

The atmosphere of expectation was also being influenced, as always by fictional elements in the culture – in, for example, films and tales.

The first of Isaac Asimov's robot stories appeared in 1941, and a flood of further yarns appeared in the years that followed. The Asimov robots contained 'positronic' brains which sometimes, malfunctioned, requiring at such times the services of a 'robo-psychologist'. Again, albeit at a fanciful level, the idea was nurtured that it was possible to view certain types of artefacts in anthropomorphic terms.

In Asimov we found that robots could have intentions, affections, fears and all the rest – fully fledged psychologies with which their human friends and colleagues had to deal. But fiction is one thing, fact another.

In the real world, there were parallel efforts to devise functional robots. M W Thring, Professor of Mechanical Engineering at the University of London, for example, describes (1983) how he studied robot possibilities in the 1950s and 1960s.

In 1963 he delivered a paper on the theme of a domestic robot to the Royal Society of Arts; and other writers were beginning to speculate on the similarities between the human nervous system and the control systems of robots (see, for example, McCulloch, 1965). The first patent application for an industrial robotic device was filed by George Devol in 1954.

It is clear that many factors were now combining to raise the profile of artificial intelligence. Parallels were drawn between biological and artificial systems, purely theoretical concepts were being developed in such areas as logic and semantic processing, and industrial artefacts – following the great strides in twentieth-century automation – were now increasingly being viewed in anthropomorphic terms. Theory, practice and fiction were combining to encourage the design and construction of artefacts that could be said to be capable of intelligent activity in the real world. We need to highlight some of the contributing elements in more detail, prior to offering a brief profile of particular AI efforts in particular fields.

CONTRIBUTING ELEMENTS

General

The various elements that contributed to the expansion of AI accomplishment were necessarily, in the first instance, theoretical and speculative: only later could functional real-world systems be grounded in the spectrum of adequate co-operative theories that were developed.

Some of the theoretical advances related to logic and mathematics: researchers worked to build on Boole, Turing's 'computable number' theories and other developments. Prawitz (1965), for example, introduced a natural deduction system with particular innovative features. Newell and Simon (1956) had already discussed the Logic Theorist deduction system for propositional logic at the celebrated Dartmouth College conference; and Minsky was working on idea that would come to be used in Gelernter's theorem prover for elementary geometry (see Gelernter, 1963). Many aspects of information-handling theory were being expanded; and new schools of psychology – heavily influenced by the newly-emerging categories of information processing – were being developed, as *cognitivism* or *cognitive psychology,* and used to dispel the old stimulus-response (S-R) behaviourism.

In this fertile and highly influential climate, particular contributing elements were of prime importance. It is worth providing a brief profile of:

- emerging hardware and software;

- communications theory;

- linguistic analysis;

- cognitive psychology;
- heuristics and fuzziness;
- Wiener and cybernetics
- Turing and AI.

These are some of the principal elements that combined, in a mutually fructifying concoction, to stimulate the AI efforts of the 1950s and 1960s, and to lay the basis of future AI work.

EMERGING HARDWARE AND SOFTWARE

The evolution of computer hardware has already been described for the 1950s and 1960s (Chapter 7). Through this period machines were becoming faster and, relatively, more economic. The rapidly developing technological base meant that information storage was rapidly increasing, reliability was improving, and new computer architectures were being designed. Today we often hear strictures against the limitations of von Neumann architectures (and it is true that today there is a departure from mainstream sequential processing), but von Neumann himself proposed parallel architectures and the first parallel processors appeared in the late-sixties. The Illiac IV, developed at the University of Illinois in the years 1967–71, was a parallel machine comprising sixty-four independent processing units that could operate simultaneously. This computer could execute 200 million instructions per second. At the same time there was massive development of integrated circuits, with the first large-scale integration (LSI) chips – individually carrying the equivalent of thousands of transistors – appearing also in the late-1960s.

Such hardware developments were of obvious importance to the progress realisation of AI circuits. It was rapidly becoming clear that – whatever intelligence was – it needed high levels of storage capacity and a fast processing capability. Machines without such features could only strive after intelligence in the most mundane sense.

There was also significant development in programming techniques and practice, changes that were to help to define the character of the newly-emerging computer generations. In particular, from the point of view of AI, in 1958 John McCarthy invented LISP, the main programming language used in AI research throughout the world. Large development systems have been built to support the language, and it is universally regarded as having important features that are uniquely suited to the investigation and implementation of AI possibilities. The later logic-programming language PROLOG was adopted for the Japanese fifth-generation project but it has not displaced LISP in most of its traditional applications areas. (A detailed description of LISP is given in Barr and Feigenbaum, 1982.)

Such developments in programming – refinement of traditional methods and innovations particularly relevant to AI – were able, in conjunction with the simultaneous hardware developments, to dramatically expand the scope of intelligent artefacts.

COMMUNICATIONS THEORY

The task of handling information depends directly on the existence of an adequate theory of communications. In this field, information is essentially a quantitative element, somewhat removed from the popular idea of information as something contained in conversation or books. In 1949 C E Shannon and W Weaver published a seminal work, *The Mathematical Theory of Communication,* in which it was argued that information was a concrete measurable quantity. This approach suggests that information can have both a quantitative and a semantic aspect. Thus Dretske (1981) was later to observe that the technical (mathematical) theory of information 'deals with amounts of information – not, except indirectly and by implication, with the information that comes in those amounts'. In the same spirit, other researchers have distinguished between information in its technical sense from the *value* of the received information (Miller, 1953) and from its *importance* or *truth* (Bar-Hillel, 1964).

The early mathematical theory of information was important to the development of computing and so to the evolution of AI (it was also of crucial importance to the rapidly changing field of telecommunications). Soon, however, it became obvious that artificial intelligence was concerned with more than a quantitative definition of information. Semantics too was a vital, and directly relevant, subject area. Part of the later progress of AI – in, for example, natural language processing – was the direct result of developments in semantic theory. Such topics also relate to the question of linguistic analysis.

LINGUISTIC ANALYSIS

Developments in linguistic analysis in the 1950s represent a further contribution that was to influence psychology, the expanding field of AI and other areas. These advances are largely associated with the name of Noam Chomsky, MIT Professor of Modern Languages and Linguistics. His book *Syntactic Structures,* published in 1957, is a seminal work that encouraged a new scrutiny of syntax. (This book was anticipated in 1955 in Chomsky's lengthy monograph, *The Logical Structure of Linguistic Theory*. Some of the ideas were to be revised in his 1965 text, *Aspects of the Theory of Syntax*.)

A central purpose was to establish the existence of a universal grammar for all possible languages. It is argued that the principles of grammar are so deep and complex that only an organism 'preset' to their complexities could learn vocabularies and use language in a coherent way. This has implications for understanding the nature of the human mind on the one hand and the character of linguistic utterances on the other. The interpretation departs from earlier linguistic theories that tended to emphasise that linguistic forms were the result of environment (including teaching), not defined by a preprogrammed structure.

Chomsky's work – in, for example, developing the theory of *generative grammar* and *transformational grammar* – was a principal impulse behind the newly-emerging cognitive psychology and behind the development of computer-language theory. At the same time new computer languages and new data structures were being developed by computer specialists. We have already mentioned the invention of the AI language LISP in 1958; ALGOL – less important for AI but containing some LISP like features (lists, recursion facilities) – was invented in 1960. Again a number of advances were combining to shape the rapidly developing computer science, a psychology increasingly influenced by information processing, and other disciplines.

A further summary of Chomsky's standard theory is offered in his 1971 text, *Deep Structure, Surface Structure and Semantic Interpretation* (in Steinberg and Jakobovits, 1971; and see also the popular account of Chomsky in Lyons, 1970). In brief, the theory proposes that the generation of sentences begins with a context-free grammar producing a *sentence structure*. The structure is then supplied in a formal fashion with words selected from a *lexicon*. The grammar and lexicon together constitute the *base* of the grammar, its output being a *deep structure*; and the base and the *transformational rules* (used to translate between deep and surface structures) comprise the *syntactic component*. Other elements – *phonological component* and *semantic component* – determine, respectively, sounds and meanings.

Chomsky aimed to provide a comprehensive and generalised theory of language structure; and it was seen that this had relevance to psychology, sociology, computer science and politics. It is no accident that Chomsky is America's leading dissident, accusing the intellectual establishment of supporting unjust power structures by focusing only on trivial surface matters rather than addressing fundamental problems. Chomsky's thought is multifaceted, though nicely integrated in a formal sense. Here we need to stress his impact on cognitive psychology and computer science.

COGNITIVE PSYCHOLOGY

In Chomsky's *Syntactic Structures* there is a determined effort to identify and describe the various structures that are essential to language usage: for example, the theory is concerned with such aspects as sentence construction, the creation of a spoken utterance, comprehension, the transmission of meaning, and the response of a listener. It was inevitable that such a focus should encourage speculation on the mental structures that together define the human mind: this was a radical departure from the simple 'black-box' model of naive behaviourism.

Workers in other disciplines also were interested in the question of mental structures. For example, Jean Piaget (1954) speculated on the growth of mental structures (and their associated processes) as a means of explaining the developmental changes in psychology of the growing human beings. In such a fashion the biological orientation of Piaget was linked, in direction of focus, to the linguistic preoccupations of Chomsky. Hence a conflux of factors – linguistic analysis, Piaget's developmental psychology and the rapid advances in computer science – was encouraging the development of an information-processing model of *Homo sapiens* on the one hand and a growing interest in artificial intelligence on the other.

At the same time other researchers were making proposals that, in other characteristic ways, reinforced these two important preoccupations. A book by Miller, Galanter and Pribram (1960) drew attention to the idea of the mental *plan,* a behaviour-generating system analogous to the rapidly-developing electronic computer. The plan, like the computer, uses feedback loops, a common mechanism in cybernetic systems (see Wiener and Cybernetics, below). Neisser (1967) was another researcher who worked to develop a general information-processing model of the human mind. Again the influence of computer science is plain: the model relies upon such elements as memory stores, information transfer, and input/output processes. And in 1971, another researcher, Earl Hunt, was asking: 'What kind of a computer is man?' Here an effort was made to describe a computer that 'thinks like a man'; and the AI programme was also set yet more securely on the agenda.

Even as early as the 1950s and 1960s there was a growing reciprocal influence between human psychology and artificial intelligence. Minsky (1968) identified three areas of activities that he saw as linked by their respective roots in cybernetics: 'the search for simple basic principles'; 'an attempt to build working models of human behaviour'; and 'an attempt to build intelligent machines'. At the same time it was emphasised that the machines need not be 'simple, biological, or humanoid' - which suggests that intelligence need not necessarily be human.

HEURISTICS AND FUZZINESS

During this period particular concepts were being framed that would come to influence, to differing degrees, the development of AI in subsequent years. At this stage it is worth mentioning *heuristics* and *fuzziness.*

AI researchers have been concerned at the seeming discrepancy between the traditional well-formed (algorithmic) processes of mainstream computing and the less rigorous 'rule of thumb' methods that characterise much human mental performance. It was seen that computing methods were needed that more closely resembled those used by human beings. One result was the development of the heuristic concept. A classic definition is given in Newell, Shaw and Simon (1957): 'A process that *may* solve a given problem, but offers no guarantees of doing so, is called a *heuristic* for that problem' (original italics). Minsky (1963), however, was keen to emphasise that 'heuristic' should not be regarded as the opposite to 'foolproof' ('this has caused some confusion in the literature'). And Feigenbaum and Feldman (1963) saw a heuristic as 'a rule of thumb, strategy, trick, simplification, or any other kind of device which drastically limits search for solutions in large problem spaces'; this is a method of obtaining 'solutions which are good enough most of the time'. The concept of *heuristic search,* a specific AI method, was introduced in the mid-1960s. Nilsson (1971) makes an important distinction between heuristic search and blind search.

The heuristic strategy may be regarded as one in which a solution to a problem is sought in circumstances where it is impossible to obtain exhaustive information for the complete solution to be predictably obtained. This is in fact how human beings operate. They build up heuristic methods through experience and approximate solutions to problems are usually sufficient. One factor is that the information manipulated by human problem solvers is often partial and inexact: awareness of this information *fuzziness* has inspired some researchers to explore the possibility of introducing fuzzy methods into computer processes.

One of the first efforts to develop a fuzzy logic (a theory of fuzzy sets) was made by Zadeh (1965). There is now a FUZZY language, designed to aid reasoning with fuzzy sets; and the fuzzy concept has been incorporated (as, for example, as the 'uncertainty factor' in MYCIN) in expert systems (see Chapter 14). Both heuristics and fuzzy methods can be seen as effective ways of enabling artificial systems to evolve an intelligence that more closely approximates to that of human beings.

WIENER AND CYBERNETICS

We have already highlighted efforts to compare the features and behaviour of biological systems with those of artefacts. A principal way in which this can be done is through the science of cybernetics. Cybernetics (the Greek word means helmsman) applied equally to the hierarchy of biological systems (cells, organs, organisms, societies, etc) on the one hand and to the various types of adaptive artefacts (usually computer-based systems using feedback, homeostasis, etc) on the other. Today the word *cybernetics* is often used to denote only artificial systems: this debased usage is unhelpful.

In the immediate pre-war years there was growing interest in comparing the operating and engineering principles of living systems with those of (actual and possible) artefacts (we have seen that Turing and von Neumann were keen to compare biological brain architectures with designs for possible electronic computers). In 1946 Warren McCulloch at MIT organised a meeting of about twenty scientists in different disciplines. The conference, Mechanisms Underlying Purposive Behaviour, was attended by specialists in psychiatry, psychology, neurophysiology, sociology, mathematics, electronics and other subjects. The discussions took place in a New York Hotel on 8 and 9 March, 1946; and one writer (Steve Heims, 1980) observes that John von Neumann and Norbert Wiener were the star performers.

Von Neumann was interested in the current state of computer design (then of course scarcely into first generation), and Wiener was concerned to emphasise the importance of purposive behaviour in both biological and artificial systems, and how such elements as feedback and information were crucial to their operation. Wiener's contribution prefigured his seminal text, *Cybernetics: Control and Communication in the Animal and the Machine,* published in 1948. The group of specialists first dubbed itself the 'Conference for Circular Causal and Feedback Mechanisms in Biological and Social Systems'; but fortunately Wiener's inclination prevailed and the group became known as the 'Conference on Cybernetics'.

It was soon realised that efforts to develop mathematical models of biological nervous systems were fraught with difficulty (von Neumann observed that the problems 'reside in the exceptional complexity of the human nervous system, and indeed of any nervous system'). Nonetheless, progress was made: already Wiener and others had managed to develop mathematical models of primitive nervous systems, and particular simple organisms (eg the bacteriophage) was of interest because it could reproduce. Wiener remained a leading light of the group, and was later to apply cybernetic principles to the development of aids for the disabled (whereas von Neumann became committed to weapons research). He observed: 'It is easy to put pressure gauges into the artificial fingers, and these can communicate electrical impulses to a suitable circuit. This can in turn activate devices acting on the living skin . . . .'

Early cybernetics may thus be seen as an attempt to understand living systems in term of the engineering principles of control and communications. The corollary was that, once this sort of understanding has been gained, it would be possible to design artefacts that could either supplement human performance with a direct physical connection (as with prostheses for the disabled) or that could function intelligently, able to originate purposes of their own. By the early 1970s there was much speculation about the possibility of autonomous artefacts. For example, W Ross Ashby (1972) was asking whether it was possible for the cybernetician to 'make a machine that can choose its own goal'. And the relevance of cybernetics to many seemingly non-computational activities was increasingly being perceived.

Thus Jasia Reichardt (1971) presents an anthology of essays exploring how cybernetic principles can inform such areas as art, music and poetry (Japanese haiku). It was now being proposed that even artistic creativity could be properly viewed as a cybernetic matter, with such elements as feedback, information handling and computation being the key considerations in any creative enterprise. The later Gaia hypothesis of J E Lovelock (1979, for a subsequent summary) proposed that the Earth itself is a vast cybernetic system, able to adjust the conditions of the biosphere to maintain an effective homeostasis.

Cybernetic forces were, it seemed, ubiquitous phenomena. In particular, for our purposes, an understanding of how they operated provided further clues for the design of intelligent artefacts.

TURING*

In 1950 Turing published a startlingly prophetic paper, *Computing Machinery and Intelligence,* on AI. Here he comments on whether machines will be able to think:

> ' ... I believe that at the end of the century the use of words and general educated opinion will have altered so much that one will be able to speak of machines thinking without expecting to be contradicted.'

He begins the paper with what he calls the 'imitation game', a ploy that is today known as the *Turing test.* Here an interrogator is separated from a person (or a machine) under interrogation, and communication is only possible using a teletype. The idea is that if the human cannot tell, through the interrogration, whether the communication is with another person or a machine, then the machine – if indeed it *is* a machine giving the answers – may be regarded as intelligent. Turing was well aware that many people would find absurd the notion that a machine could be intelligent. So he anticipated some of the objections and answered them. He presents nine objections to the idea that machines could think, and presents counter-comments in each case:

- *the theological objection* suggests that no animal or machine can think because God has only given souls to men and women (Turing: 'I am unable to accept any part of this ... I am not very impressed with theological arguments whatever they may be used to support');

- *the "heads in the sand" objection* suggests that the consequences of machines thinking would be too dreadful ('I do not think that this argument is sufficiently substantial to require refutation');

- *the mathematical objection* cites Gödel's theorem to show that there are necessary limitations to the power of artificial systems (' ... it has been stated, without any sort of proof, that no such limitations apply to the human intellect');

---

*This section originally appeared in *Introducing Artificial Intelligence* (NCC Publications, 1984)

- *the argument from consciousness* as represented, for examination in Professor Jefferson's Lister Oration (1949): 'Not until a machine can write a sonnet or compose a concerto because of thoughts and emotions felt ... could we agree that machine equals brain ... No mechanism could feel ... pleasure at its successes, grief when its valves fuse, be warmed by flattery, be made miserable by its mistakes, be charmed by sex, be angry or depressed when it cannot get what it wants'. Turing comments that this argument relies upon a solipsist posture ('... the only way to know that a *man* thinks is to be that particular man'), and he concludes: 'I think that most of those who support the argument from consciousness could be persuaded to abandon it rather than be forced into the solipsist position';

- *arguments from various disabilities* suggest that however competent machines become they will always be unable to do particular things, like 'be kind, resourceful, beautiful, friendly ... have initiative, have a sense of humour, tell right from wrong, make mistakes ... fall in love, enjoy strawberries and cream ... make someone fall in love ... learn from experience ... use words properly, be the subject of its own thought ... have as much diversity of behaviour as a man, do something really new ...'. Turing observes caustically that no support is usually offered for these statements and that they mostly boil down to forms of the argument from consciousness;

- *Lady Lovelace's objection* ('The Analytical Engine has no pretensions to *originate* anything. It can do *whatever we know how to order it* to perform') implies that machines are mindless slaves, incapable of any degree of intelligence. After a slight detour, Turing arrives back at the argument from consciousness ('It is a line of argument that we must consider closed'). Today we are sufficiently aware of computers accomplishing new things not to attach much weight to this objection;

- *the argument from continuity in the nervous system* suggests that, since a small error in the information about the size of a nervous impulse impinging on a neuron may significantly affect the size of the outgoing impulse, it is impossible to

mimic the behaviour of the nervous system with a discrete
state machine (Turing: ' . . . if we adhere to the conditions of
the imitation game, the interrogator will not be able to take
any advantage of this difference');

– *the argument from informality of behaviour* suggests that it is
impossible to provide a set of rules to indicate what a person
should do in every conceivable set of circumstances, and so
people are not machines. Here Turing emphasises that we
will only find such rules through scientific observation, and
we know of no circumstances where we may claim to have
searched enough. Moreover would anyone expect to be able
to understand totally a computer program by examining a
limited number of computer responses. Talking of computer
output, Turing comments: 'I would defy anyone to learn
from these replies sufficient about the program to be able to
predict any replies to untried values';

– *the argument from sensory preception* suggests that human
beings have powers not available to machines. Perhaps
surprisingly, Turing finds this argument 'quite a strong one'
('If telepathy is admitted it will be necessary to tighten our
test'). Later AI workers (eg Hofstadter, 1979 – 'My own
point of view . . . is that ESP does not exist') have been less
impressed than Turing by this sort of argument.

By the time Alan Turing came to write *Computing Machinery and
Intelligence,* his reputation – resting on his mathematical work,
the proposal for universal ('Turing') machines, the cracking of
the Enigma codes, the design for the ACE machine, etc – was
well established. When he threw his weight behind the newly-
emerging discipline of AI (not yet called such), he gave significant
credibility to the idea that human beings would be able to design
intelligent artefacts.

At the same time there were many important efforts to develop
AI systems. It is useful to indicate such efforts briefly in the
present chapter (most of the topics are dealt with in more detail in
Part 6).

EARLY AI EFFORTS

General

The first working AI systems were usually dedicated to a specific type of application. There was always the lure of an artificial system able to adapt a flexible intelligence to problems in different domains; but such a scheme was rarely attempted, the aim being to mimic, simulate or duplicate specific aspects of human mental performance. We will find (in Part 6) that this focus has persisted in modern times: AI systems are individually directed at this or that task, rarely expected to manifest anything resembling a general-purpose intelligent capability.

Memory and Learning

Some of the earliest electronic AI systems were designed to simulate aspects of human memory and learning. For instance, in the period 1954 to 1964 Edward Feigenbaum and Herbert Simon developed the EPAM (Elementary Perceiver and Memorizer) program. This was the first model of human verbal-learning performance, using nonsense syllables in various ways to explore verbal responses to verbal stimuli. In a performance mode, EPAM was expected to produce responses to stimulus syllables; and in a learning mode, the system was able to discriminate and to associate stimuli and responses.

During the 1950s and 1960s A L Samuel studied how a computer might learn to play checkers (draughts). He used three specific learning methods: rote learning, polynomial evaluation functions and signature tables. The system improved its perform-ance with experience, a notable early AI success.

John McCarthy (1958) produced one of the earliest papers on machine learning: here he suggested the design of an advice-taking system that could use proferred advice to plan and perform activities in the world. This idea prefigured modern experts that are expected to accumulate information as a necessary condition for expert performance in the real world. McCarthy declared (in 1958): 'Our ultimate objective is to make programs that learn from their experience as effectively as human do.'

Pattern Recognition

Efforts were made thirty years ago to enable computers to recognise patterns of various sorts. Such endeavours continue today to achieve a wide range of objectives (for example, face recognition for security systems, vision capability in industrial robots). It was soon perceived that pattern recognition was relevant to many human problems. Thus, in a classic paper, Selfridge and Neisser (1963) emphasised that man's ability 'to solve problems, prove theorems and generally run his life depends' upon being able to abstract relevant patterns from a welter of data.

Another researcher, Murray Eden (1968), noted that there had been 'success in performing pattern-recognition tasks by mechanical means', but at the same time emphasised the limitations of current systems (the methods could be used to classify only a few well-defined patterns, 'but are likely to lack any significant value for classifying any other set of patterns'). The early systems were dedicated to particular tasks of pattern recognition, as indeed are some of the most impressive pattern-recognition systems in the modern world (eg fingerprint-identification systems, the Wisard face-recognition facility, etc). Here, as elsewhere, there were early successes that nonetheless revealed important limitations.

Natural Language Processing

Interpreted in the widest sense, natural language processing (NLP) can be taken to include translation, voice and speech recognition, voice and speech synthesis, voice and speech understanding, printed- or handwritten-word understanding, etc (though today these various topics are separated out – see Chapter 10).

Anthony Oettinger was the first researcher to produce (in 1955) a program able to carry out a word-for-word translation of Russian into English. In 1963 he observed: 'The notion of … fully automatic high quality mechanical translation, planted by overzealous propagandists for automatic translation on both sides of the Iron Curtain and nurtured by the wishful thinking of potential users, blossomed like a vigorous weed.' The atmosphere of the time was well conveyed by Bar-Hillel (1960): he pointed out that the problems that had been solved were only the simplest ones whereas the 'few' remaining problems 'were the harder ones – very hard indeed'.

Other early work in natural language processing included:

- Daniel Bobrow's STUDENT program, a system for solving algebra word problems (Minsky has dubbed this 'a demonstration *par* excellence of the power of using meaning to solve linguistic problems');

- Ross Quillian Semantic Memory Program;

- Robert Lindsay's SAD-SAM (Syntactic Appraiser and Diagrammer – Semantic Analyzing Machine), able to accept information in English and then answer questions about its accumulating corpus of knowledge;

- BASEBALL, able to answer questions about its data store;

- Joseph Weizenbaum's ELIZA, able to function as a non-directive therapist in its conversation with the user.

Efforts to achieve isolated-word recognition systems necessarily preceded work on speech understanding. The idea with word recognition (Vincens, 1969) is to compare an incoming speech signal with an internally-stored representation of the words' acoustical patterns. Typically the store of acoustical representations is small and the results are far from perfect. Today some impressive results have been achieved with relatively large vocabularies, but in the 1960s the systems were primitive and unreliable.

The problems are obvious: difficulties with interference; different articulations of the same word by the same person at different times; imperfect match between incoming signal and the stored 'template', etc. In the early–1970s, to overcome these and other difficulties, the Advanced Research Projects Agency (ARPA) of the US Department of Defense funded a five-year programme on speech understanding, and a number of important systems developed out of this work (see Chapter 10).

Language is often represented as central to human intelligence: we use language in thought, and intelligent behaviour is manifested usually in a social environment in which verbal intercourse is a prime requisite. Computers have always been adept at handling their own characteristic language structures – from machine code to the most high-level symbolisms. But there are obvious subtleties in *natural* language with which computers are at present poorly equipped to deal. Perhaps when computer-based systems can handle the complexities of natural language with some proficiency* there will be no debate about whether artefacts can be intelligent.

Game Playing

The possibility of designing game-playing machines has interested researchers from the earliest times, not least because *gaming* can be seen as an analogue or metaphor for many real-life situations (eg industrial negotiations, human relationships, war making, etc). In this spirit it may be argued that the lessons learned from a chess or poker program may enable a person to conduct his/her affairs more intelligently, may enhance the security of the state, etc.

In 1912, Leonardo Torres Quevedo (1852–1936) built an automatic electromagnetic machine capable of playing an end game of chess; and in 1951 Leonardo's son, G Torres Quevedo, operating the machine at the Cybernetic Congress in Paris, was challenged by Norbert Wiener. It is reported that the machine won every game. (Leonardo had commented: 'The ancient automatons . . . imitate the appearance and movements of living beings, but this has not much practical interest, and what is wanted is a class of apparatus which leaves out the mere visible gestures of man and attempts to accomplish the results which a living person obtains, thus replacing a man by a machine.')

With the first generation of electronic game-playing systems, the various electromagnetic and electromechanical devices were finally routed. Von Neumann became interested in game theory;

---

*It is worth remembering that a comprehensive verbal proficiency must span *all* areas of human verbal expression (eg transfer of facts, exhortation, emotional expression, literary creation, etc).

and Turing, with David Champernowne (who later worked on how computers might compose music), wrote one of the first chess-playing programs, 'Turochamp'. (The early automatic chess players were very primitive, but today they are beating international specialists: for example, International Master David Levy beaten by the Chess 4.7 program; Grandmaster John Nunn beaten by Chess Champion Mark V.)

In 1956 Shannon highlighted some of the problems in designing a chess-playing computer and made specific design proposals (though he did not actually write a chess program). He suggested that a computer programmed as described 'would play a fairly strong game at speeds comparable to human speeds'. In 1955 Allen Newell declared that the mechanisms required for an automatic chess player 'are so complicated that it is impossible to predict whether they will work' (see Sayre and Crossons, 1963). But soon he was to declare, with J C Shaw and H A Simon, that 'we have at least entered the arena of human play – we can beat a beginner' (Feigenbaum and Feldman, 1963). By 1957 a program designed by Alex Bernstein for the IBM 704 played two 'passable amateur games'.

We have already cited the Samuel checker player (as an example of programmed learning). Samuel himself calculated that even for checkers, a relatively simple game, the size of the search space was around 10 40 – a daunting prospect for any programmer aiming to cover every option. At the same time efforts were being made to program computers to play every imaginable game (blackjack, casino, bridge, go, etc). In 1968 Donald Water wrote a computer program to play draw poker, a game of imperfect information in which psychological factors are crucial. And, before long, the world champion backgammon player would be a computer.

Problem Solving

There is a sense in which all AI programs are designed to solve problems, but usually the problems are specific and well defined and dedicated programs are produced. As we have seen, the idea of a general-purpose program, able to deploy a flexible intelligence in different situations, has always attracted AI researchers.

In 1957 the Logic Theorist of Newell, Shaw and Simon, using a heuristic search, managed to prove 38 out of 52 theorems in *Principia Mathematica* (by Russell and Whitehead). By 1960 their celebrated General Problem Solver (GPS), using means-ends analysis, had solved the 'cannibal and missionary' problem and various other problems in other areas. Newell and Simon declared in 1961 that GPS 'provided a rather good first approximation to an information processing theory of certain kinds of thinking and problem-solving behaviour'.

GPS was developed over a period of ten years, and various versions of the program were produced. It succeeded in solving problems in symbolic integration, resolution theorem proving and puzzles of various types (eleven different kinds of problems in all). There is general recognition that GPS could only solve relatively simple problems in limited domains: what it gained in generality it lost in depth of competence (it could not, for example, compete with the problem-solving competence of special-purpose programs). Part of the reason for GPS's limited scope was the size of its memory, a limitation that prohibited lengthy searches: the generation of new data structures quickly exhausted the available memory.

It has been emphasised (Barr and Feigenbaum, 1981) that GPS was not intended to be a 'performance program'. Instead, as Ernst and Newell (1969) pointed out, it provided 'a series of lessons that give a more perfect view of the nature of problem solving and what is required to construct processes that accomplish it'.

Mathematics

The 1950s and 1960s saw the emergence of various mathematical programs, dealing with geometry, equation solving and other matters Herbert Gelernter wrote the Geometry Theorem Machine in 1959 at the New York IBM Research Centre. The main aim was to provide a program able to solve the problems in high-school textbooks and final examinations in plane geometry. Researchers were pleased to note early successes (as with the *pons asinorum* theorem), but again the early triumphs only occurred in relatively simple areas and a Gelernter prediction in 1960 ('machines will be proving interesting theorems in number theory three years hence') was found to be unduly optimistic.

This period also saw work on the first expert systems (Chapter 14), with DENDRAL (see below), MACSYMA and others. The original specification for the MACSYMA mathematical system was drawn up by Carl Engleman, William Martin and Joel Moses in 1968. The system, able to perform a prodigious range of mathematical tasks, has evolved over the last twenty years and today comprises nearly a quarter of a million words of compiled LISP code and as much again written in the MACSYMA programming language. MACSYMA is able to perform more than 600 different types of mathematical operations including differentiation, integration, Taylor series expansions, matrix operations, order analysis and vector operations. It is accessed via the ARPA Network.

A key factor in the design of MACSYMA was the belief that high-performance systems of this sort should be based on a large body of stored information. This principle, first explored in the 1960s, was to stimulate the later proliferation of *knowledge-based systems* (typically expert systems) in the 1970s and 1980s.

Chemical Analysis

The DENDRAL algorithm was developed in 1964 by Joshua Lederberg to aid chemical analysis: when a set of constituent atoms are specified, the algorithm is able to compute all the possible acrylic molecular structures that could be formed. The Heuristic DENDRAL program, developed via a project that began at Stanford University in 1965, exploited the derived algorithm, data from mass-spectrographic analysis, and rules obtained from expert chemists. As a further development, the Meta-DENDRAL project in 1970 focused on how to derive the rules of mass spectrometry from molecular structures already analysed by human beings. In 1976 the CONGEN program, without DENDRAL's acyclic limitation, became a principal concern.

Education

Systems able to provide individualised instruction were first developed in the 1960s – with emphasis on the idea of 'branching' on the basis of student response. A second type of computer-aided instruction (CAI) – today known as knowledge-based or intelligent CAI – was also being developed by the late-1960s. Some early systems relied on *generative* CAI, a large database being used to generate appropriate problems. Later intelligent CAI systems included SCHOLAR (a geography tutor), WHY (a rainfall causation tutor), SOPHIE (an electronics troubleshooting tutor), GUIDON (a diagnostic problem-solving tutor) and EXCHECK (a logic and set theory tutor).*

Vision

Efforts were made by L G Roberts in 1965 to explore the automatic recognition of three-dimensional objects (earlier work had focused on two-dimensional forms). Roberts chose a hypothetical world comprising cubes, rectangular solids, wedges and hexagonal prisms. The program that he developed was able to analyze a photograph of a scene to identify all the objects. Moreover it could ascertain their orientations and locations in three-dimensional space.

This 'blocks-world' approach has been adopted also by other researchers. A Guzman designed a program in 1968 to recognise cubes and wedges, but unlike the Roberts program Guzman's SEE was not intended to offer a three-dimensional description. G Falk was one of a number of later researchers to work on the identification of three-dimensional objects. (The work of Guzman and Falk was significant for using heuristic techniques.) Such research was to lead to, amongst other things, the provision of visual faculties in robotic systems (Chapter 13).

Robots

In 1954 George C Devol filed a patent application for what was then called Programmed Article Transfer; and in 1961 the patent (No. 2,988,237) was issued by the US Patents Office. Devol anticipated such robotic requirements as program control and positional feedback, and coined the word 'Unimation' to describe

---

*These systems and others are described in detail in Barr and Feigenbaum (1982).

this new type of equipment. Soon after, Joseph Engleberger founded Unimation Inc., the first company to focus solely on robotics: it installed a robot manipulator in 1961 to tend a die-casting machine. Kawasaki Heavy Industries, in Japan, produced their first industrial robot, under licence from Unimation, in 1968. Robots were first controlled by minicomputers in the early-1960s.

At the same time robotics research was being conducted that would lead to the proliferation of robots in the modern world (see Chapter 13). One important experimental device was the Shakey robot, developed in 1968 at the Stanford Research Institute. This device was a mobile system incorporating a television camera (to provide a visual faculty), an optical rangefinder, bump detectors and a radio link to a computer.

SUMMARY

This chapter has profiled the principal elements that combined to lay the basis for the modern AI age. Attention has been given to such aspects as communications theory, linguistic analysis, cognitive psychology, heuristics and cybernetics. It is emphasised that there are many contributing components – in theory, social attitudes, engineering, etc – that have together stimulated the emergence of an important new area of computer science. Brief attention has also been given to such key pioneering thinkers as Alan Turing, John von Neumann and Norbert Wiener.

A brief profile has also been given of early AI efforts, the imaginative first attempts to build intelligence into electronic artefacts. Here we have focused on such areas as memory, learning, pattern recognition, language processing, game playing, mathematics, chemical analysis and education. And we have also sketched some of the first steps in robotics and expert systems (covered in more detail in Chapter 13 and 14 respectively).

It is important to emphasise a key feature of the trends and developments outlined in this chapter. We have seen a progressive convergence of theoretical and practical aspects to facilitate the growth of the AI enterprise and the AI culture. And this phenomenon is also discernible in the context of specific research efforts: so enquiries into problem solving are relevant to many particular research programmes; natural language processing (NLP) research and vision studies are relevant to robotics; and game playing is relevant to the financial and military expert systems that are emerging, in circumstances of some controversy, in the modern world. Increasingly the AI agenda will be perceived to be 'of a whole', though a host of technical and philosophical problems will remain unresolved.

PART 6
1970 TO 1990

9 Cognitivism and Simulation

INTRODUCTION

The emergence of cognitive psychology encouraged the decline of naive behaviourism and forced researchers to speculate about possible mental structures: whereas the behaviourists had been content to regard the mind as an intractable 'black box', attended only by information inputs and generated outputs, the cognitivists were keen to explore the character of the intermediate processing. In this context there was a growing and reciprocal influence between cognitive psychology and AI. Nothing could be accomplished in AI unless researchers were prepared to venture inside the black box, to devise information-processing structures that would be able to produce the appropriate 'mental' performances.

One of the main aims of artificial intelligence is to mimic, model, simulate or duplicate* psychological phenomena; and congitive psychology offers an information-processing interpretation of mental events that is highly sympathetic to realisation in computer-based systems. In this interpretation it is clear that artificial intelligence and cognitive psychology have common interests, a common frame of reference: both are intereted in how mental (or 'mental') performances can be produced by information-processing structures. Thus Zenon Pylyshyn (1981), a celebrated AI researcher, has emphasised that 'the field of AI is coextensive with that of cognitive psychology ... as intellectual disciplines (not applied technologies), both fields are concerned

---

* These verbs are not intended as synonyms. 'Mimicry' implies an illusion of identity, 'duplication' than the identity has been achieved.

with the same problems, and thus must ultimately be judged by the same criteria of success'. In particular, the ultimate goal in each case is 'a better understanding of intelligence'.

Developments in computer science have encouraged psychologists to interpret the mind in terms of computer categories; and, in turn, the new psychological insights have stimulated the 'mental ambitions' of certain types of computer-based systems (Pylyshyn: 'I believe that AI is just the medicine that cognitive psychology needs at this stage in its development'). The information-processing model of the human mind, encouraged by AI as a subclass of computer science, has opened up new lines of enquiry in psychology and related disciplines; and some researchers see this development as of the utmost importance – thus Allport (1980) suggests that 'the advent of Artificial Intelligence is the single most important development in the history of psychology ... it seems to me not unreasonable to expect that Artificial Intelligence will ultimately come to play the role *vis à vis* the psychological and social sciences that mathematics, from the seventeenth century on, has done for the physical sciences'.

Various earlier schools of psychology (eg gestalt) worked to uncover internal mental structures, but lacked the theoretical equipment to do so. Mayer (1981) stressed that the gestaltists asked many of the same questions that are asked by today's cognitive psychologists, but now there are the tools 'to answer at least some of them successfully'. We have already indicated (in Chapter 8) some of the influences – associated with such names as Shannon, Chomsky and Piaget – that helped to shape cognitive psychology and the rapidly developing science of artificial intelligence. In 1972 the psychologist George Miller summarised the new situation: 'Many psychologists have come to take for granted in recent years ... that men and computers are merely two different species of a more abstract genus called "information processing systems".' This had the implication that 'The concepts that describe abstract information-processing systems must, perforce, describe any particular examples of such systems'. So if the human mind (and the minds of any other biological systems) could be described *in toto* in terms of information processing, then any machine that could be induced to process information in the requisite ways would thereby have mental properties. In such a fashion, it was proposed, artificial minds could be built into electronic computers.

One consequence was that efforts to find similarities between natural and artificial systems were redoubled. It was useful, for example, that both humans and computers had memories, problems with information retrieval, channels for information input and output, etc. And soon there was speculation about the information-processing nature of sleep, intuition, and common sense, emotion, etc (see Cognitive Simulation, below). In this way, there were fresh attempts to draw analogies between biological systems and 'intelligent' artefacts. Stevens (1984), for example, considered how it would be useful to build 'motivation-al' features into AI systems; and the familiar game of comparing brains and computers continued – Michie (1971) compared the storage capacity, speed and data transfer rates of the human brain with those of a CDC Star 100 computer.

Efforts were also made to understand the neural networks of simpler biological systems. Thus Andy Clark (1987) suggests that 'perhaps we should concentrate on problems that even slugs can solve' – as an approach to comprehending the structural features of particular information-processing systems. And at the same time, efforts were made to compare human and machine performance in specific areas: Marcus (1983), for instance, compares the effectiveness of humans and computers as search intermediaries.

However the rapidly-developing interest in the AI/cognitive psychology symbiosis did not, in the 1970s, carry all before it. There were sceptics who rejected the proposed similarities between natural and artificial systems. Benson (1971) suggested that AI scientists were corrupting the word 'intelligence', and disputed the whole analogy between human mental processes and machine operations. In the United Kingdom an important (perhaps now notorious) report was produced by Sir James Lighthill (1972) for the Science Research Council, declaring AI work unfruitful and undeserving of government funds. (A belated effort was made, under the 1983/84 Alvey initiative, to remedy what came to be seen as this colossal blow to AI research in Britain.) And it is also worth highlighting such AI sceptics as Searle, Dreyfus and Weizenbaum.

This chapter outlines the basic ideas of cognitive psychology, profiles some simulation aspects and highlights some working systems. Particular practical ways in which AI and cognitive psychology are exerting a reciprocal influence are indicated, and some current research activities in this area are cited.

COGNITIVE PSYCHOLOGY

The Basic Model

The cognitive approach to human psychology assumes that every human being is equipped with the same basic information processing system, and that all mental processes can in principle be explained in terms of the operation of this system. (As the term 'cognitive psychology' suggests, this approach is strong on such *cognitive* elements as remembering, recalling information, comparing data items, etc; but weak on such *conative* elements as willing and desiring.) The basic information-processing model is shown in Figure 9.1. It can be expanded to accommodate the various associated theories of perception, information retrieval, etc.

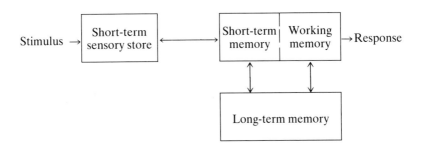

Figure 9.1   Basic Cognitive Model of Mind

Information from the outside world impringes on the sense receptors. These are similar, but not identical, from one biological species to another, and are likely to evolve peculiar characteristics in artificial systems. The typical receptors rely on changes in natural phenomena, such as air pressure, temperature, distribution of molecules, and electromagnetic radiation. (It should be remembered that biological systems have internal receptors as well as those associated with the familiar five senses.)

At first the information is held in a short-term sensory store (sometimes called a 'sensory buffer'). It is generally assumed that this store has a large capacity and can hold all the information presented to the sensory receptors but only for a short time. Some researchers suggest that there is a short-term sensory buffer for each sense.

Attention is paid by the individual to only a small proportion of the information that reaches the short-term store: vast amounts of information fade without being noticed. Where attention *is* paid, it is likely that some of the information will be transferred to the short-term (conscious) memory. Here a few items can be held for a few seconds unless 'pushed out' by other incoming items. Information can be 'rehearsed', if the person wishes, in order to preserve it in consciousness; and 'chunking' techniques can be employed, partly to compensate for the relatively small capacity of the short-term memory, in order to increase the spectrum of current awareness.

The short-term memory has the working memory as an affective appendage, this latter having only limited storage capacity and intermediate-term storage capabilities. The working memory functions as a mental scratch pad to facilitate conscious intellectual tasks. As with short-term memory, information is quickly lost from working memory unless a rehearsal strategy is adopted. Information can also be transferred from the short-term memory to long-term memory, allowing vast amounts of information to be stored for lengthy periods. Blocks may prevent information from being retrieved but the information is still present. In the absense of preventive blocks, information items are retrieved using search strategies (search is a principal AI concern).

Two points need to be stressed. In the first place, the fact that every individual is equipped with the same basic information-processing system does not mean that there are not considerable cognitive differences from one person to another. It is a matter of simple observation that people vary enormously in their cognitive performances. In the second place it should be emphasised that the model is extremely simple: it explains nothing about searching, retrieval, problem solving, decision making, remembering – the principal cognitive concerns. The development of more sophisticated models, essential for any genuinely elucidatory task, is part of the task of cognitive researchers, encouraged by the development of functional software systems in artificial intelligence. Neisser (1976) has caricatured some of the early cognitive models for their evident lack of elucidatory potential (see Figure 9.2).

Figure 9.2   Neisser Caricature of Cognitive Models

It is clearly unhelpful to cite 'processing' as a supposed *explanation* for mental performance. The task is to show *how* the processing takes place: until this is done it is impossible to code mental faculties into software systems (see Working Systems, below). In fact the basic cognitive model has been developed in various ways to illuminate particular psychological problems: see the examples of the cognitive approach described in Mayer (1981).

Memory Mechanisms

An obvious way of expanding the basic cognitive model is to develop the various memory elements (in fact the basic model contains nothing more than proposed memory components). A common ploy, for example, is to regard memory in terms of a spatial metaphor: memory is an effective reservoir to be filled with appropriate items (Plato compared the mind to an aviary, with modern researchers preferring to talk about switchboards, gramaphones, libraries, conveyor belts, underground maps, etc). Not surprisingly, in the computer age, the traditional spatial metaphor has been reshaped by the categories offered by electronic computation.

It is likely that actual memory mechanisms vary according to the types of information being stored. For example, verbal memory will have different requirements to visual memory; and there will be corresponding differences in capacity, accessibility, duration, etc. Detailed discussions of memory options are given in, for example, Eysenck (1986); and Lindsay and Norman* (1977). Of particular value are the efforts to produce working systems that model important aspects of human memory performance (see Working Systems, below).

Current Status

Cognitive psychology, propelled in part by the modern successes of practical computer-based systems, is today the dominant school of psychology (though there are various species of cognitivism in modern academic circles). Unless there is a reaction against progress in computer science in general and AI in particular (and, since hype often outruns practical realisation, such a reaction is not hard to envisage), some form of cognitive psychology is likely to remain dominant for the foreseeable future. At the same time there are a number of voices declaring that all is not well in the cognitivist world.

It has long been suggested that the basic cognitivist agenda rests on a distorted model of the human being. Claxton (1980) expresses this well enough. Here cognitive psychology is seen to deal, not with whole people 'but with a very special and bizarre – almost Frankensteinian – preparation, which consists of a brain attached to two eyes, two ears, and two index fingers'. It is to be found inside 'small, gloomy cubicles', staring 'fixedly at a small screen', its fingers resting 'lightly and expectantly' on microswitches. The entity does not feel hungry, tired or inquisitive; nor does it 'think extraneous thoughts or try to understand what is going on. It simply *processes information*. So the human being is reduced to a speciman made in the image of the 'larger electronic organism that sends it stimuli and records its responses'.

---

* These authors suggest that extensions of the area of information processing research can help to illuminate 'many if not all human phenomena'.

This interpretation was hinted at earlier. The cognitive model, nominally interested in internal mental structures, in fact only focuses on possible mechanisms that serve the paradigm. There is interest in manipulating stored information, but seeming indifference to such matters as feelings, hopes, ambitions, attitudes and all the other paraphernalia that is supposed to define the singular mental equipment of *Homo sapiens*.

There are also particular criticisms of the cognitivist approach; for example, those proposed by Newell (1973) and discussed by Eysenck (1986) – to the effect that research strategies are inappropriate and hypotheses badly conceived. One problem is that empirical data can be explained adequately by various incompatible cognitivist theories, and it is not obvious how to choose between them.

Such concerns are of importance to the development of AI, not least because of the reciprocal influence between AI and cognitivism. Theories in cognitive psychology affect AI research programmes and the development of specific systems intended to function in the real world. For example, the development of man/machine interfaces (see below) may be unduly influenced by a too narrow view of human beings as simple information processors.

There is considerable debate about how far AI can go in offering explanations about human mental processes, and this is relevant to the development of (for example) expert systems that purport to function with competence in various specialist areas (see Chapter 14). Sharkey and Pfeifer (1984) discuss AI and cognitive psychology as 'uncomfortable bedfellows' – and this interpretation should be borne in mind when considering the various efforts to simulate cognitive behaviour.

COGNITIVE SIMULATION

General

The principal purpose of cognitive simulation is to design and build an artefact that mimics the behaviour of a natural system deemed to have a cognitive capability. This can be attempted at many different levels. The behaviour of a single nerve, an

element in a cognitive network, can be simulated – at a primitive
level – by a simple electrical circuit. More complex forms of
cognition, presumably similarly rooted in neurological configurations*, cannot be simulated on a nerve-by-nerve basis (the
neurological architectures are not adequately understood and in
any case the combinatorial explosion would make the logic and
the software impossibly complex). Here cognitive simulation is
attempted by designing software to mimic a particular feature, or
small set of features, in a cognitive system. Having designed and
coded such software its mode of behaviour might then provide
clues for the interpretation of how natural (ie biological) systems
work.

The main cognitive tasks – for example, perception, interpretation, information storage, information retrieval, reasoning, explanation, goal setting, learning, decision making, etc – are highly
relevant to the broad question of intelligence; and they are
difficult to simulate in artificial systems. One problem is that they
are not well understood in biological systems and simulations are
inevitably based on partial knowledge. At the same time
cognitive simulation is now a widely acknowledged mode of AI
research (see Current Research, below). It is commonplace, for
example, in knowledge-based systems.

Scope

Efforts to achieve computer simulations of mental processes are
extremely wide ranging. Today systems are being design to
mimic, albeit with inevitable simplification, many of the behavioural manifestations of the human mind. And sometimes it is
suggested that particular aspects of computer performance are
effective simulations, without this being a prior design intention.
One example of this is the theory of Christopher Evans (1983) to
the effect that what happens in the human brain during sleep is
strictly analogous to what happens in a digital computer during
particular phases of its operation.

---

* Neurological information processing is described by Lindsay and
Norman (1977), Chapter 6.

In conventional computer usage there is the familiar task of 'program clearance', carried out to allow a computer-based system to adapt to new circumstances. Here computer programs are updated in the light of changed information, ie they are pruned, expanded or otherwise modified to enable the system to continue functioning effectively in what is in effect a fresh environment. And this process is compared with what a human brain may be doing during sleep: clearly every human being needs to adapt constantly to a changing fabric of information (much of this adaptation goes on in the waking state but perhaps certain types of updating can only be managed when the biological system is 'off line').

This suggests that typical computer activity (program clearance) may be regarded as a simulation of human information processing, of certain types, during sleep. Again the theory is only sketched, not framed in a detailed way that would encourage testing and evaluation.

Other forms of simulation are directly designed to focus on an aspect of human mental performance. Thus Eden et al (1980) discuss a simulation approach in the context of human learning; Oren (1987) considers how cognitive simulation may evolve towards cognizant simulation; and various researchers explore how such human mental states as consciousness can be interpreted in cognitive terms and simulated in computer based systems. Thus the philosopher Daniel Dennett (1979) considers a cognitive theory of consciousness; E W Kent (1980) considers the evolution of consciousness in machines (to mimic or simulate biological consciousness); and Syndetic Corporation, in Omaha, claims to have developed a computer algorithm that can enable a mainframe computer to reproduce the processes of the human subconscious mind.

It is also possible to build cognitive simulations of decision making, political activity and other human activities normally assumed to depend upon value judgements. Greene (1987) describes how international decision-makers and international stability can be modelled; and Boden (1977) considers the simulation of ideological beliefs and neurotic mental states. K M Colly, over a period of several years, developed a simulation of a neurotic process to represent a woman undergoing pys-choanalysis.

Simulations have thus focused on the standard cognitive functions (learning, remembering, etc) and on such matters as the holding of beliefs (there are Tony Benn and Barry Goldwater 'machines') and the existence of abnormal mental states. In principle, any mental state or mental process can be simulated by a computer-based system. In this way, cognitive simulation can be represented as a principal AI concern.

Working Systems

Particular software systems intended to simulate cognitive func-tions are necessarily based on explicit psychological theories. Thus the associationist theory of human long-term memory (in, for example, Anderson and Bower, 1973) has been used for the HAM* simulation system designed to parse simple propositional sentences and to store (memorise) the parsed sentences. The system can also answer questions, a capability that requires storage, information retrieval and parsing functions. HAM carries knowledge, represented as propositions and encoded in binary trees. When the system accepts knowledge it then builds associative structures in memory.

The system has been used to derive various predictions that were tested using standard methods of cognitive psychology. It has been demonstrated that a wide range of memory tasks can be simulated using an associationist theory.

The ACT system, following work on HAM, aimed to model a wide range of cognitive tasks. It contains short-term memory, long-term memory, and ways of modifying them in particular circumstances. Again various associative devices are used. It has been shown that, for example, ACT can be programmed to perform specific memory-scanning activities (Sternberg, 1969). The system is capable of shifting its focus of attention, of

---

* The working systems profiled in this section are fully described in Cohen and Feigenbaum (1982).

exploiting probabilistic events, and of learning (in four different ways). ACT is a flexible system, not designed to accomplish only a specific task. The MEMOD system represents another general model of human long-term memory.

MEMOD is intended to be a general knowledge-representation system (it began by representing linguistic knowledge but was designed to accommodate knowledge of any type). Thus Norman et al (1975) observed that the system 'has to be capable of handling the representation and processing issues in syntactic and semantic analysis of language, in memory, perception, problem solving, reasoning, question answering, and in the acquisition of knowledge'. MEMOD is seen to embody various powerful notions (for example, the system is designed so that concepts with similar meanings are structured in a similar way).

The various working systems are usually intended to simulate relatively straightforward cognitive functions – learning, memorising, recalling, etc. Such functions have often been associated with the operations of the left hemisphere of the human brain. Ranzino (1982), for example, argues that it is to be expected that computer performance should begin with 'left-brain activity', before evolving to mirror the more esoteric functions of the right hemisphere ('the products of the right brain are generally nonverbal – a painting, a symphony, an initiative flash . . . many right brain functions cannot even be expressed in left brain terms . . .'). In such circumstances, the progressive evolution of artificial systems for mental simulation may be expected to approach right-brain activities (in principle, any brain function, once adequately understood, can be simulated by computer-based systems).

MAN/MACHINE INTERFACES

For a number of years efforts have been made to consider congitive factors when designing artefacts intended to work with human beings on a day-to-day basis. In particular, where people are expected to interact with computers there are various cognitive factors to be addressed. Such factors are involved even in simple keying tasks (emphasised by Allen, 1982, with citations); and such topics as programming techniques, command languages, data-base access and editing are now assumed to have cognitive overtones. Awareness of theories about short-term memory, long-term memory, information recall, problem solving, etc are expected to influence the design of computer-based man/machine interfaces (Allen describes various empirical studies relating to directing a computer's actions, cognitive factors in programming, problem solving, document preparation, visual displays, and interaction with computers by voice and other non-visual modalities). It is assumed that, as artificial systems become ever more complex, the importance of designs that take cognitive factors into account will increase.

Some discussions on the nature of the human/computer interface focus on the precise relationships between human beings and computer-based systems. Goldes (1983), for example, asks:

'1. What is the relationship between humans and machines?

2. How are humans and machines different?

3. Who is in charge of whom?'

In such matters the provision of AI facilities, incorporating cognitive awareness, may be deemed to be particularly important. Increasingly, interface design is focusing on the advantages that can be achieved using AI input (see, for example, Lawrence, 1986; Harris, 1987 – focusing on the use of natural language; Nemes, 1987; and Berry and Broadbent, 1986 – dealing with expert-system interfaces). Here, as elsewhere, the development of AI as a key element in the design of working systems is increasingly important.

AI AND PSYCHOLOGY

This chapter has so far considered the reciprocal influence of AI and cognitive psychology. Before citing some current research in the linked area of cognitive simulation it is worth highlighting again some principal concerns of modern researchers.

Since the early days of GPS (see Chapter 8), the search for systems that can embody a *general* intelligence continues. Laird et al (1987) describe SOAR, an architecture for general intelligence: the system is able to work on a wide range of tasks, from routine procedures to difficult open-ended problems; employ a wide spectrum of problem-solving methods; and learn about the tasks as they are performed. (John McCarthy, 1987, discusses the on-going problem of generality in artificial intelligence. In particular, he discusses the representation of knowledge in logic.)

Aspects of information retrieval continue to be researched as prime considerations in the design of computer-based systems (database facilities, natural language systems, expert systems, etc). Here too cognitive models are recognised as vital tools in illuminating the needs of artefacts intended to store and retrieval knowledge. Daniels (1986), for example, evaluates the various approaches to cognitive simulation in information retrieval.

Such broad topics highlight the wide-ranging ambitions of AI and cognitive researchers (Cherniak, 1988, even considers the design of a computer program that 'approximates all human mentality'). Much work on cognitive simulation focuses, by contrast, on small matters, the detail of this or that perception, the significance of an isolated parameter (and it has sometimes been criticised for preoccupation with such narrow affairs). It is worth indicating, without comment, some recently published research.

RESEARCH INTERESTS

The following papers are cited at random to indicate some specific research interests:

> Webb (1987) explores student understanding of domains as relevant to the design of intelligent tutoring systems.

> Barnard et al (1986) explore the modelling of cognitive activity using psychological constructs and an expert system.

> Vessey (1987) investigates programmer knowledge structures as relevant to progammer performance.

> Courbon (1987) considers the features that should characterise the interactive dialogue of a decision support system.

> Wielinga and Breuker (1986) explore how expert knowledge can be defined to preserve the flexibility of the human expert.

Hirsig et al (1987) consider interactive computer games as a strategy for research into cognitive psychology.

Dubois and De-Rycker (1987) consider how AI research can help the evaluation of educational methodologies.

Shank (1987) explores cognitive modelling as a route to programming a computer to be capable of creative thought.

Reif (1987) considers cognitive issues as relevant to the understanding of scientific or mathematical concepts.

SUMMARY

This chapter has profiled some of the reciprocal effects of AI and cognitive psychology. In particular, modern psychology has been influenced heavily by the information-processing paradigm of the electronic computer; and AI specialists have been encouraged by the idea that mental processes can be interpreted in information-processing terms. In this atmosphere, impetus has been given to efforts to compare artificial and natural (ie biological) capabilities, and cognitive modelling has emerged as one of the fruits of the doctrine that mental features can, in an important sense, be mimicked by artefacts.

Some indication has also been given of important cognitive modelling systems (HAM, ACT, MEMOD, etc); and of current research interests. In summary, modern research can be seen to have two basic (and complementary) thrusts. On the one hand, artificial systems are being used to throw light on possible interpretations of human pyschology; on the other, knowledge of human psychology is being used to improve the design of computer-based artefacts that are intended to interface and interact with human beings (this concern is central to what is today known as *software ergonomics*).

It has also been emphasised that the old controversies about AI persist in the modern world. Some observers (Dreyfus, Searle, etc) suggest that the AI enterprise is basically ill-conceived, that efforts to mimic or duplicate human mental qualities in artefacts can only result in a 'reduction' or distortion of human beings, an antihumanist programme. To some extent the question will be settled in an empirical fashion: we will see whether cognitive simulation, for example, helps to illuminate aspects of human mental performance. For the rest we will have to wait to see whether machines will be able to evolve right-brain capabilities (Ranzino, 1982). At present there is no doubt that cognitive considerations are influencing the shape of artefacts (eg man/ machine interfaces).

10 Language and Speech*

INTRODUCTION

There are many ways in which speech and language relate to AI interests. There is growing emphasis on making computers more 'user-friendly', ie more able to interact with human beings without the people needing to be computer specialists (or typists). One obvious ploy is to design computers to respond to human language – in its various written, printed and spoken forms. It would obviously be convenient to be able to tell a computer what to do and then to receive its spoken comments on the practicality of the order. The provision of user-friendly interfaces that would allow this degree of two-way communication is a central aim of much current research: in particular, it is a key objective of the Japanese fifth-generation-computer programme.

Research devoted to developing the conversational abilities of computers is central to work in artificial intelligence. For example, it is a key design aim for expert systems (Chapter 14) that they be able to converse with human beings, explaining lines of reasoning, making other comments, offering advice, etc. Moreover it can also be assumed that progress in language understanding will directly affect how computers can *think* about problems in different fields. There has always been philosophic

* This chapter is based partly on Chapter 7 of *Introducing Artificial Intelligence* (NCC, 1984) and partly on Chapter 8 of *Management Guide to Office Automation* (NCC, 1986). Up-to-date information is added.

debate about the relevance of language to thought, about the importance of the various linguistic symbols to the mental powers of human beings. It is now highly significant that computer research into syntax and semantics is not only concerned with the artificial computer languages but also with the various natural languages. Psycholinguistics, programming theory and various logical formalisms are coverging to develop a generalised framework for mental information processing ('cognition', 'thought') that is equally relevant to human beings and machines.

It is interesting that the year (1968) that saw the publication of Arthur C. Clarke's *2001: A Space Odyssey,* which features the famous conversational computer Hal, also saw the emergence of a number of programs for understanding natural language. In the 1960s, computers were already able to accept and answer questions in English in many different subject areas (for example, algebra, medicine and kinship relations), and could conduct a rudimentary psychiatric interview in English, Welsh or German. Such systems relied upon teletype facilities – and even with this limitation they invited anthropomorphisation. Today, with the rapid development of voice recognition and speech synthesis facilities, it is even more tempting to personalise computers.

BIOLOGY AND LANGUAGE

As in other areas of AI work, research into speech and language understanding is likely to profit from appreciation of relevant biological phenomena. We have already seen how prior assumption, probably genetically programmed into the mammalian brain, is essential for the correct interpretation of visual information. It is likely that analogous pre-established cerebral structures are equally essential for the adequate interpretation of other complex data in nonvisual fields: for example, in the area of speech and language understanding.

We may expect a study of language to throw light on aspects of brain structure and behaviour. Thus Lashley (1950) has observed that 'Speech is the only window through which the physiologist can view cerebral life . . . the problems raised by the organisation of language seem to be characteristic of almost all other cerebral activity'. This highlights again a central feature of AI research –

that there is a characteristic merging and interdependence of different cognitive phenomena and activities. We cannot usefully consider any single aspect – memory, learning, problem solving, language understanding, knowledge representation, etc – without giving attention to at least some of the others.

It is now widely believed that the human brain is structured to predispose it to accept linguistic relationships and linguistic information. Brain programs manipulate linguistic data, ordering it for storage and other purposes (and it can also be convenient to regard the brain programs as written in a language, though not in the way that speech or thought depends upon language). And we would expect the various brain programs to relate to earlier evolutionary structures. 'Biological causes run deep. One does not find complex, highly evolved life processes showing no evidence of their origin from much simpler adaptive functions. To explain language one must therefore attend to apparently unrelated aspects of intentional performance' (Trevarthen, 1974). In this sense it is convenient to regard the brain as producing language as it produces other forms of behaviour to aid the survival potential of a biological system. Language serves *international purposes,* working as a device to influence human behaviour – either in the originator of the language-supported thoughts or in an agent who evaluates the information being conveyed from another person. Young (1978) therefore defines language as 'any species-specific system of intentional communication between individuals'. (We can speculate on how systems developed through AI research may be deemed 'intentional'.)

In *Homo sapiens,* language has immense syntactic and semantic complexity, and no other species has a comparable system for communication. It has been suggested that other primates may be able to handle several dozen distinct signs, but compared with human language this is a very primitive ability. The syntax and semantics of computer languages are less complex than those in natural languages (Russian, English, Japanese, etc) and they are evolving for computer-specific purposes, but the requirement that computers be ever more user-friendly will have implications for the future of computer languages: they will, in short, become more humanlike.

Structure is a key element in any sophisticated language system, and the notion of structure implies relationships between symbols, group hierarchies, rules for substitutions and transformations, etc. Again we can emphasise how such structural aspects are mediated by the awareness of purposes that language is supposed to serve. For example, a person sees danger and wants to warn a friend: visual perception provides the input to the linguistic system. In such a circumstance it is reasonable to infer structural and causal links between the neurons that are interested in, say, line detection and those that are involved in the structuring of sentences. The intelligence system is an integrated network, a feature that we may aim to duplicate in sophisticated AI systems.

It has been suggested that 'many properties of grammar are present in some form in prelinguistic perceptuo-motor behaviour' (Osgood, 1971). This neatly illustrates how language in man evolved from earlier nonlinguistic modes of behaviour, and today represents a range of encoding and decoding abilities that developed from related skills that had evolved for other purposes. Many of the linguistic computational abilities are concerned with manipulating the relationships that define the linguistic structure, and such abilities – because of the evolutionary background – are at least partly preprogrammed into the human brain. Human infants, before they can speak or understand, have special detectors that are uniquely sensitive to speech sounds (and the early 'burblings' and 'gurglings', seemingly meaningless, are already influenced in their character by the prevailing language of the infant's environment).

A study of how language is learned can help to uncover its complexities. We may, for example, trace the development of linguistic usage in the child, moving from early babbling, through the acquisition of simple 'label words' (*mama, dada,* etc), to the use of first-order relationship symbols that begin the acquisition of a structural linguistic ability. The gradual development of comprehension can be examined in the same way – from both the passive end (where the child gives behavioural evidence of understanding given linguistic statements) and the active end (where the child generates a statement to signal intended action or to influence the behaviour of other people in the environment).

The decoding of speech depends upon the person (or machine) being able to make reference to a body of stored knowledge. A word is interpreted within a spectrum of expectations influenced by the context of the linguistic experience. If a friend is talking we are unconsciously (sometimes consciously) anticipating both the words that will be used and their intended meaning. This suggests constant reference to a knowledge base, a circumstance that has implications for the design of artificial systems that are capable of understanding language. Speech cannot be decoded without a store 'of *a priori* knowledge about the language.... Every speaker or listener carries in his cortext a vast store of information about any languages he uses' (Fry, 1970). It is one of the tasks of the neurophysiologists to find out how this linguistic knowledge is encapsulated in brain structures.

The more complex the stored knowledge, the most difficult it is to access it quickly for pattern-recognition or thinking processes. A sequential search of *all* the knowledge would obviously be highly inefficient, and various search strategies are employed to allow a person to 'home in' on the specific areas of knowledge that are relevant to the task in hand. In human beings there are also a variety of psychological constraints that influence how effectively a piece of language is understood. For example, the speed of understanding must keep pace with the rate of speech; and sentences must be understood as the words are delivered chronologically (sometimes several words must be given before the analysis can get started). People, like computers, vary in their language-understanding competence: this may or may not indicate the existence of both common and disparate linguistic mechanisms from one person to another.

The mechanisms for understanding printed and spoken words are closely related to the mechanisms for perception and pattern recognition. As with other forms of perceptual processing, language is analysed by a combination of two sorts of mechanisms:

- with *data-driven, bottom-up* mechanisms, the relevant processes are stimulated by signals arriving at the system (in the case of language processing human beings, at the eyes and ears). 'Bottom-up' signifies that the analysis begins with the lowest level of information – sensory data;

- with *conceptually-driven, top-down* mechanisms, the analysis begins with the expectations and cues that are always available. Conceptually-guided processing helps to frame expectations about the subject matter, about the information that is likely to arrive ('I knew what she was going to say next'). Here analysis is from high-level structures to low-level data.

It is generally assumed that both data-driven and conceptually-driven approaches work together in human language understanding and other perceptual acts. Again there are clues as to what we may expect in an AI system designed to cope with language. One requirement is likely to be software routines variously equipped to handle individual words, grammatical classes (noun, preposition, etc), and specific sentence components (noun phrase, verb phrase, etc). Other routines can be devoted to integrating the findings of routines, using the knowledge base for comparison purposes, and other semantic matters. The top-down sentence and meaning routines allow the overall system to work quickly and in a way that is relatively insensitive to errors in the sensory analysis. But the system may come to expect things that will never happen, and so must be amenable to correction by data-driven routines. In human language-understanding systems, and ideally in the analogous AI systems, there is scope for abandoning one procedure, if seen to be fruitless, and trying another.

Cognitive psychology describes the language-understanding task in information-processing terms that can be interpreted in a computer context. Thus there is talk of how language enables human beings to encode the structural networks in their memory systems and to express them using (written or spoken) symbols. The human being, trying (usually) to be 'person-friendly', adapts the symbolic expressions deemed most likely to be accessible to the other person. The intelligent computer, aiming to be user-friendly, will evolve a similar adaptive potential.

Miller and Johnson-Laird (1976) suggested that understanding a sentence is analogous to running a program on a computer. Just as a program is *compiled,* and then *run* (with respect to the relevant data), so the person *translates* the natural-language input into a set of mental instructions and then *decides* how to respond.

In essence, this approach may be regarded as offering a procedural semantics. The important consideration is that this approach offers an information-processing analysis of language understanding that does not depend upon any specific type of hardware. The corollary is that language can in principle be understood as an array of neurons, an array of silicon chips, or an array of anything else – provided that the necessary procedures and protocols are embedded in the configuration.

The study of the relationships between computer languages and the computers on which they are used indicates how brain structures may be revealed by a study of natural language. Thus Sampson (1975) asks: 'what is to human language as the internal mechanisms of a computer are to the computer's language ... what mind of a computer would use languages of the kind we have identified as natural languages?' This again illustrates the reciprocal influence of cognitive psychology and computer science: a study of language understanding in *Homo sapiens* helps us to frame analogous procedures for computers, and a study of computer languages gives clues about possible brain structures.

The biology (and psychology) of language understanding in people will continue to influence attempts to define artefacts with similar powers, and psychological theories will be mediated by what we know of computer performance. Sampson suggests it is possible to develop a theory of the human mind based on Chomsky's theory of language, using the strategy of comparing 'Man with another type of organism which uses complex languages, namely the digital computer'. The approach to language understanding in artificial systems, described below, has been influenced by what we know of language understanding in *homo sapiens*.

LANGUAGE AND PRODUCTS

A growing range of voice facilities is being developed to improve communications between people and computer-based systems, and between people and people (using computer-based systems for the purpose). We are increasingly seeing reference to how computers can 'talk to' other items of electronic equipment, a metaphor that is now beginning to assume literal proportions.

There are obvious advantages in computers being able to recognise and understand human speech, and being able to generate appropriate speech responses: such facilities would offer a most effective ('humanlike') interface between man and machine. However, researchers have uncovered immense semantic and syntactical difficulties in attempting to design computer-based systems able to converse, using speech, with human beings.

We all know that voice systems in human beings can function in either input or output modes, ie we can hear and speak. One purpose of current research in artificial intelligence (AI) and related areas is to enable computers to recognise the voices of people speaking to them. Here a computer is trained by allowing it to analyse a number of speech performances (usually several utterances of the same word or phrase) by the same person, after which the computer recognises the person's voice when it hears it. However, *recognition* is not the same as *understanding*. To understand any group of related sentences in, say, a monologue or paragraph requires a high level of semantic competence; and computer abilities in this area are rudimentary, though steadily developing.

Once a computer has framed a reply to a query (which may or may not have been spoken) it may be useful for the reply to be given in aural terms, ie it may be helpful for the machine to speak – in a way that has significance for the human hearer. In fact it is relatively easy for computer-based systems to synthesise speech, and to deliver it in a male or female voice, in any of several languages, or with a French, Welsh, Russian accent, etc. Voice *synthesis* – which again does not imply voice *understanding* – has been likened to squeezing the toothpaste out of the tube, voice recognition to pushing it back in.

Voice-recognition and speech-synthesis systems will increasingly feature in commercial products, including those destined for the office environment (we can see the advantages of being able to speak to a word processor or facsimile machine, and to hear a meaningful reply). For some years it has been suggested that the speech technology industry is ready for major expansion, though it is obvious that there are still major theoretical and technical problems to overcome if anything but the most simple speech systems to be made commercially available. There are already many speech systems on the market (some are mentioned later): speech recognisers, speech synthesisers, voice store-and-forward systems (where spoken words are stored for retrieval by other system users), etc. These and other facilities will progressively improve the man/machine interface in the years to come. It will be possible to speak to computer-based office equipment and for it to answer back. Already, in various commercial and industrial environments there are devices that use a combination of speech input and speech output to aid communication with human users. For example, Henthorn and Dawson (1983) described an electropneumatic robotic device, formerly speech controlled, that now carries a voice response unit; and successful research in one industrial or commercial sector can quickly feed through to affect the design of systems in other environments, including the modern office.

It is expected that speech recognition/generation technology will progressively enhance existing telecommunications facilities. Text messaging has already been very successful where people have access to terminals and the associated computers, but voice messaging could be even more effective since there would be no requirement for standard terminals. Many organisations are now exploring the possibilities for development in these areas. For example, for some years the Bell-Northern research/INRS-Telecom team has been researching the efficient coding of speech for digital transmission, and looking at the design of man/machine communication systems. Such research includes the development of techniques for the computer recognition of spoken information, the computer production of speech, and the design of communications protocols that integrate these techniques for practical applications.

Again we can emphasise that it is not equally problematic to design systems for speech recognition and systems for speech synthesis. One of the main problems with speech input (ie when the computer is being required to recognise and/or understand what is being said to it) is that the human voice – variously affected by emotion, alcohol, fatigue, etc – is an extremely inconsistent transmitter. Factors such as volume, accent, and ambient noise can also make it extremely difficult for a computer to derive any sense from what human beings are saying in its environment. It is rare from a computer to recognise lengthy connected speech with any consistency.

Many commentaries and reports (eg McCarten, 1985) have suggested that the commercial applications of speech technology will expand in the coming years, a main benefit that a wide variety of system-based functions will be accessible with minimum effort. Already particular speech implementations are in operation, and others will follow. In 1984 French Railways (SNCF) launched an automatic information system in Tours which involved computer synthesis of speech from recorded syllables (an operator keys in messages, whereupon the computer contacts signal boxes to tell staff about problems). In 1984 the British government expressed its support for research into the development of voice-controlled equipment. This included, for example, support for the work of the Alvey directorate in developing a voice-operated word processor, of obvious relevance to the electronic office.

LANGUAGE UNDERSTANDING

General

Soon after computers first became available in the 1940s it was obvious that they would find application in many linguistic areas. The evident ability of the computer to handle symbols allowed it to compile indexes from text and to generate concordances (indexes than included a line of context for each entry). These tasks were computationally simple, requiring the computer to do nothing more than count and arrange data in particular ways. It was soon felt that computers might perform more ambitious linguistic tasks.

Machine translation (see below) was one of the first application areas that extended the linguistic activity of computers. One of the early researchers, Warren Weaver, suggested in 1949 that computers might be useful for 'the solution of world-wide translation problems'. Initially the task of machine translation seemed relatively straightforward – which led to an optimism later found to be unfounded. The idea was that the computer would look up the words in a bilingual dictionary and process the findings to produce suitable sentences in the output language. In fact many problems afflict these seemingly simple tasks.

It was soon recognised that computers might do better at translation if they had a degree of understanding of the texts they were handling. Such a facility would enable them, it was thought, to cope with the peculiarities of individual languages. The approach to helping machines to understand the textual material they were handling is a central feature of work in artificial intelligence. Some of the AI work in this field involves the use of knowledge-based systems to model human language and the development of computer programs that would serve as functional implementations of such models. Barr and Feigenbaum (1981) have identified four historical categories of natural language programs:

- some programs (eg BASEBALL, SAD-SAM, STUDENT and ELIZA) aimed to generate limited results in narrow domains. By keeping the processes simple, many of the problems of natural language could be ignored;

- in some early systems (such as PROTO-SYNTHEX I), a representation of the text was stored, indexing devices being employed to aid retrieval of particular words or phrases. Since the stored text could cover any subject the systems were not restricted, by virtue of their structure, to a particular domain. However, such systems were weak on semantics and had no deductive powers;

- limited-logical systems (eg SIR, TLC, DEACON and CONVERSE) aimed to translate input sentences into the formal notation used in the database. Here the aim was to allow deductions to be made from information held in the database, even though only a few of the processes used in everyday conversation could be exploited;

- knowledge-based systems (eg LUNAR and SHRDLU) most closely linked to current work in artificial intelligence, use information about the particular subject domain to understand the input sentences. Such programs, some of which are expert systems (Chapter 8), have various deductive and other powers.

The main difficulty in developing programs to understand natural language is the sheer complexity of everyday communication. It has long been possible to formalise aspects of everyday discourse but such efforts have only related to a small proportion of the processes that occur in natural-language usage. It is still true that we do not understand the complexities of natural language, and so we cannot write compilers for English or Japanese. At the same time, various strategies are being developed to enable computers to handle natural-language discourse. Most of these strategies rely upon modelling how human beings cope with linguistic communication. For example, people need to store information about the meanings of words (how words relate to each other, how words relate to particular behavioural manifestations), about how to transcribe one linguistic expression into another logically-equivalent one, and about how new (more up-to-date) linguistic information can be used to modify or replace existing stored information.

By the 1980s much attention had already been given to how knowledge could be stored to aid linguistic understanding in computer systems (see, for example, Tennant, 1978). Subsequent work has focused on developing his knowledge-based approach with the aim of making it easier for human beings to interrogate intelligent machines. Already modern database management systems often include query languages to augment programming language access, but in general such languages can only be used by specialists. The user of a typical query language must have a good idea of what is in the database, must know how the knowledge is formalised and encoded, and must be able to cope with the specialised syntax and semantics of the query languages. Clearly this degree of expertise will not be found in the typical everyday user wanting to converse with a computer. There are obvious advantages in giving computers their own understanding of natural language. There are already commercial natural-language systems available, but many of the problems associated with linguistics have not yet been solved.

It is still true that users are mostly expected to communicate with computers using highly structured, computer-imposed techniques. A few familiar English (or French or German, etc) words are allowed but only within specific (unnatural) formats. At the same time, progress in natural-language processing is influencing the character of commercial products. For example, the Intellect system, developed by the Artificial Intelligence Corporation

(AIC) and now marketed by IBM, is able to translate typed English requests into formal database query languages and to present the requested information to the enquirer. Intellect can respond effectively even if semantically equivalent requests are written in different ways. It has been suggested that a natural-language system should be able to answer users' requests well over ninety per cent of the time (Harris of AIC claims that Intellect easily meets that requirement – 'No one cares why it doesn't work. When people sit down to use the system, it's got to deliver').

Most natural-language processing systems run on large-scale computers. Intellect, for example, runs in IBM 4300 systems and larger mainframes, with one version for Prime Computer superminicomputers (it requires up to 1M byte of memory for the load module). At the same time it is suggested that Intellect will not need to lose much of its power to run on microcomputers operating with less-complex data (though it will require a fair bit of 'technological shoehorning' – Harris). There are in fact a number of natural-language systems available for microcomputers, with others planned.

The Symantec spin-off from the Machine Intelligence Corporation aims to develop language-processing systems for micros, with the IBM Personal Computer in mind. The company is now incorporating AI features in software that will have a natural-language processing capacity. It is recognised that successes on large machines have led to the feasibility of scaled down versions of AI programs for smaller machines. Another company, Cognitive Systems, is developing systems that will have extensive domain knowledge and knowledge also of natural language. Here the products will include natural-language 'front-ends' for database query systems and also expert systems that can advise users on specific topics. And in 1984 the American Frey Associates software house (in Amherst, N.H.) began delivery of a natural language database query language that makes use of AI techniques to enlarge its vocabulary without any help from a programmer.

The Themis package from Frey, intended initially to run on Digital Equipment Corporation's VAX family of superminicomputers, can be easily expanded by a human operator ('We'll deliver Themis with a base vocabulary of over 900 words, and the ease with which users can add new ones means it can then be tailored for a variety of special applications' – Eric D Frey). Themis is written in InterLisp and requires up to 2M bytes of main memory. It can translate conversational-English queries into a 'language-understander module', the language understander again being used to translate the retrieved database information for display on the terminal screen. (Themis responds 'politely but firmly' to expletives.)

We can expect the range of commercial natural-language products to increase in the years ahead. Japan marked out natural-language systems as a central theme for its ten-year fifth-generation project; and Western companies are increasingly active in this field. Already many US companies (eg Bolt, Beranek and Newman of Cambridge, MA and SRI of Palo Alto, CA) have many years development experience in natural-language systems, work which has yielded such systems as RUS and Dialogic. In Europe there are various University projects (eg the Hamans system at the University of Hamburg and the database-access facility at the University of Cambridge). More initiatives may be expected from the centrally funded ESPRIT and Alvey programmes.

Syntax, Semantics and Logic

The study of both machine and natural language has traditionally focused on *syntax* and *semantics*. The syntax of a language defines how the strings of symbols that comprise the sentences of the language are formally structured, without at this stage considering what the sentences mean. *Grammar* is often regarded as a synonym for syntax. It is important, when studying syntax, to ascertain which strings of symbols are grammatical within the language. *Semantics* is concerned with what the symbols and sentences actually mean.

Linguistic analysis usually involves exploring first the syntax of an expression and then the semantics, a chronology that was adopted in the early work on automation translation from one language to another. But it was quickly seen that, in natural language, syntax and semantics often merged in inconvenient ways and that it became impossible to study the semantics of a natural language without considering also the structure of the language in question. This discovery was to have various implications for the study of computer languages and the use of AI techniques for linguistic purposes.

Particular research programmes also influenced the approach to AI work in computational linguistics. For example, Chomsky's theory of generative grammar radically affected work in linguistics, including attitudes to how computers could be given an understanding of linguistic expressions. One approach is for language-processing programs to use grammatical rules to *parse* the input sentences, ie to analyse the symbolic expressions and to provide thereby clues as to what the various parts of a sentence might mean. Parsing components are virtually universal in natural-language-processing systems, but it has so far proved impossible to explore all types of natural-language expressions using parsing processes.

Today increasing attention is being directed at exploring the underlying logic (or logics) of language. Chomsky's linguistic analysis, for example, is virtually an enquiry in symbolic logic and the various ways of exploring language-related knowledge representations depend upon symbolic formalisms of various sorts. The syntax (grammar) of a natural language is a patterned structure that can also be formalised in symbolic terms. It is the possibility of formalising aspects of natural language that allows linguistic understanding to be modelled in artificial systems.

Research highlighted by Webber (1983) and others shows how logic and deduction are relevant to the generation of natural language. For example, producing a successful sentence may require reasoning about the competence of other people: we take into account what a person is likely to know before we make a remark. Ideally a computer would do the same when addressing a human user. Moreover the limitations of first-order logic, concerned as it is with eternal truths, suggest that other formalisms need to be developed to cope with a changing world. Model logic is interested in relating knowledge to action as a means of exploring the characteristics of 'possible worlds'. This approach is also relevant to the task of language generation.

Everyday language relies on a range of reasoning techniques that can handle simple first-order relations, the properties of a changing world, common sense, fuzzy information, etc. The complexity of these disparate techniques is one of the reasons why it is difficult to build a sophisticated conversational ability and language understanding into computer programs.

SOME EARLY SYSTEMS

The ARPA SUR (speech understanding research) project yielded a range of linguistic programs designed to demonstrate various automatic language-understanding abilities. Under the terms of the overall programme five different speech projects were initiated and various subcontracts placed for developing components for speech systems. Bolt, Beranek and Newman produced SPEECHLIS and HWIM (Hear What I Mean). By 1976 Carnegie-Mellon University had produced a number of different programs: HEARSAY-I, DRAGON, HARPY and HEARSAY-II. And SRI International also developed a speech understanding program in collaboration with SDC. (These programs are described in detail in Barr and Feigenbaum, 1981.)

The LUNAR program, rated by many observers as one of the most successful language-processing systems, was developed to help human users to analyse the rocks brought back from the moon. The system first works out the meaning of the user's query, and then answers the question. This language-processing facility is essentially a type of expert system: it assesses enquiries against a detailed knowledge-base, in this case in the field of geology, and then provides a specific detailed response.

The SHRDLU program, again much publicised, represents a robot that shows its understanding by replying to a human user and by behaving in certain ways at the human's command. Here the simulated robot contains an internal representation of its own acts and a model of the external world. This enables the 'robot' to cope with questions that would otherwise be unmanageable. SHRDLU, like other AI programs (see Chapter 8), is interested in the 'blocks world'. It can carry on a conversation with a human user, the program answering questions, pointing out when a query is ambiguous or obscure, declaiming 'OK' when it carries out a command, and quite likely to say 'You're welcome!' when finally thanked by the human user.

Application	Definition	Status in mid-1985	Active companies and products
Database interfaces: mainframes and minis	Portable or integrated front-ends to DBMS and other applications software	Several 100 commercial systems installed, starting in 1981; prices from $13,000 to $70,000 IBS	Artificial Intelligence Corp. (Intellect); Mathematica, (Ramis II English); Carnegie Group;
Database interfaces: micros	PC or similar interfaces to application software or online services	First product in 1982; several in 1984 and 1985, with some 10,000's sold; prices from $75 (standalone) to $395 (package)	Excalibur (Savvy); Microrim (Clout); Microdata; Safeguard Business Systems; TI's Natural-Link is an NL menu system
Dialogue interfaces	Conversational interface to complex system, eg expert system or ICAI	Prototype include investment adviser, ICAI systems, none known to be operational	Cognitive Systems; several research programmes, including British Telecom, Logica, U of Cambridge in UK Alvey Programme
Content scanning	Processing messages or other semi-format texts to decide action or routeing	A prototype for shipping messages due to be operational in 1985; systems for international banking telexes in progress	Cognitive Systems; Carnegie Group; Small AI
Text editing	Checking style and grammar of text and suggesting improvements	At least one system undergoing extensive field trials by 1984	IBM (Epistle); AT&T's Writer's Workbench has some NLP features; other office systems cos. believed to be interested
Machine translation	Computer translation of texts from source to target natural language	Some mainframe systems have been in use since the 1960s; since 1983 mini and micro systems have been appearing	Systran Institute (mainframe systems); ALPS, Logos & Weidner are main suppliers of office systems
Talkwriter	Transcription of spoken input into computer text	Hardware under development; some promising demonstrations; product trials expected in 1986	IBM; Kurzweil; Speech Systems; major DARPA and Alvey research projects at MIT, CMU, Edinburgh

Figure 10.1   Applications of Natural Language Processing (*Source: Johnson, 1985*)

APPLICATIONS AND DEVELOPMENT

Applications of natural language processing are shown in Figure 10.1 with an indication provided of the progress towards operational systems. The applications can be divided into interfacing applications for human/computer communication, and text processing applications to support human-to-human

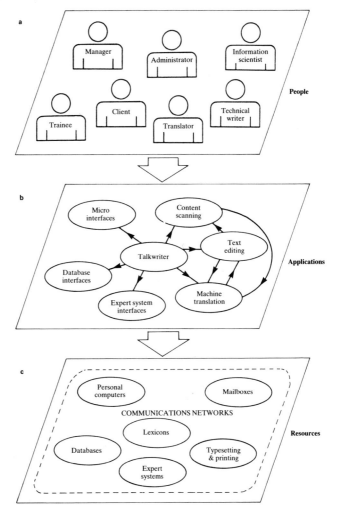

Figure 10.2 Levels of Corporate Language Systems
(Source: Johnson, 1985)

communication. Some of the applications are currently operational; others will emerge in the future. One suggestion is that
organisations could have integrated natural language processing
(NLP) systems (structured as shown in Figure 10.2). A future
scenario for the development of NLP applications is shown in the
two parts of Figure 10.3.

Year	Tools and techniques	Database interfaces: Mainframes & minis	Database interfaces: Micros	Dialogue interfaces
1986		Demos, of intergrated talkwriter/db interfaces	Numerous products with NL menu interfaces;	Telephone enquiry systems of field test
1987	Advanced PSG parsers implemented in systems;	Interface-building tools show proven results; Commercial new-generation interfaces on test	NL interfaces common options on applications software	Expert systems interfaces on field test
1988	Eurotra research MT system implemented			Telephone enquiry systems begin operational use; Moderate performance ICAI systems demo'd.
1989		New-generation interfaces in operational use	NL interfaces on a steady minority of packages sold	
1990		Demonstrations of integrated corporate language systems (CLS)		Expert systems interfaces operational
1991				Moderate performance ICAI systems operational
1992		New-generation interfaces increasingly supersede 4GLs		
1993		CLS in operational use	True new-generation NL available on personal computers	ICAI systems on personal computers
1994				
1995		Integrated CLS begins to become standard practice in large organisations		

Figure 10.3i   Scenario for NLP Development
(Source: Johnson, 1985)

Year	Content scanning	Text editing	Machine translation	Talkwriters
1986	Products for banking messages in field test (Atrans)	First NLP products on beta-test	Several WP suppliers announce integration with MT products	Field tests by IBM, Kurzweil, Speech Systems begin
1987		First NLP products on general release; further WP suppliers announce products	Major IT suppliers (IBM?) announce own products	Phoneme recognition task largely solved; CMU continuous recognition demo'd
1988	Message scanning systems operational in banks and other applications	Integration with full MT demonstrated	Operational systems for all major language pairs (Eng, Fr, Ger, Ital, Jap)	
1989	Abstract scanning systems, integration with MT, both demo'd		Well established in technical translation for productivity and quality benefits	Some machines in operation use for limited applications
1990		Text-editing/MT integration operational		Alvey project completed
1991				
1992	Abstract scanning systems operational			
1993	Abstracting systems demo'd, relying on large term banks		Eurotra-based systems in operational use; MT becoming essential to top-quality translation	High-performance machines with wide capability available
1994				
1995				

Figure 10.3ii   Scenario for NLP Development
(Source: Johnson, 1985)

VOICE SYSTEMS

General

Voice systems in human beings can function in either input or output modes, ie we can speak and hear. One purpose of AI development is to enable computers to synthesise voices (male, female, young, old, in any known language) and to recognise the voices of people (or computers) replying to them. Voice-recognition and speech-synthesis systems will increasingly feature in commercial products, and such facilities will be commonplace in the interface provisions of new-generation computers. A number of observers (eg Kirvan, 1984) have suggested that the speech technology industry is now ready for major expansion.

Voice input can conveniently be divided into speech recognition and speaker verification (it is one thing to recognise a voice, quite another to understand what a person is saying). Similarly, voice output can be seen as comprising speech coding and speech synthesis. In one type of specialised product (called a voice store-and-forward system), spoken words are stored for future retrieval by other users. These and other facilities will progressively improve the man/machine interface in the years to come. It will be possible to speak to computers, in any language, and for them to answer back. Already there are a number of experimental devices that use a combination of speech input and speech output to aid communication with human users. For example, an electropneumatic robotic device (Henthorn and Dawson, 1983), formerly speech-controlled, now also carries a vocal response unit. The aim of such work is to explore the feasibility of using speech input and output to control a robotic system.

It is also anticipated that speech recognition and generation technology will enhance existing telecommunications facilities. Text messaging has already been very successful where people have access to terminals and the associated computers, but voice messaging could be even more effective since there would be no requirement for standard terminals. Many organisations are now exploring the possibilities for development in these areas. The Bell-Northern research/INRS-Telecom team, for instance, is now researching the efficient coding of speech for digital transmission and also looking at the design of man/machine communication systems. The communication research includes the development of techniques for the computer recognition of spoken information, the computer production of speech, and the design of communication protocols that integrate these techniques for practical applications.

As we would expect, there are different research problems in speech input and speech output. It is relatively easy, for example, to define the requirements of speech synthesis, though voice intonation can bring problems. Without a detailed knowledge of semantics – beyond the grasp of current machines – computers cannot decide, in any convincing way, when to emphasise a word or when to raise or lower their voice. In speech input (ie when the computer is required to recognise what is being said) a main problem is that the human voice, variously affected by emotion, alcohol, fatigue, etc, is an extremely inconsistent transmitter. Factors such as volume, accent and ambient noise can also make it extremely difficult for a computer to derive any sense from what human beings are saying in its environment. Artificially synthesised sentences can now be produced in a variety of contexts, but it is extremely unusual for a computer-based system to be able to recognise connected speech with much consistency.

Voice Recognition

People have speculated, for at least two thousand years, on the possibility of artefacts being able to recognise and understand human speech. (There is an intriguing reference to machine understanding of speech in Samuel Butler's *Erewhon,* first published in 1872.) The possibility of machines recognising spoken words has been practically researched for a few decades, though until recently with little success.

In human beings, the ear detects sound waves which are then converted into nerve pulses for transmission to the brain. Similarly, a microphone converts sound waves into electrical pulses for subsequent interpretation. It is this interpretation task that is at the heart of the speech-recognition problem. An early step towards solving it was taken by an acoustics engineer about thirty years ago. He built a box of electronic equipment with a red light on top and linked to a microphone. Whenever anyone in the vicinity mentioned the word 'watermelon' the light would flash! Unfortunately this engagingly successful device did not point the way to effective speech-recognition systems. There are around 10,000 words commonly used in conversation, and 'watermelon', apparently is unusually easy to recognise. The ensuing spate of bigger and better watermelon boxes only led to about 100 words ever being recognised, and only if these were pronounced very carefully, one at a time, and by a speaker whom the system had been tuned. A different approach was needed.

One approach relied on integrating various acoustic techniques with the most successful linguistic and question-answering techniques. The aim was to develop a speech understanding system that contains a range of acoustic, syntactic and semantic elements tailored to a particular subject domain. One such subject domain is the game of chess, used in speech-understanding system developed at Carnegie-Mellon University in 1971. Here it was found that the system could not easily distinguish between the words 'queen' and 'king' – an evident limitation! By the mid–1970s a few experimental speech-understanding systems were being developed, and it became clear that systems already able to handle, albeit slowly, more than a hundred words would be capable of enhancement to provide much more competent systems.

It was obvious that voice-recognition and speech-understanding systems would need to model at least some of the processes occurring in the analogous human systems. The computer uses an analogue-to-digital converter to digitise the voice information received (this is equivalent to how the ear converts sound waves into electrical pulses). When the data stored is a mathematical translation of a three-dimensional waveform, the information can serve as an effective template. Template-matching is the most common approach to voice recognition.

Most voice-recognition systems are speaker-dependent (ie they can only cope with words spoken by the same person), so the person must first speak each word of the required vocabulary to allow the system to generate reference templates. The larger the vocabulary, the larger the memory required by the computer. Once the reference templates are in place, the speaker can utter a word: the computer system 'hears' it, via a microphone, converts it into pulses, and makes reference to the stored template for that word, whereupon a match is found and the computer responds accordingly. The technique of *Linear Predictive Coding* (LPC) has been developed as a system of mathematical analysis that enables the computer to use fewer numbers when storing template details, so facilitating significant memory savings. It is also possible to use *features analysis* to enable a sound's phonetic characteristics, instead of waveform data, to be stored.

There are many speech elements that can be used to aid the tasks of voice recognition and speech understanding. We have already mentioned such elements as phonetics, syntax and semantics. There are also *phonemics* (where pronunciations vary when words are spoken together in sentences), *morphemics* (combining *morphemes,* units of meaning, to form words, as with plurals, conjugations, etc), *prosodics* (where stress and intonation vary), and *pragmatics* (where conversation may be influenced by the speaker's intentions). Underlying the security of such speech elements is the holding of relevant information, not only template data but also the domain-specific knowledge without which a computer could not aspire to semantic understanding.

The various theoretical and research programmes have yielded a growing range of practical products. For instance, the Nippon Electricity Company launched the Voice Data Input Terminal in 1978, a device able to recognise up to 120 words, spoken continuously in groups of up to five words. This followed the voice recognition units introduced in 1976 by the US firm Threshold Technology Inc. IBM researchers at Yorktown Heights used a computer in 1980 to transcribe spoken sentences from a 1000-word vocabulary read at normal speaking pace (91 per cent accuracy was claimed). At the same time the Scott Instruments Corporation was introducing the Vet–1 voice-entry terminal, to be followed by a Vet–2 model with enhanced performance.

Typically the NEC terminal included a voice analyser, a reference pattern memory, and three microprocessors required to perform programming, input/output, and control functions. In this configuration the pattern-matching processor, a high-speed bipolar assemblage of mostly transistor-logic (TTL) devices, matches the patterns of incoming speech with those stored in the reference pattern memory. The I/O processor is the interface between the voice recognition system and remote-control units serving two operator positions. This processor also handles input from a tape reader that provides the words to be stored. Recognition in this system is complete 300 milliseconds after the end of the word group, allowing an input of up to 60 words a minute. The Threshold 600 achieved recognition in a similar time

LANGUAGE AND SPEECH165

with a vocabulary of less than 100 words but required up to one second when the full 512 word vocabulary was used.

The smaller the required vocabulary, the easier it is to design a reliable and effective recognition system. If a large vocabulary is needed for a particular application the user must be prepared to spend time teaching the machine how to respond. And even then, with current technology, there are various impediments to accurate recognition. *Word verification* methods have been developed to improve the efficiency of the recognition process.

The verification approach is based on the 1-word vocabulary, ie only one word or phrase is acceptable at a time, the aim being to verify the active word, not to select the correct word from among many, as is attempted in most speech recognition systems. More processing time and more interpretive data can be focused on the single word, with limitations on the total vocabulary size determined by the amount of mass storage available. An experimental system called voice-aided wirewrapping (described by Scott, 1983) uses the word verification approach.

In the Scott Instruments VBLS system, which also uses word verification, training the system is regarded as an essential part of the user's learning process. For instance, the system can be trained in foreign languages by functioning in a conventional way in a language laboratory: when a student hears a word from a tape recorder, he repeats it and the utterance is used by the computer as a training template. This type of application is one of many that will influence fifth-generation research into the development of intelligent interfaces.

By the late–1970s it was obvious that speech recognition systems were a practical possibility for various applications. Voice control in the industrial environment was seen as particularly useful where:

- the worker's hands are busy;
- mobility is required during the data entry process;
- the worker's eyes must remain fixed upon a display, an optical instrument, or some object to be tracked;
- the environment is too harsh to allow use of a keyboard.

Specific industrial applications for voice-recognition systems were identified for such areas as quality control, incoming inspection, receiving accountability, part and serial number verification, warehousing and sorting. In the early 1980s, voice data entry was being used in such CAD/CAM applications as text annotation in printed circuit board component layout, preparation of program tapes for NC machine tools, and generation of wire lists, civil engineering drawings, structural drawings, and bills of material. Voice input was also being used in the office environment.

In general the performance of word-recognition systems has been measured by three parameters:

- *accuracy*. It has been found that poor accuracy quickly discourages user involvement, without which it is difficult to improve operating systems. Word-recognition accuracies below 95 per cent cause frustration and, in practical terms, the data flow may be seriously impaired. Various working systems in the early–1980s boasted accuracies greater than 98 per cent;

- *vocabulary size*. With an increase in vocabulary size it is often difficult to maintain accuracy. In fact, accuracy is at its best in speaker-dependent, isolated-word systems operating with small vocabularies carrying few similar-sounding word pairs ('confusing pairs'). It is easier to extend the vocabulary if most of the words are polysyllabic, making it easier to avoid confusion;

- *data entry speed*. Many applications, in industry and elsewhere, require vocabularies of 50 words or less, but available systems may offer data entry speeds that are marginal or even inadequate. In general, continuous-speech recognition systems provide faster throughput than isolated-word systems, but often at the expense of accuracy. In fast continuous speech, adjacent words modify each other, an effect termed 'coarticulation', so that individual words may no longer match the reference templates.

In 1980, IBM researchers at Yorktown Heights, NY, used a computer to transcribe spoken sentences from a 1000-word vocabulary read at a normal speaking pace. The sentences were transformed into hard copy with 91 per cent accuracy, believed at that time to be the best obtained under complex experimental conditions. Use was made of an IBM System/370 Model 168 computer with high fidelity equipment. The user talked into a microphone, and the words recognised by the computer appeared on a screen.

This work, reported by Dr Frederick Jelinek at the 1980 SAE Congress in Detroit, was based on a 1000-word natural vocabulary drawn from sentences used by lawyers in submitting US patent applications in the laser field. The entire laser patent text embraced a vocabulary of 12,000 words, reduced by computer search to the most frequently used 1000 to enable the recognition experimentation to be carried out.

Progress towards cost-effective voice-recognition systems has been influenced by the development of high levels of computer power at reducing costs. In common with other electronic systems, recognition units are beginning to exploit VLSI technology to achieve high-performance, relatively low-cost results. By the late–1970s a voice preprocessor used to convert an analogue signal from the microphone into a digital signal for processing might have occupied a 15-inch square board, whereas today such a preprocessor can be incorporated on a couple of VLSI chips.

The emergence of 32-bit and 64-bit microprocessors will also influence the development of speech-recognition systems. The increased computer power will be linked to enhanced algorithms to achieve higher levels of performance and reliability. There will be growing pressure for the development of an accurate continuous-speech algorithm, which in turn will require increased computer power. In currently available systems, trade-offs are inevitable between performance (eg vocabulary size) and cost (eg the amount of storage available), with the result that systems range from small-vocabulary, speaker-dependent units to large-vocabulary multi-user facilities. And speech output units (see Speech Synthesis, below) generate sounds ranging from robot-voice stereotypes to the most persuasive male and female voices. In 1982 it was reckoned that several thousand computer installations were using voice data input. One prediction is that by

1990 the market for speech recognition units will have reached $100 million worldwide.

In 1983, Intel developed its entry into voice-recognition markets with three levels of products; a development system, a speech transaction board and a chip set. The Intel board allowed up to 200 discrete utterances to be enrolled, each lasting up to 2.2 seconds, and recognised discrete utterances only, with 80 to 240 milliseconds' pause between commands. The Votan 6000 recognition unit was initially marketed for a language profile that Stu Farnham, director of international marketing, called the American dialect.

At the (December 1982) Midcon show in Dallas, Texas Instruments described work on a single-board, speaker-dependent word recogniser, a prototype indicating (for example) the algorithms that TI deems to be important. The prototype could recognise about 50 words, the average item lasting 0-6 second. It was possible to string words together to form phrases: a single utterance could contain a string of up to 21 connected vocabulary items.

The TI approach uses the digital extraction of linear-predictive-coding parameters, based on a model of human speech. The parameters are used to characterise words and data is passed into the memory for future reference. The system extracts the parameters from heard speech and performs computations to determine similarities between the spoken words and the stored templates. The algorithm, in common with algorithms in other systems, also carries out nonlinear time-warping to compensate for speed variations in human speech. As with other systems, software is a key consideration.

One of the most successful voice-recognition systems is the Logos system, developed by Logica using techniques designed by the Government's Joint Speech Research Unit (JSRU). Logos, designed for continuous speech, allows extensive real-time processing to take place according to word sequence rules adapted to particular applications. A Logica brochure highlights various Logos features:

  – continuous recognition of natural speech in real time for vocabularies of up to several hundred words;

- fully user-programmable word sequence rules (syntax) also allowing the incorporation of error correction strategies;

- special 'wildcard' templates to permit keyword spotting, and to eliminate spurious input (such as coughs);

- sophisticated acoustic analysis which reduces sensitivity to variations in microphone position and background noise;

- a powerful microcomputer to run applications-specific programs in high- or low-level language and to handle interfacing to the user and host machines;

- highly modular design allowing flexibility in configuration for small or large vocabularies and simple or complex applications.

Logos represented a significant advance over most other word recognition systems, allowing continuous recognition of spoken phrases of any length from a predefined vocabulary. This requirement demands extensive resort to parallel computing; otherwise, the recognition process, unable to keep pace with the speech rate, would not be able to operate in real time. To handle large vocabularies, a split is made so that central sets of computing for sections of the vocabulary are individually handled by a separate dynamic programming processor, each being based on a standard Intel 8086 microprocessor working on a 16-bit basis. Similar micros are used for the control processor, designed to handle interactions between templates and to supervise first-stage signal capture and analysis.

The word-sequencing rules (syntax) can be used to reduce the number of word choices at any point in a phrase, so reducing the amount of computation needed and in some cases improving the recognition accuracy. The syntax also includes error-correction strategies. Rule 'nodes' are each connected to a word or groups of alternative words allowed at that point.

Nodes can be looped together to allow the words between them to be recognised any number of times: in a simple case all the digits may be allowed between two looped nodes, thus allowing the operator to speak a digit sequence of any length. Recognition results are fed out either at the end of a phrase or on a continuous basis a word or so behind the current utterance.

Logos can be controlled by a VDU or host computer. Users are individually required to train the machine by speaking one example of each word in the defined vocabulary; where a VDU is used, the operator is prompted with each word when the training mode is selected. The reference patterns obtained during training can be stored. The functional operation of Logos is shown in Figure 10.4 (spectrum analysis being initially performed on microphone input).

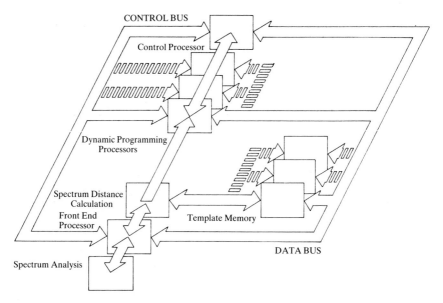

Figure 10.4   Functional Operation of Logos
(Source: Logica brochure)

Logos uses algorithms developed at JSRU and includes a facility for programming syntax in the form of a finite state grammar with loops. The method of acoustic analysis incorporates such features as noise compensation, spectrum shape normalisation and variable frame rate analysis designed to improve the recognition performance. The high degree of flexibility and the programmability make Logos a powerful tool for applications requiring connected or continuous speech input.

There is scope for extending Logos for multi-speaker use. It is expected that the system will be increasingly relevant to applications in such areas as information retrieval from computer databases, data entry to computers, programming of NC machine tools, CAD, office automation, and the direct control of training simulators.

Today there is a growing range of voice-recognition systems available as commercial products. The range has expanded through the 1980s and will have a growing impact on office practices in the years ahead. Newton (1985) highlighted two important voice-recognition products:

- **The Texas Instruments Speech Command System (SCS)**
  The TI Professional Computer now offers voice recognition by means of the speech command system (SCS), comprising a card that plugs into one of the Professional's slots, software, and a headset. The software can set up a user-defined vocabulary of up to 50 words (or more by switching to lower-level vocabularies), whereupon spoken words are associated with a string of up to 40 ASCII characters. The software also offers functions such as dictation, calendar/tickler facilities, telephone management, autodialling, call forwarding, telephone directory management, and selectable pre-recorded greetings;

- **The Votan VPC 2000 Voice Card**
  This adds voice input/output and telephone management capabilities to the IBM Personal Computer and compatible systems. The vocabulary of 75 words can be exchanged with other vocabulary subsets as required. The Voice Key software enables the user to drive application programs by voice commands; and incorporates voice output for operator prompting, feedback and messaging. Telephone interfacing capabilities include auto-answer and autodial.

These were two of a growing spectrum of voice-recognition facilities. Vacca (1985), for example, profiled the IBM Talkwriter and Kurzweil Applied Intelligence's Voicewriter. Such types of products will become increasingly common in the electronic office.

Voice Synthesis

Speech synthesis is the other side of the aural communication coin. We have seen that many companies specialising in voice recognition systems are also interested in speech synthesis. In fact various techniques – for example, linear predictive coding (see above) – are common to both.

In 1978 a speech synthesiser chip, the TMC 0280, appeared with the TMC 0350 read-only memory and the TMC 0270 controller in the Speak & Spell learning aid from Texas. This was one of the first speech synthesis chips based on the (then) recently discovered voice-compression technique of linear-predictive-coding. When the system produces speech, the controller specifies to the synthesiser the starting point of a string of data stored in the memory. The 131,072-bit ROM can accommodate 165 words, its output providing the pitch, amplitude and filter parameters from which the synthesiser chip constructs the speech waveform.

The TMC 0280 system (described by Wiggins and Brantingham, 1978) was one of a number heralding 'yet another phase of electronic wizardry'. In 1978 it was easy to see the practical possibilities of speaking clocks, machines that could explain their operations in spoken words, and computers with which conversation would be feasible using natural language. And at that time it was discerned that voice recognition (see above) would prove a weightier problem than speech synthesis.

The late-1970s saw a range of products that could synthesise their own speech in response to queries or other inputs. Votrax of Michigan, a division of Federal Screw Works, developed portable speech synthesisers for the vocally impaired, and began manufacturing a Business Communicator which was able to translate up to 64 telephone Touch-Tone inputs into an audio response. A multilingual voice system, at first synthesising English and German, was also developed. Master Specialities Company, California, manufactured a talking calculator and a variety of word-oriented announcement products. Similarly, Telesensory Systems Inc, again in California, launched a talking calculator for the blind.

By 1980, IBM had launched an Audio Typing Unit, using voice synthesis techniques to provide a variety of functions for blind typists. The speech was created when basic speech sounds (phonemes) were combined according to an extensive set of pronunciation rules stored in the units memory. In theory this allowed for an unlimited vocabulary: sounds could be synthesised in any combination. Furthermore, the unit blended and modified the phoneme commands for transitions, pauses and rhythm (see *Software Digest*, 8/11/79).

Some early speech synthesisers were intended as commercial products for education or domestic use. We have mentioned Speak & Spell as a learning (and teaching) aid, and talking calculators have been available for several years. Linggard and Marlow (1979) described a low-cost, programmable digital speech synthesiser used for research purposes: this device has a general-purpose architecture which enables it to stimulate formant-type synthesisers as well as vocal-track models, and all in real time. Two hundred integrated circuits were used at a cost (in 1979) of £350. A principal use of the machine was to compare different synthesiser types.

In 1980 Votrax announced a single-chip synthesiser, the SC–01 having as major features unlimited vocabulary and minimal memory requirements. With this product, neither the chip supplier nor a human speaker is required to assist in generating a vocabulary. Phonemes are stored as 6-bit words in a separate memory chip, with the speech integrated circuit containing the circuits for selecting the phonemes and connecting them to generate the necessary words (and other sounds).

In some applications, the synthesiser chip independently accesses the stored phonemes. When the reproduced phrases reach a certain complexity (eg if words to be spoken go beyond a simple phrase), a microprocessor is used to control the synthesis task. The LSI chip was designed for Votrax by Silicon Systems Inc and Intelligent Systems Corp, maker of small business systems, developed a voice-synthesis peripheral based on the SC–01 circuit. 1980 also saw the launch by National Semiconductor Corp of its first speech-synthesis chips.

By the early-1980s, speech synthesis applications were evident in a wide range of industrial, commercial and educational sectors. Samuel (1981) described the use of a microprocessor and a speech synthesiser which together can detect system faults and then make a telephone call to summon assistance. Research has suggested that voice response is more effective than flashing lights or video displays. In this system the vocabulary is limited to about 1000 words (larger vocabularies are possible but involve some loss of speech clarity). Speech synthesis of this sort allows effective contact to be maintained at all times with a remote operator. This is of particular value where system monitoring is required in hostile environments and in other circumstances where it is not convenient for an operator to be present. And, inevitably, the military has had an eye on what can be done with voice-recognition and speech-synthesis techniques. Today, partly under the stimulus of the fifth-generation programme, a number of approaches to speech synthesis are being researched. In summary, it is now possible to produce practical speech output by means of waveform synthesis, constructive synthesis or analysis synthesis.

With *waveform synthesis,* the original speech waveform is recreated by sampling the input at suitable intervals (eg at a sampling rate of 8 KHz, yielding data rates ranging from 64K to 96K per second). The typical rates tend to make unaided waveform synthesis impractical because too much data needs to be stored. Storage requirements can be significantly reduced by developing an electronic model of the vocal tract controlled by parameters derived from raw input data. The Texas Instruments LPC technique, for example, models the vocal tract by means of a 10-pole, time-varying, digital lattice filter. Here the bit rate of the coded data for pitch, energy level and the filter parameters is up to 100 times lower than that required for waveform synthesis. (The LPC approach is highly suited to representing the human vocal equipment.)

In *constructive synthesis,* speech output is generated from a library of token sounds under the control of a set of stored rules. For example, American English can be broken up into 42 'building-block' sounds (*phonemes*), though it can be difficult to assemble such elements into natural-sounding speech. A TI approach, using the constructive synthesis method, expands the 42-phoneme family to 128 allophones, fine variations of the basic sounds. Allophonic speech is a better approximation to human speech, and there is scope for further refining the allophonic rules to achieve higher levels of naturalness.

Analysis synthesis relies on generating speech from human input. An initial step in this method may be to write the complete vocabulary for a product into a script: all the words, including ther repetitions in various contexts, are used. Then, during a recording session, data is extracted from a speaker's reading of the script. During LPC analysis, data is transformed from direct analogues of speech waveforms to LPC–10 parameters which are then fed into a synthesiser chip. The data can be edited to improve the final sound quality. In this way, the analysis-synthesis approach accurately preserves the character of human speech.

There are many actual and potential uses of voice synthesis in the office environment (for example, electronic mail, database enquiry, proof-reading, optical character recognition, training, etc); and a growing range of products to meet such specific application requirements. For instance, Rosenberg (1985) pro-files some of the products demonstrated at Speech Tech '85 (forthcoming releases included the Multiple Rate Voice Terminal from GTE Government Systems, and systems from IBM, Speech Systems and Kurzweil); and Shapiro (1985) and Newton (1985) profile DECtalk and other products.

TRANSLATION

In the early days of computing it was believed that certain syntactic transformations could be applied to natural language without distorting the meaning. One of the results of this belief was a great effort in the 1950s to have computers translate text from one language to another. Multilingual dictionaries were set up on computer tape, and grammars were developed to indicate the differences (in word order, noun cases, etc) in the various natural languages. This work, however, was largely unsuccessful, the generated translations being usually unreliable and inaccurate. (One example often quoted is the translation of 'The spirit is willing but the flesh is weak' into Russian and then back into English to give 'The wine is agreeable but the meat has spoiled'.) A central lesson learned from the early failures was that the line between syntax and semantics is extremely hazy, a difficulty that is less evident in the artificial languages developed for the writing of computer programs.

Today there are well over a dozen translation systems (WEIDNER, LAGOS, ALPS, etc) that serve as aids for the professional translator. Few automatic systems would be trusted to provide unaided translations with an acceptable degree of accuracy. Some systems produce a raw translation which is then edited by a human being; and some are interactive, able to ask the human translator for help when they encounter problems. But the task facing both human and machine translators should not be underestimated: there are around 5000 languages and dialects spoken in the world, and with increased communication across national boundaries there will be a growing requirement for translation services.

Some observers view the prospect of automatic translation with great optimism. Thus Rouvray and Wilkinson (1984) declare: 'we are convinced that, for particular applications, all major languages will be translated by computer by the early 1990s'. The possibilities for machine translation developed rapidly in the 1960s following the work of Zellig Harris and Noam Chomsky. It became possible to devise logical rules for the analysis of language, a development that aided the computerisation of linguistic acts. Today millions of words a year are translated, with the help of computers, by such organisations as ITT, Xerox, General Motors and the Commission of the European Communities in Luxembourg. The most successful translations are in the fields of science, technology, law and administration: computers cannot yet master the subtleties of creative writing.

One of the most successful translation packages is SYSTRAN, first installed nearly a decade ago and today running on an IBM 370/158 computer. Already this type of system is handling around 20 per cent of the French-to-English translation and about 50 per cent of the English-to-Italian for the European Commission. Rouvray and Wilkinson (1984) highlight some of the most effective translation systems, including SYSTRAN, WEIDNER, ALPS, SPANAM, TAUB, CULT, SMART and SUSY. Efforts are made to reassure human translators that computers are unlikely to replace large numbers of employees, but some observers (eg Durham, 1983) acknowledge that machine translation with *no* human involvement is the long-term research goal. Already the European Eurotra project is aiming to dramatically reduce the amount of initial translation and post-editing required by human beings. (The research may also overcome SYSTRAN's habit of translating 'hydraulic ram' into the equivalent of 'water goat'.)

Machine translation was originally viewed as a simple matter of replacing words in one language by words in another. It was only later that the many syntactic and semantic problems became evident. Progress in artificial intelligence, helping machines to understand language, will increase the effectiveness of computer translation, particularly in the areas were subtleties and ambiguities characterise the texts in question.

CURRENT APPLICATIONS AND RESEARCH

Today we witness multifaceted research on natural language processing, speech recognition, translation, voice synthesis, etc. Some of the developments are linked to new (often parallel) computer architectures; others to new algorithms or software. The architectural features of transputers, for example, are being exploited to provide enhanced speech recognition (Vaughan et al, 1987). Here use is made of a dynamic time warping algorithm ('each part of a word may be expanded, compressed or left unchanged' to facilitate template matching), and the system is configured in such a way that it could be expanded relatively easily to a multitransputer environment (the authors discuss the single template comparator and the multitemplate comparator). The dynamic time warping algorithm has been implemented in OCCAM to achieve effective speech recognition, albeit for a small number of words.

According to one estimate (Gartner Group Inc, cited in Lalonde and Donnelly, 1988), the 1987 North American market for voice recognition and voice synthesis systems was between

$50 million and $70 million, with an expected compound annual growth rate of 50%. Thus the market is expected to be around $400 million by 1991. Today there are voice technology applications in such areas as telecommunications, inventory control, office automation and security. Computer-based language translation is expected to find a range of market applications, as effective systems become commercially available. British Telecom, for example, has demonstrated a system for the instantaneous translation of speech. This configuration is based on two Merlin 5200 PCs, and is able to recognise and translate around 400 phrases. The prototype equipment can handle English, French, German, Spanish, Swedish and Italian.

The Intellect natural-language system, already mentioned was developed in the late-1970s by AIC and is now represented as a leading IBM mainframe product (Jones, 1988). A central aim is to offer users 'an ultra-friendly way of querying and manipulating data within corporate databases; and the system can even cope with language idiosyncracies. A competing product, DataTalker from Natural Language Inc (NLI), is similar to Intellect but includes an expert system facility to help users to construct queries. These and other systems are continuing to develop in the context of wide-ranging research. For example, a recent issue of the *IBM Journal of Research and Development* (March 1988) carried articles on spelling assistance for compound words, discrimination between word senses, large-vocabulary speech recognition, Japanese sentence analysis, sentence generation, etc.

Again it is worth highlighting, without comment, some research interests that focus on speech and natural language:

Haddock (1987) considers the 'incremental' interpretation of language as a route to comprehension.

Carbonell et al (1987) explore the acoustic-phonetic decoding of sentences as a major bottleneck in continuous speech recognition.

Zue (1987) surveys aspects of automatic speech recognition and understanding with attention to human speech and perception processes.

Schmandt (1987) explores the use of non-lexical acoustic cues as an aid to listener comprehension in a dialogue with a computer.

Finin (1987) considers the relevance of natural language to the effective use of expert systems.

Aggoun (1987) explores how the SYNTHEX system can handle prosodic information in speech synthesis.

Kayser et al (1987) describe an approach to reasoning in natural language (focus on the 'caricature' pattern-matching technique).

Jullien and Solvay (1987) consider the development of dialogue for a financial advice giving system.

Dalta (1987) describes a scheme for organising expert systems for automatic speech recognition.

Rich (1987) presents the procrastination approach to ambiguity, with focus on natural-languages interfaces.

SUMMARY

This chapter has profited some of the principal areas of interest relating to the automatic handling of speech and natural language. It is emphasised that language is frequently an assumed component in intelligent behaviour: it is essential for much human/human and human/machine intercourse, and assumed to underlie the characteristic thought processes of *Homo sapiens*.

Attention is given to some of the theoretical concerns that bear on speech and language research, and particular products are mentioned. We see that, as is common throughout AI, one area of interest soon evokes another. Thus natural-language systems often rely upon database structures and the effective storing of knowledge; and the manipulation of speech and language is often able to exploit the strategies and techniques developed for expert systems. Here, as elsewhere, we are encouraged to view AI as a coalescing whole, despite the necessary formalism whereby various topics are treated separately. This again suggests the growing parity between artificial and natural systems.

11 Theorems, Deduction, Automatic Programming

INTRODUCTION

Many of the specific formalisms associated with AI can be linked to achieve particular results. For example, methods of reasoning can be exploited to facilitate the manipulation of knowledge via logic programming; and strategies evolved for deduction and theorem proving can be applied to facilitate automatic programming. We have already seen that the Logic Theorist (developed in 1956) was able to prove 38 of the first 52 theorems in Chapter 2 of *Principia Mathematica* (by Russell and Whitehead); and that Gelernter's program was able to prove that the base angles of an isosceles triangle and equal.* Thus by the 1960s it was clear that computer-based systems could, using deduction and other methods, prove a range of theorems of different types (for example, purely formal demonstrations and familiar geometrical relations). Such developments were to influence the evolution of automatic programming, ie the automatic derivation of practical software systems from formal specifications (see below).

Today AI research into automatic programming is concerned with such aspects as the development of high-level languages that can, for example, generalise from examples, correct syntactical errors, detect misprints, offer interpretations of ambiguous descriptions and ask questions if statements are confused. One aim of automatic programming is to develop systems that can

---

* The celebrated 'pons asinorum' proof, discovered independently by the program, was first stated by Pappus (c. 300 AD).

provide English descriptions of algorithms; another is to evolve AI programs equipped to 'learn by experience' (here they would use fresh data to modify their own code to achieve unprecedented behaviour). A key objective is to provide semiautomatic and automatic software-development systems – to overcome, for instance, the many quality and resource problems that currently afflict the development of new software applications. Thus we can see that automatic programming is directly relevant to various AI topics that might be discussed under different heads: automatic deduction, learning, the human/machine interface, the evolving computer autonomy, etc.

We have already cited the Samuel program that can learn in the world of checkers. In an analogous way Sussman's HACKER program can learn general lessons from particular experiences in the much-exploited world of simulated blocks. In fact HACKER is able to learn by constructively criticising its own attempts to achieve an objective; and the system can be represented as a device for automatic programming – it is able to write and improve programs, and can learn to perform better with practice. Again we can see how such evident talents could relate to another area of AI; namely, expert systems. If artificial systems could be designed to learn more rapidly it would be easier to construct the knowledge bases without which expert systems are nothing more than empty shells (see Chapter 14).

This chapter highlights a few key aspects of automatic deduction and automatic programming, emphasising at the same time how such concerns relate to many seemingly disparate AI topics. It is also worth stressing that automatic programming is necessarily linked to the development of new artificial languages and that this is a central AI concern: thus Hofstadter (1979) observed that 'AI advances are language advances'. The topics indicated here are of prime concern to the growing spectrum of AI specialists researching in different fields.

AUTOMATIC DEDUCTION

General

The perennial and contentious question about whether computers can think is obviously related to their reasoning power.

Perhaps reasoning is a necessary, but not sufficient, condition for thinking. It may be argued that consciousness is another necessary requirement, that even though the human mind may at times manipulate information in an *un*consciousness manner it may not in such circumstances be said to be *thinking*. Such debates are partly semantic and need not detain us. What we need to emphasise is that automatic reasoning, in which automatic deduction is an important element, is an increasing crucial AI concern with many ramifications for the 'mental performance' of artefacts.

A central task is for computer-based systems to be able to draw conclusions from supplied information. Such information can be, for example, sensory information in robotic systems (see Chapter 12) or domain information in expert systems (Chapter 14). It is necessary, for reasoning to proceed, that the information be represented in a useful way and that methods be developed to allow conclusions to be drawn. There is also a growing awareness that artificial reasoning should be able to proceed in circumstances in which the supplied information is hazy or incomplete. Human beings are often obliged to draw conclusions from partial information, and if computer-based systems are to think with a similar sophistication they will have to learn to make deductions from fuzzy premises. This is another concern of AI specialists, not least in the rapidly expanding field of expert systems.

Automatic deduction, often taken as synonymous with automatic theorem-proving, was discussed at the celebrated Dartmouth College conference in 1956. Here the Logic Theorist was represented as a deduction system for propositional logic (Newell and Simon, 1956), and ideas were being developed that would form the basis of Gelernter's theorem prover and deductive systems in other fields (Wang, 1960; Gelernter, 1963). Soon after, Robinson (1965) described a method for proving theorems in first-order predictive calculus, and this was to influence attitudes to both commonsense reasoning and mathematical theorem-proving.

As with other areas of AI, great enthusiasm was shown in the early days for efforts to achieve automatic deduction. However, the emphasis shifted when the problems became apparent, and the early-1970s did not witness the expected advances in automatic reasoning. The late-1970s and early-1980s saw a new interest in this field: researchers were finding many problems that perhaps could not be solved in any other way.

Inference

It should be stressed that deduction is not the only type of inference (for centuries philosophers have speculated about the role of *inductive* logic as a means of obtaining new empirical knowledge). Moreover, even within deductive logic there are many approaches, devices, strategies, etc that can be used to derive conclusions, prove theorems and solve problems. Cohen and Feigenbaum (1982), for example, consider Robinson's resolution procedure as a method of automatic theorem-proving, a time-consuming strategy that has nonetheless yielded various extensions.

Resolution procedures rely on the fact that, if a theorem follows from its axioms, then the axioms and the *negation* of the theorem must together lead to a contradiction. The axioms and the negated theorem are used to produce new clauses, *resolvents,* which are then combined with the clauses from which they were derived – to generate new resolvents. The procedure is repeated recursively until a contradiction emerges, at which stage it is concluded that the theorem is proved.

In addition to developing nondeductive forms of reasoning (eg inductive methods, statistical methods, etc), researchers have also worked to expand the scope of the early deductive schemes. Nonmonotonic logic is seen as one of the most important extensions of deductive reasoning (logics based on the nonmonotonic approach are described in detail in Cohen and Feigenbaum, 1982). Here assumptions are made that might have to be abandoned in the light of new information. This is in contrast to traditional ('monotonic') deductive logic where the number of theorems grows as axioms are added. Various modes of nonmonotonic reasoning (eg reasoning by default, reasoning by circumscription, etc) have been described.

It is clear that AI systems can exploit a wide range of inference methods. The straightforward first-order reasoning method of the

Logic Theorist has today been supplemented by various nondeductive methods and by extentions to the basic deductive
approach. One tack is to identify the characteristic logics that
regulate human thought processes and to build these into artificial
systems. There is also the possibility that an effective 'logic of
emotion' may be uncovered, making it possible to build motivational states into AI systems. (The philosopher Spinoza claimed
that the emotions obey laws, much as do lines, planes and bodies;
and Pascal proclaimed that 'the heart has its reasons . . .') For the
present, the spectrum of logics are concerned essentially with
such matters as expert systems, theorem proving and automatic
programming.

Theorem Proving

We have already seen that theorem proving can be of many
different types. It may involve proving the theorems of Principia
Mathematica, the geometrical theorems of Euclid, other
theorems of logic and mathematics, etc. The aim may be for the
computer to 'discover' known proofs of to invent fresh proofs for
familiar theorems (much as a program may be designed to
discover a fresh chess end-game solution). In general, a theorem
prover may be expected to deduce a theorem (the effective
conclusion) from an axiomatic body of knowledge. This of course
suggests that the knowledge can be in any domain, and computer
theorem provers can in principle work as happily with geometry
and algebra as with medicine and imaginary 'blocks worlds'.

The SHRDLU program of Terry Winograd (1972), a 'blocks-
world' system, is an effective theorem prover, able to exploit
particular problem-solving stategies using deductive logic. One
early mathematical theorem prover is described by Guard et al
(1969). This program, SAM (Semi-Automated Mathematics) was
able to solve an open problem in lattice theory. Here, on contrast
to programs that work unaided to prove a theorem, SAM relies
on human assistance: 'Semi-automated mathematics is an
approach to theorem-proving which seeks to combine automatic
logic routines with ordinary proof procedures in such a manner
that the resulting procedure is both efficient and subject to human
intervention in the form of control and guidance.'

Again we can identify various approaches to automatic and semiautomatic theorem-proving. Resolution strategies can be used, and also the nonresolution (goal-directed) methods that are natural for human beings. (In this latter approach the inference methods are devised to mimic human reasoning.) Another approach, exploited by Boyer and Moore (1979), uses recursive function theory and heuristic techniques: a central purpose of the Boyer-Moore Theorem Prover (BMTP) is to automate induction proofs.

AUTOMATIC PROGRAMMING

General

Automatic programming, an increasingly important subclass of AI, represents the effective automation of some part of the overall task of program development. At present the aim is to help programmers with their tasks, relieving them of burdensome activity and bringing a higher level of efficiency to the business of program design, coding, etc. Already there is speculation that automatic programming will make various classes of programmers redundant, while adding greatly to the levels of computer competence in the traditional programming environment. It is hard to overestimate the importance of automatic programming for the AI enterprise. Thus Barr and Feigenbaum (1982) declare that: 'In a sense, all of AI is a search for appropriate methods of automatic programming.'

The early development of compilers has been represented as a first step in automatic programming. For example, Backus and Herrik (1954) described the first FORTRAN compiler as an 'automatic programming' system. In general, the task of automatic programming may be seen as 'raising the level' at which useful instructions can be given to a computer-based system. For this to be accomplished, it is essential for computer software to be able to reason about itself, to generate appropriate code for particular purposes (LISP, for example, has the valuable talent of being able to manipulate programs as data). Once software can function is such a way, it can assume various interesting features: it can, for example, become self-adaptive, able to evolve in new environmental circumstances without human intervention. Such an ability may be viewed as a significant enhancement to computer autonomy.

The central practical task of automatic programming is to ease the programming burden. Computers, in this scenario, can be induced to write their own programs – so, for example, saving human beings from the onerous task of system coding. And automatic-programming systems can be evaluated according to the time and effort that they save, the reliability of the generated software, the ease with which future modifications can be added, the range of tasks that can be handled, etc.

Specifications

An automatic-programming system needs the actual program requirement to be *specified* in a way that it can understand (it is also necessary to identify the *target language,* the *problem area* and the *method of operation*). Various ways of specifying program requirements to automatic-programming systems have been devised. *Formal* specification methods – very high-level programming languages – are often intended to list exhaustively the required program features; or there may be an interactive capacity, to enable the human user to supply extra information as necessary. Some automatic-programming systems can build programs following scrutiny of examples of what the programs are expected to achieve; or by interpreting natural-language instructions.

Thus there are various ways in which specifications can be formulated to provide comprehensible input to automatic-programming systems. The ideal must be to design systems that can cope with the higher-level input: this is an effect analogue of what happens in human verbal intercourse, when we ask someone 'in so many words' to do something. The most sophisticated automatic-programming system therefore is one that can construct appropriate goal-directed programs when, in everyday language, we tell it to do so.

Reasoning from Specifications

Various different methods are employed in automatic-programming systems to build programs from the supplied specifications. Where the input and output conditions can be specified in the formalism of the predicate calculus, then a theorem-proving approach can be adopted. Here the required program can be defined as a statement to be proved, and the actual program is achieved as a product of the proof generated by the theorem prover. The proof produces statements and axioms of various types (conditional statements, sequential statements, loops, recursions, etc), and these can be exploited to derive the required program.

With this approach the input and output features of the program must be specified *in toto*. Similarly the domain must be axiomatised completely – to guarantee that the theorem prover is able to generate the requisite proof. And it can be very difficult to achieve such exhaustive specifications (sometimes it is easier to write the program!). Different methods are employed in circumstances where it is possible to provide only a partial specification.

Techniques can be employed for the automatic transformation of simple programs into more efficient complex ones, and appropriate data-structure implementations can be selected for programs specified in high-level terms. Heuristic methods and inductive inference can also be used to influence program generation in various ways. Program induction can be achieved from examples of input/output pairs and from a set of traces (this latter, 'very similar to inferring a description of a finite-state machine from a set of sequential states that the machine might pass through' – Barr and Feigenbaum, 1982, p 321). Again the overall purpose is to replace human programming effort by automatically generating programs from higher-level descriptions or specifications. Today there are many commercial and experimental systems available to generate programs systems at various levels.

Actual Systems

The PSI automatic-programming system was developed by Cordell Green and co-workers (see, for example, Green et al, 1974; Green, 1975; and Green, 1976). The research has been carried out at Stanford University, Systems Control Inc, and the Kestrel Institute in Palo Alto. PSI is a knowledge-based system that can cope with partial specifications. Use is made of interacting modules ('experts'). In common with other automatic-programming systems, PSI first accepts the specification of the required program and then sets about synthesising the program code.

Work on PSI led to the development of the CHI programming system at the Kestrel Institute. Here the aim was to provide a high-level programming environment in addition to the synthesis system: this represents an enhanced man/machine interface (the 'V' language is used to specify programs and programming knowledge, and to facilitate interactions with the programming environment).

Other systems* include SAFE (developed by Robert Balzer and colleagues at the Information Sciences Institute of the University of Southern California); the Programmer's Apprentice (Charles Rich and colleagues at MIT; PECOS (Barstow, 1979); DEDALUS (Richard Waldinger and Zohar Manna at SRI International); Protosystem I (William Martin and colleagues at MIT); NLPQ (George Heidorn at Yale University and the Naval Postgraduate School); and LIBRA (independently developed by Elaine Kant as one of the PSI modular 'experts').

Such systems tend to have a mainly experimental significance. Available commercial systems tend to be limited in scope, but provide useful automated facilities in well defined areas. There is, for example, a growing family of tools and methods designed to assist in software development and indicated by the growing portfolio of automated and semiautomated facilities being developed by the NCC Software Tools Demonstration Centre † (see Figure 11.1).

---

* described in detail in Barr and Feigenbaum (1982)

† Refer also to the STARTS (Software Tools for Application to large Real-Time Systems) national programme, created to improve the UK real-time software supply industry.

Software Tools
Demonstration Centre

SOFTWARE ESTIMATING

These tools support the project management activity by assisting in the estimating of software development timescales and costs. Features include: code size estimation, using, for example, comparison with existing productivity measurement, analysis of risk; estimation of development effort, costs and timescales.

PROJECT SUPPORT ENVIRONMENTS

An integrated project support environment (IPSE) is a complete set of software engineering tools, which together provide all of the facilities necessary to execute a project with a high degree of automation of the activities involved in the life cycle. A project support environment (PSE) provides a subset of the tools provided in an IPSE. The tools may be only partially integrated. PSEs provide support for the definition and design phases, for overall technical management, and for the automatic production of documentation, source code and test data.

FOURTH GENERATION SYSTEMS

A fourth generation system (4GS) is an integrated set of software engineering tools, which has evolved to provide an environment for the support of the production and development of interactive transaction processing applications, and for ad hoc access to an applications database. Among the key characteristics of 4GS are interactive use via terminals and workstations, will support for multi-user access, and rapid response to queries and applications processing; a data dictionary and a database; high level end-user facilities; applications generation features possibly interfacing to COBOL or FORTRAN; free from formal and conversational features.

IKBS

Tools for building intelligent knowledge based systems (IKBS) are now quite common. IKBS techniques are starting to be used in the tools used for building other software systems.

PROJECT MANAGEMENT TOOLS

Project management tools are used to support the activities involved in planning projects, and the manager's need to monitor and control actual projects, and produce reports. Typical tools allow estimating, scheduling and analysis of time and effort. They allow critical-path analysis and 'What-if' analysis, as well as financial analysis. Interactive use and multi-project use are valuable features. Fourth generation features are becoming common. Project management tools should be integrated with other tools, such as IPSEs and configuration management.

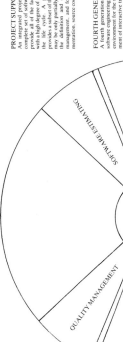

QUALITY MANAGEMENT

These assist in the management and control of product quality during software development. Quality planning and quality control are the two aspects that need to be supported. Quality planning involves planning documentation and recording, and planning distribution. Quality management involves adherence checking for project standards, for specification standards, and for coding standards. There should be support for quality milestones, quality reviews and inspections, and effectiveness measurement for V and V for testing. Integration with other tools and interactive use for desirable features.

CONFIGURATION MANAGEMENT

Configuration management tools assist in the control of products generated during the development life-cycle – such as documents, code, and computer media. The tools also assist in control of externally produced products, such as operating systems and software tools. The three major aspects are configuration control, software configuring, and documentation control.

ANALYSIS AND DESIGN

Specification of requirements and actual design performed before creation of actual code are the subject of the analysis and design phases of the life cycle. Tools support requirements specification and analysis, including the stages of requirements acquisition and requirements expression. Design specification and analysis are covered, including design expression, design derivation and design analysis and checking.

IMPLEMENTATION

These tools support the implementation of the final software product, starting with the lowest level (unit or module) of design specification. The code and unit test phase, the integration and final test phase, and final acceptance testing are included in implementation.

There are six activities. Code production and maintenance; generation of executable code; generation of test environments; generation of software test configurations; test execution and monitoring; and test results analysis.

VERIFICATION AND VALIDATION

Verification and validation tools support specification analysis at all levels, including requirements, design and code itself. There are five activities; dynamic specification analysis; static specification analysis; source-code data analysis; correctness proving; and quality control. V & V tools have much in common with analysis and design tools and with quality management tools.

GRAPHICS TOOLS

Graphics are now an essential component of many business systems, because the cost of high-quality graphic devices has fallen so dramatically. Software developers need a whole variety of graphic tools, both for ordinary plotting and charting, and for high quality presentation graphics developments.

Figure 11.1   Categories of Avaliable Software Tools

The availability of such tools has rapidly developed through the 1980s. Myers (1985), for example, identified 275 programmer productivity packages, with new products arriving on the market every week. Some are today relatively sophisticated packages and require extensive staff training. 'Fourth-generation systems' are often taken to denote any modern software system that aids programming and software development. The celebrated consultant James Martin has commented: 'A 4GL is a language whose basics can be learned in two days and that offers at least a ten-to-one productivity gain over COBOL.' This suggests that there can be 4GLs and linked tools that may have automated features.

AI AND SOFTWARE ENGINEERING*

The potential relevance of AI techniques to software development has been evident for some years. For example, Robert Kowalski (1984), in his SPL-Insight Award (1983–84) lecture, explores various ways in which logic programming can offer software designers a shortcut through the traditional development process ('I shall argue here that ... in some cases artificial intelligence can render systems analysis efficient enough to remove the need for separate specifications and programs'). In this way it is suggested that the application of AI technology to software engineering can revolutionise the software life cycle. At the same time it is acknowledged that intelligent tools can help to preserve the conventional development approach. The new technology can provide:

- intelligent front ends to otherwise opaque computer programs;

- knowledge bases to support traditional development methods;

- expert systems that contain software engineering expertise.

Kowalski points out that it may be useful to promote AI support for the conventional development process if this is the

---

*This section formerly appeared in *Introducing Software Engineering* (NCC, 1987).

'only way we can convince the software engineer to experiment with AI technology'. Emphasis is given to the relevance of AI to the formal computer-assisted derivation of programs from specifications (as an example of automated life-cycle activity), and to the reciprocal AI/SE influence ('I have talked about the applications of AI to SE. What about the applications of SE to AI?').

There are clues here to the ultimate aim of computerising all phases of the life cycle, though it is inevitable that the goal will be approached in a piecemeal and cumulative fashion. The strategy of Reasoning Systems Inc (mentioned above) is to work from the specification level to produce a new way of supporting the software life cycle. The aim here is for the system to validate all designs and upgrades at the specification level – with a view to identifying design errors before the software is coded (implemented). This suggests an integral approach to specification, design, coding and documentation – in contrast to many traditional error-prone techniques.

Today various companies are developing tools able to support the full life cycle. Thus Mike Kendall, DEC (Maynard, Mass.) marketing manager, observed: 'We're expanding our focus to look at tools which support the entire life cycle.' Wolfe (1985) profiles US developments in this area, citing individual tools and particular company philosophies. For example, attention is given to 'eye-catching' tools that automate the first (or development) phase of the software life cycle. These have been dubbed visual programming and visual simulation tools. And there is reference to the system from MCC's Software Technology Program, the horrendously named Leonardo (Low-cost Exploration Offered by the Network Approach to Requirements and Design Optimization).

In 1984, Information Architects Inc (Needham Heights, Mass.) employed AI technology to develop a customised, transaction-processing package for a distribution company. Use was made of COBOL as a standard business language, but parts of the package were written in Prolog, a leading AI language (it was found that parts of the application were best tackled using Prolog and AI concepts). The programmers also employed Datatrieve, a query language able to simulate human decision-making in procedures that embody simple data structures. Wess (1984) indicates some of the factors involved in this development approach.

Such examples illustrate the growing links between software engineering and artificial intelligence. AI guru Herbert Simon (1986) has commented: ' . . . software engineering and artificial intelligence are either going to have to join hands or . . . software engineering people are going to have to reinvent artificial intelligence.' And he identifies key concerns that bear on the software engineering strategy. For example, there is a need for a wholly formal specification language; natural-language under-standing – a key AI concern – will be given increasing attention; and there is a need for a database of data representations ('so that the program itself can analyse properties of alternative repre-sentations and can select representations for particular tasks and for particular needs').

A central aim is to automate more of the software development process as a means of avoiding the rapidly escalating software crisis ('Everyone points in panic to the burgeoning software tasks that face us'). Automatic programming has a relatively long history, and has always been a central AI concern. It is only quite recently however that the relevance of automatic programming to new-fangled software engineering (to certain types of tools and methods) has become widely appreciated in the software-development fraternity.

Today there is increasing attention to the application of expert systems, knowledge-based facilities and other AI-linked techni-ques to the task of software development. Harandi (1986), for example, describes the structure and design principles of a knowledge-based programming-support tool, the Knowledge-Based Programming Assistant (KBPA). This facility is being developed at the University of Illinois at Urbana-Champaign in conjunction with IBM. The aim is to address a range of software-development activities, from relatively low-level issues involving design, implementation and the maintenance of algor-ithms and procedures to higher-level issues of specification and design.

It is pointed out that software design, normally carried out by expert software designers, depends upon a reliable knowledge base built up through work on similar systems. This 'stereotypical' nature of software design renders it highly suitable for treatment in terms of knowledge-based technology. Here software design can be viewed as a 'mapping of the domain-oriented high-level requirement specification into an implementation-oriented model of the software system' (Harandi, 1986). And attention is also given to such aspects as the KBPA system architecture, software design, the components of the knowledge base, program coding and features of intelligent debugging (this latter involving deep and shallow models of debugging, program analysers, heuristic methods, etc). By 1987 it was clear that the KBPA system could become a useful programming support system (its design, decoding and debugging aid units are being implemented as prototypes).

The emerging picture is one in which AI strategies and techniques (for example, exploiting expert systems, knowledge-based procedures, heuristics, etc) are being increasingly directed at the various phases of the traditional software development life cycle. We have already seen how expert systems can function as diagnostic 'engineers' for detection of faults in electronic equipment and other hardware. It is a small step to apply such diagnostic competence to the requirements of software maintenance, debugging, etc. We can envisage a time when all phases of the life cycle are automated, when a range of AI-based tools can generate required software systems rapidly and within budgets. Such a 'total solution' is not yet on the horizon, but there is little doubt the computer-based facilities with AI-content (however 'AI' is defined) will increasingly aid the software developer who is equipped to exploit them.

RESEARCH INTERESTS

We have seen that research in this area bears on many topics of direct relevance to artificial intelligence. Under such heads as 'automatic programming', 'theorem proving' and 'logic programming' areas of research interest are highlighted in abstracting publications (eg the Turing Institute *Abstracts in Artificial Intelligence*) and elsewhere. Again it is worth highlighting a few topics of research interest:

Benzinger (1987) offers a mathematical foundation for the stepwise development of verified programs.

Dershowitz and Lee (1987) describe a method of automating the debugging process by reasoning about programs and their specifications.

Pearce (1987) presents a prototype Integrity Checker for validating the knowledge base of an expert system.

Abadi (1987) describes a proof system for temporal logic.

Kennedy (1987) offers a means of translating from one high-level language to another.

Lowry (1987) describes a means of synthesising algorithms through reformulating problems.

Taylor and Shapiro (1987) describe a compilation method for concurrent logic programs where procedures are compiled into a decision graph.

SUMMARY

This chapter has highlighted some topics of concern in automatic programming, theorem proving and automatic deduction. One aim has been to show how techniques developed in one AI domain can often be effectively exploited in another. For example, the development of automated reasoning techniques can be used for theorem proving and program generation; and such facilities are soon seen to be relevant to the creation of specialised problem solvers in real-world subject areas, the familiar provinces of expert systems (Chapter 14).

It is a cliché of our times that increased automation is likely to impact on job security. This can be discerned in the area of automatic programming, as elsewhere. The early-1980s saw a growing interest in program generators ('programs that write programs') and there was speculation on possible programmer redundancies. Thus Chris Naylor (writing in Computer Talk, 27 February 1984) asked 'Will program generators put you out of a job!'; and Ferguson (1984) began an article with the words: 'We, as users, understand the high-level objectives for application generators: to develop applications faster, *with less experienced personnel* and lower maintenance costs'. And in the same spirit,

Romberg and Thomas (1984) consider how a computer-based expert system can be used to produce 'more reliable software in less time *with fewer people*'.

We have seen that automatic programming is intended to replace, to a degree, some of the human activities in the familiar software development life cycle. This was a clear intention in the early days of automatic programming, and – with the development of tools, methods, 4GLs, etc – the idea is gaining increasing weight in the modern world. This should not surprise us. A central aim of artificial intelligence is to mimic, duplicate and replace human activities in particular areas. The development of automatic programming as an important sector of artificial intelligence brings the AI enterprise particularly close to the heart of the computer specialist.

12 Sensor Systems

INTRODUCTION

The design and manufacture of sensors provides a range of products able to mimic and duplicate the analogous facilities in biological systems (we choose to say that certain artefacts have *sensors*, whereas man and other animals have *senses*). This further extends the analogy between artificial and natural systems, and so indicates how sensors are relevant to artificial intelligence (see below). We have seen (in Chapter 8) how efforts were made to identify the similarities between computers and the human brain, and how Norbert Wiener regarded cybernetics as applying equally to control/communication in man and machines. The provision of artificial sensors helps to emphasise the continuity between artefacts conceived in anthropomorphic terms and the zoological systems which they are intended to resemble.

This chapter highlights the spectrum of sensors that is being developed for robotic and other purposes. Key aspects are indicated and biological allusions are included where appropriate. It is also emphasised that there is continuity between the design of the earliest scientific instruments (eg thermometers) and the design of sophisticated sensor systems to operate in conjunction with modern computer-based configurations.

A principal purpose of sensor systems is to serve as an interface between robots (and other artefacts) and the environment in which they work. In this way the 'artificial senses' of robots facilitate the performance of artefacts in the real world (other robot features are profiled in Chapter 13). First it is necessary to indicate the relevance of sensor systems to artificial intelligence.

SENSORS AND AI

Sensor systems are rarely given full attention in surveys of artificial intelligence. Attention *is* given to such matters as the computation or programming of artificial vision ('sight') and to the phonetics and semantics of voice recognition and speech understanding ('hearing'), but there is usually little effort to profile the full range of sensor options. Tactile sensing ('touch'), for example, is well covered in the robotics literature but much less frequently examined in AI literature. Historical and other reasons have contributed to this pattern of emphasis.

In fact it would seem appropriate that all the sensor options be dealt with as important AI topics: AI facilities are increasingly being incorporated in sensor systems, and it is to such systems that computer-based configurations will increasingly look for development of their own autonomous decision-making capabilities in the real world. Sensors collect information from the environment and feed it to the linked system for processing. They therefore make it easier for computer-based systems to operate without human intervention.

Artificial sensors have a long history in science and technology. We have seen, for example, that artefacts in ancient China and ancient India were sensitive to water pressure and air temperature. Galileo built a thermoscope – a glass bulb containing air, connected to a glass tube dipped into reservoir of coloured liquid – to detect temperature and atmospheric pressure; and in 1612 constructed the first of many thermometer-like devices – a tube connected to a reservoir containing alcohol. Later, Gabriel Daniel Fahrenheit was to substitute mercury for the alcohol. And soon a vast range of sensors, many of them dedicated to particular purposes, had emerged to detect appropriate events in physics, chemistry, biology, geology, meteorology, etc. With the development of information processing in the modern age the route to intelligent ('smart') sensors and AI-linked sensors was clear.

In the 1980s it became increasingly clear that real-time control systems could be developed to exploit sensor-supplied information. In an article entitled 'Artificial intelligence: sensors need it', Stephen McClelland (1987) suggests that 'the next leap of faith for artificial intelligence will be to implement fully-operative real-time control systems, with the processing of sensory information immediately followed by analysis, followed by the proposal of decisions, followed by the execution of those decisions'. It is emphasised that such facilities would require prodigious computational abilities, not least in the collection of information from the outside world. Again we are not surprised to see considerable military interest in such options. In a later article, McClelland (1988) emphasises that intelligent sensors are essential if control loops, containing expert systems, are to be closed and thereafter fully operated by AI.

What we see is the increased feasibility of sensors designed to incorporate AI features. Here information about real-world events is gathered and interpreted according to some dedicated objective. Then sensor outputs are fed to other processing systems to facilitate control, communication and other activities. This is a nice analogue of how human beings function in the world.: we take in information via the senses, carry out some initial processing, and then feed the results to appropriate cerebral centres for final interpretation and storage.

VISION

General

It is clear that a computer-based system with a visual faculty would offer many advantages. It would be able to acquire information through its own 'eye(s)' without having to wait for human operators to key-in the necessary details; it would be able to acquire *more detailed* information (any formalism adopted for human communication purposes may be assumed to convey only *part* of a visual scene); and it would be able to combine detailed visual information with information acquired via other sensory routes. In computer research, attention has been given to such aspects as pattern recognition, brightness, hidden-line detection, template matching, etc. In all this there is the assumption that sensory systems (eg the biological senses) can be understood *in toto* according to the well-defined principles of information processing.

Biology and Computation

One consequence of the growing impact of computer science on the interpretation of sensory processing is that it is increasingly realistic to talk about 'programs for seeing', a phrase that happily combines the computing and biological realms. Such visual programs can interpret incoming information so that the system, of which the programs are a part, is provided with an adequate picture of the outside world. This generalised point is true whether the vision programs exist in a bee, a shark, a hawk or a human being. In all cases the 'seen object' (which may be a complex panorama) has emitted or reflected light of a certain frequency, which then causes photochemical changes to occur in the retina, resulting in appropriate neural impulses to be fed down the optic nerve to the sight centres in the brain. In such a fashion the nerve impulses are effective symbols representing the perceived object: they are decoded in the brain to enable the visual construction of the object to be achieved by information processing (philosophers have long debated how closely the visual 'construction' in the brain resembles the real-world object that is perceived).

Scrutiny of biological organs (in particular, the sensory organs and the brain) has always provided clues for the design of intelligent artefacts. It is interesting, for example, that the typical human eye contains a retina comprising an array of rods and cones, each of which detects a tiny part of an image thrown on it by the lens. This causes minute electrical and chemical changes that facilitate both digital and analogue computation. The retinal nerve cells can generate yes/no responses and also produce graded changes that are able to influence the computational activity of the associated systems.

It is obvious that the visual act can only be accomplished by the system passing through a number of processing stages (remember the parody of cognitive psychology: processing → more processing → yet more processing). This means that an effective algorithm is required to specify the computational steps that are needed to accomplish the visual (or any other perceptual) objective. And it is obvious, for biological systems, that there has been a parallel evolution of visual algorithms and visual hardware (either is useless without the other), and that this simple fact should inform the design of 'seeing programs' intended to be realised in artificial real-world systems.

One approach is highlighted by Poggio (1984) who explores a sequence of algorithms that first extract information (edges or pronounced contours in the intensity of light) from visual images and then calculate from those edges the depths of objects in the three-dimensional world. Light is reflected from the world onto the two-dimensional retinal array, and one aim in AI is to explore ways of constructing an effective image of a three-dimensional scene from two dimensional data. For example, solid-state sensors can generate an array of 1000 by 1000 light-intensity values, with each value a pixel (or picture element), in a way that is strictly analogous to the operation of the rod and cone receptors in the human retina. It is obvious that various computational processes have to be carried out before an accurate picture of the external world can be constructed. In fact, modules work in parallel and in series to construct the various aspects of the required picture. The modules variously derive shape from shading, from motion, from occlusions, etc, and from the information supplied by stereopsis. Some work on the raw incoming data, others on symbol arrays which are themselves the results of earlier processing. A central task for AI research is to identify the computational requirements of the various co-operative modules. This task is well represented in studies of stereopsis.

This requires an analysis of the information received from each eye (in a binocular vision system) to construct an effective image of a three-dimensional world. Four steps have been identified: select space location from one retinal image; identify the same location in the other retinal image; measure their positions; and from the disparity between the two measurements calculate the distance to the location. Work at AT & T Bell Laboratories on random-dot stereograms has helped researchers to formulate the computational goal of stereopsis. In fact the brain makes pragmatic assumptions about the world that usefully constrain the problem, and again there is a clue here to how artificial systems might be designed to achieve visual perception. In the mid-1970s, David Marr and Tomasco Poggio, working at MIT, identified constraints that could facilitate the development of stereopsis algorithms that were within the scope of a computer. Thus, well over a decade ago, computers were able to perform like biological systems equipped with binocular vision.

Work on stereopsis emphasises a key point in connection with the design of artificial vision systems: *prior assumption* can reduce a problem to manageable proportions, though care should be taken to avoid distortions in such circumstances. What we *know* (or *assume* we know) determines what we *see* (or hear, etc). It is clear that this has many implications for the design of AI systems intended to have a perceptual competence. Again we can emphasise the complex computational steps needed to accomplish even the simplest visual act. To recognise an item in a visual field requires the performance of many tasks, including:

- discerning points of different intensity;

- deciding how to group features;

- deciding which features to ignore;

- making inferences about hidden parts;

- using inconsistencies to acquire new data;

- using clues to decide between scene interpretations, all of which are consistent with the evidence;

- recognizing that 'obvious' interpretations may be wrong.

Characteristic computations are required by all these tasks (and the list is not exhaustive). Prior knowledge is important to cognitive performance – a fact emphasised by the philosopher Emmanuel Kant in the eighteenth century; and this may be taken as crucial to the design of vision (and other perceptual) systems for intelligent artefacts. In fact there is already a lengthy history of vision-system research for investigative and practical purposes. This has variously impinged on such topics as cognitive psychology, artificial intelligence, robotics and factory automation.

Artificial Vision

Artificial vision, like all other AI-related subjects, can be represented as the information-processing task of interpreting projected images to generate an understanding of a scene. Cohen and Feigenbaum (1982) have identified three overlapping fields of vision research: *signal processing* (where an input image is converted into another, more useful image); *classification,* or *pattern recognition* (where images are grouped into categories); and *understanding* (where a description is generated for image and scene). Vision research tends to address an information-processing hierarchy. First, in *low-level vision* or *early processing,* basic features (such as intensity levels, edge orientations, etc) are extracted. Then *intermediate-level processing* focuses on regions and shapes. And finally, using *high-level processing,* descriptions of scenes are constructed using relevant knowledge and aims. The various software systems designed over the last three decades have operated at one or more of the levels in the hierarchy.

Early AI vision research grew out of developments in image processing; for example, automatic character recognition recognition, researched in the 1950s and early-1960s, highlighted some of the topics that future vision researchers would be forced to address. Some of the most significant early vision research was carried out by L G Roberts (1965) in an effort to develop a program that could cope with a world inhabited by square or rectangular boxes, wedges or pyramids (or various combinations of these elementary shapes). Attention was given to basic geometric properties of the object types to predict how they would appear in a picture, and then the presented line drawing was investigated to verify the predictions. The program could analyse a photograph, identifying all the visible objects and determining their positions in three-dimensional space.

The Roberts approach has greatly influenced later efforts in scene analysis, and other researchers have adopted different approaches. For example, Adolfo Guzman's SEE program, interpreted as a more general approach to analysing straight-line drawings, relies neither on intensive mathematical processes nor on theories used to identify the three-dimensional objects encapsulated in a two-dimensional representation. Guzman was influenced by awareness of how human beings can look at a line drawing of a jumble of solid objects and quickly identify the various components of the scene. How can a computer be made to perform the same feat?

The SEE program (developed in 1965) looks for junctions and regions in the picture, at the same time searching for clues that indicate that two regions form part of the same body. Junctions, points where two or more lines meet, are classified according to the geometry of their incident lines. The regions around the junctions are than analysed to suggest heuristics for assigning regions to one body or another. SEE was the first program to use junctions and vertices to aid the recognition of three-dimensional objects. This became a popular approach in later systems. SEE also has a daughter program, BACKGROUND, used to pick out the background in line drawings of a scene; and has been used as an integral part of an MIT robot.

G. Falk, in a similar approach to that of Roberts, developed a program (INTERPRET) that could identify the visible objects in a photograph and also determine their respective positions in three-dimensional space. However, Falk allowed for the possibility of imperfect input, in order to cope with poor views of some objects and the total absence of edges because of bad lighting. In this system, nine models were used to represent objects such as rectangular solids and wedges, and a *hypothesise-and-test* strategy was employed to identify objects in the photograph. After the objects have been recognised, a line drawing of the scene interpretation is matched with the original drawing. Use is made of heuristic procedures, as in Guzman, and later efforts (eg by Huffman and Clowes) focused on the development of a more systematic approach to scene analysis. D. Waltz expanded the work further to cope with a greater number of contingencies, and to refine the examination of adjacent junctions by means of a filtering algorithm.

These types of programs work from line drawings of scenes. By contrast, the approach of Y. Shirai is to develop systems that can *find* lines in photographs, generating lines directly from the intensity arrays. This is a difficult task because imperfections in the sensor and the photograph confuse the interpretation process: noise is interpreted by a sensitive line finder as lines, whereas a less sensitive finder misses legitimate lines.

In the Shirai approach, specific knowledge about scenes is introduced into the line-finding process. For example, if the system knows (or hypothesises) that a particular object is a block the strong lines can be used to guide a search for the weaker ones: sensitivity parameters can be adjusted to examine for suspected lines. There are ten heuristics in Shirai's program to add sophistication to the line-finding process. It is interesting that the application of particular heuristics may depend upon previous interpretations, so that the program improves with experience over time.

Another intelligent line-finder, written by G. R. Grape at Stanford, uses abstract models of the expected visual themes (convex polyhedra) to help it interpret incoming information. As with the Shirai program, use is made of a digitised TV image. The Grape system actively searches for lines that may be ambiguous in the local context but which are meaningful when viewed from a wider perspective. The program, like the other vision systems (and like human beings confused by shadows or 'spots before the eyes'), may make mistakes from time-to-time. For instance, an outline may be traced that is erroneous, deriving from unrelated items of data.

Such an event is, of course, an instance of artificial hallucination, a phenomenon that is not entirely inappropriate in the everyday working of sight systems. Hence Boden (1977): 'Only in a world that consistently offered perfect visual data would hallucination ... be totally out of place ... And predictive hallucination, or what I have called hallucination in the weak sense, is of course necessary for intelligent interpretation even of perfect data. Knowledgeable hallucination ... is an essential part of sight.'

Another line-finding program is POPEYE, written in POP-22 at Edinburgh University (and described by Sloman, 1978). Here parts of an image are sampled until unambiguous fragments can be seen as suggesting the presence of lines. Once the process has begun, the program can build on early decisions to achieve further analysis and interpretation. For example, clusters of bar-like fragments can stimulate the generation of further high-level hypotheses (eg concerning alphabetic letters), a strategy that has been recognised as useful for many different types of vision systems.

POPEYE needs to exploit an effective hierarchy of knowledge-beginning with knowledge of the two-dimensional dot array, moving through awareness of lines and bars, to the final knowledge of (for example) letters. In addition, the program is required to know how to combine various partial elements into more meaningful wholes. Again the program, like a human being, is likely to run into error if ambiguous data is presented or if the body of information is too slight to allow useful interpretations to be made.

The various vision programs tend to belong, like most technological innovation, within an evolutionary tradition. Each new vision system builds upon the features of its predecessors, and in this way refinements and new facilities are developed. Sometimes new features are incorporated at the expense of old, where a program is required to function in a specific dedicated fashion, but to a large extent new vision programs, like relatively young biological species, bear the marks of their evolutionary past. Cohen and Feigenbaum (1982) survey a wide range of vision systems. In addition to considering most of the programs mentioned above they also draw attention to (for example):

- A. K. Mackworth's POLY program used to interpret line drawings as three-dimensional scenes;

- T. Kanade's 'Origami world' and shape recovery methods;

- work on analysis of texture, motion, stereo vision, etc;

- integrated vision systems for practical applications such as robotics and aerial-photographic interpretation.

Such programs, developed mainly in the late-1960s and 1970s, were essentially research systems, design to further the understanding of biological vision faculties and what could be accomplished in artificial configurations. At the same time there was feedback into industrial (and other practical) systems, a circumstance that was quickly perceived to have commercial significance in an increasingly difficult trading environment. As we might expect, many of the practical vision systems were associated with developments in robotics.

Robotics and Vision

There are many problems in developing effective and versatile vision systems for robots. One common approach is to look to what is known about animal perception on the assumption that the chief difficulty lies in the area of pattern recognition and scene analysis. Some researchers took a different view. For example, Davies and Ihnatowicz (1979) suggested that it is the mechanical capability of the manipulative device itself which limits the amount of information that can be extracted from a visual image.

If an autonomous system is to organise mechanical operations on the basis of visual information, an adequate interpretation of the information is essential. However, this can involve finding a correspondence between elements of the real world (ie objects to be handled or avoided by the manipulator) and their two-dimensional representation within the camera image. For this to be possible, the cognitive system requires a conceptual model of its universe onto which elements of the visual image can be mapped. In research, such models are supplied by the human programmer. It is doubtful that artificial cognitive systems will be able to construct such models autonomously from visual data.

Davies and Ihnatowicz ask: 'How can information about a physical object be represented in an artificial system if it is to relate its appearance, expressed in terms of x and y coordinates of the image, with the angular velocities and forces of the mechanical arm?' We construct mental images of, say, a key in our pocket by virtue of having a large number of sensing elements distributed about our hands and by virtue of controlled finger movements. For an artificial system to work in such a way, a very precise sensing of forces (magnitudes and directions) and a very precise control of motion would be required. Interpretation of such forces in an autonomous system is not straightforward. A variety of problems relate to stability, feedback and other factors.

Particular recognition tasks, using vision, have particular problems. For example, there are two familiar difficulties in using autonomous vision systems to recognise that mechanical parts are overlapping:

- edges of overlapping parts may not be detected because of poor contrast;

- some regions of the picture, appearing as discrete entities and resulting from overlapping, may not represent any actual part.

An initial task, in developing an operational system, is to design appropriate scene lighting to allow effective contour extraction (Dessimoz et al, 1979). The edges of overlapping parts may be missed if standard lighting is used. One approach is to use several skimming lights, allowing several images to be obtained, each with a different illumination. Contours can be extracted from each image and used to provide a final two-level contour image. One problem is that artificial contour lines may be induced by shadows.

The development of autonomous vision systems demands very precise facilities for detection and interpretation. Human visual perception relies to a large degree on the perceptual sophistication of the cerebral cortex: we know which visual signals (caused through shadows, reflection or other optical effects) to ignore. These circumstances have to be precisely defined for artificial vision systems.

A team at the University of Rhode Island, under National Science Foundation grants, aimed to develop 'general methods for robots with vision to acquire, orient, and transport workpieces . . . to assist in increasing the range of industrial applications' for such robots (Birk et al, 1978). An experimental (6-axis arm) robot system was developed that uses vision to locate and pick up randomly oriented workpieces in a bin, and to determine the orientation of the workpiece in the robot's hand; whereupon the robot manipulated the piece, transported it to a site, and inserted it without collision.

The experimental system was developed in three stages. During the first stage, efforts were made to classify workpiece orientation in the bin to aid acquisition. Orientation classification by hand, used for the second stage, was more successful than efforts based on binary image analysis. Components of the third stage were the robot arm, two General Electric TN–2200 solid-state television cameras, sources of site illumination, a supply of workpieces, and the goal site. The six degrees-of-freedom arm could precisely position a workpiece. One camera was mounted on the arm, facing downwards and parallel to the Z axis: it viewed the bin and confirmed proper positioning of each workpiece at the goal site. The second camera was sited at the workstation and faced parallel to the minus X axis. The cameras were aligned to robot axes of motion to simplify transformation from camera to robot coordinates.

Data supplied by the arm camera was analysed to locate places where workpieces could be grasped by a vacuum gripper which could adapt to surfaces angled at up to 45 degrees. The workstation camera computed the orientation of the workpiece relative to the gripper. If the data was inadequate for making a decision about orientation, the arm moved the workpiece to provide another view. Two goal sites were provided so that all workpieces, irrespective of orientation, could be deposited. The researchers believed that the six-axis Mark IV arm could allow future workers or central computers in batch manufacturing applications to reprogram the system effectively for feeding a variety of workpieces to different machines. At the time of project development, the experimental unit was the first integrated system for feeding completely randomly oriented parts from a container.

Many second-generation laboratory robots were supervised by minicomputers, had sensory input, and could adapt to changing situations. In some early experiments a Unimate 2000 robot was controlled by a Data General Nova 1220 minicomputer. Data concerning the location of parts was fed to the robot from a General Electric camera connected to a Digital Equipment PDP-11/40 minicomputer which was used to determine the centre of white objects on a black conveyer belt.

The robot could pick up passing plastic cups, but could not reliably sense real parts in an industrial environment. However, the control system could adapt to a better vision system, one relying on displacement of a projected line of light to detect parts regardless of colour or reflectivity.

Another experimental prototype system was based on the CONSIGHT lighting system, where a narrow line of light was projected across the surface of a conveyor belt. Use was made of a Cincinnati-Milacron 6CH robot, considered to be one of the first robots with computer-based control that can readily accept visual guidance. Robot activity was supervised by a perceptual system that recognises the identity and position of each part, assembles instructions for new handling sequences, senses conveyor belt motion, and instructs the robot as parts move within reach. At the end of each operation the robot asks for new instructions: these are then supplied by the computer using data provided by the visual system.

One CONSIGHT production prototype used an enhanced Cincinnati Milacron T 3 robot. A Digital Equipment PDP–11/34 minicomputer controls vision, a Digital Equipment LSI–11/03 microcomputer monitors the processes, and a control inside the T 3 supervises the robot.

A prototype industrial robot which can see for about 1 metre has been developed at the NBS Centre for Mechanical Engineering and Process Technology. The robot has a small television camera mounted on its wrist, with the field of view between two fingers. A strobe light, below the wrist, flashes a narrow plane of light towards the fingers: the robot sees an object as a narrow line of light across the object. A microcomputer is used to control the strobe, to determine the distance of the object from the fingers, and to determine the orientation of the object. If the robot is not positioned to pick up the object, the computer moves the robot to another position, and the object is viewed again.

Further research is focussing on allowing the robot to locate a desired part from among various different items, and on simplifying reprogramming to allow a range of tasks to be performed. Some research is devoted to non-visual sensory elements, with recognition of three broad categories of measurement and recognition. These are typified by tactile sensors, electric measurement sensors, and image sensors (eg vidicon cameras, image dissectors, photodiode arrays, and charge-coupled devices).

As early as 1974, patents were being issued in Japan for tactile, internal measurement and visual sensors, with a discernible trend towards visual sensor research in subsequent years. Hitachi uses vidicon cameras for shape recognition and positioning of transistors in die bonding, and for remote inspection of nuclear power plants. Such cameras are also built into robots by Mitsubishi for shape recognition and positioning with assembly tasks and transistor die bonding; by Yasukawa for arc welding applications; and by Kawasaki Heavy Industries for assembly operations. Various research projects are being undertaken by these orgnisations to improve the capabilities of vision systems for industrial robots.

Research on charge-coupled devices aimed to produce efficient robot 'eyes'. Workers at Hughes Aircraft designed microelectronic devices, containing CCD silicon chips which transferred information on 'packets' of electrical charge, which could enable robots to recognise objects almost instantaneously. The CCDs, able to detect both visible and infrared light, could operate without having to convert the original analogue information into digital signals. Hence the devices can construct an image in about 50 milliseconds, whereas a digital computer would take several seconds. It had already been shown that CCD 'eyes' could detect the outlines of objects almost instantaneously (*New Scientist*, 29/11/79, p 6).

Other research relevant to robot vision was concerned with how people construct mental images of their surroundings. A team at the University of Sussex used microprocessors to investigate aspects of human perception, work that could help engineers to build visual systems for industrial robots. And another contribution from microprocessor development was the 1979 announcement from Intel that it planned to introduce a micro (the 2920) fast enough to recognise the analogue signals of the real world (*New Scientist*, 22/3/79, p 954).

The simplest experimental vision systems exhibit little more than light sensitivity: they can, for example, be configured to track or follow a light source. The more sophisticated systems have a genuine vision capability, ie they use visual perception to provide data inputs to control the carrying out of tasks. This is seen as an essential requirement if industrial robot systems are to become flexible and adaptable, able to carry out difficult tasks and to accommodate to changing industrial needs.

In one experimental system (Allen, 1978), a mobile robot had a source light as its destination. A light intensity monitor comprised three phototransistors which sensed the intensity until the device was within a foot of the light, whereupon the robot stopped. The monitoring could take place across an angle of 120 degrees, so the mobile device ('car') made its final approach moving in a forward direction.

A rotating 'eye' scanned a plane to discover a light source, eye sensitivity being adjusted for ambient light conditions. In a normally illuminated room the self-adjusting eye could discriminate between two lights if one was about three times as bright as the other. Slots on the edge of a rotating disk were counted as they passed through an optical switch. As soon as a light was spotted during the disk's rotation, the count was stored for reading by a computer. Erroneous counts were eliminated each time the disk begins a 360-degree scan. Data derived from the phototransistors is used to direct the movement of the (Tee Toddler) car.

In another experimental system (Filo, 1979), it was necessary to construct an artificial eye to allow the motion of a manipulator to be monitored closely. Use was made of a matrix of net convexity detectors for this purpose, monitoring a small bright spot of light either reflected from a retroreflector or emitted from a light emitting diode (LED) source located on the manipulator. It was deduced that at least twenty receptors were required to define motion on four axes, the matrix geometry being an array of four columns by five rows with a high-sensitivity receptor occurring in the fifth row, third column. One serious problem was in scanning and processing the information from the photoelectric devices.

The net convexity detector was represented as a good example of how a basic calculator circuit could be used for noncalculator applications. A sensory head was configured to 'push the right keys' on the calculator in response to the motion of a particular image. The net convexity detector was primarily required to define the angle and director of a small bright object.

It has long been acknowledged that the versatility of the industrial robot can be greatly improved if it is provided with the ability to make visual observations (see for example, Tsuboi, 1973). A central problem in the practical implementation of experimental visual systems is the amount of time needed by many systems for processing of the observed data. The processing problems are exacerbated if several levels of greyness need to be detected in order to distinguish similar-sized objects that differ in greyness or colour.

One approach is to limit the amount of data fed to the computer for processing. This can achieve faster operation, as well as saving memory space. A consequence of this approach is that maximal resolution is only applied where it is essential to the identification of an object. Similarly, computer processing of relatively unimportant background information should be kept to a minimum.

An industrial robot was provided with a high-resolution camera (Malinen and Niemi, 1979), the camera/computer interface being supplied with an electronic 'window' controllable by a computer program. The composite system was applied to the classification of differing, arbitrarily located objects, the catching of freely rolling objects, the recognition of differing objects, and their subsequent positioning to form a two-dimensional assembly. Fast operation was achieved by means of a somewhat coarse pictorial resolution and appropriate system programming.

The computer-controlled interface specified a high spatial resolution for those parts of the scene which include an object with its immediate environment. This data and new observations were iteratively processed until the required detailed information for each object had been collected. Quantities could then be computed which distinguished objects from each other, and also defined the locations and orientations of the individual items. The relevant data was then fed to the microprocessor memory of the robot which subsequently manipulated the objects as required.

The degree of resolution depended upon the amount of data needed for effective discrimination. If the robot was only required to sense the presence or location of an object, then the resolution only needed to correspond with the width of the object. A four-level hierarchy of discrimination was stipulated (each level requiring increasingly better resolution):

- *detection* (an object is present);

- *orientation* (the orientation of an asymmetrical or approximately symmetrical object can be discerned);

- *recognition* (the object can be broadly classified, eg as house, man, machine, etc);

- *identification* (the object can be precisely described to the limit of the observer's knowledge).

If the distance to an object decreased, the level of resolution would increase. Or the density of the lines, or raster points, in a technical visual sensor could be made variable if the robot-to-object distance was kept constant. The field of view was initially monitored by a rough scan. If the presence of an object was ascertained, the detector resolution was increased until the necessary level of discrimination was achieved. Data would then be supplied to the robot to initiate the required activities.

The provision of an electronic window allowed the 'interesting' segments in a field of view to be recognised, the selection of suitable parameters facilitating a flexible and efficient reduction of information (Malinen and Niemi, 1979). Computer control allowed each parameter to be set individually, enabling the system to adapt to any pattern configuration. The full object field was coarse-monitored, but only the data within the program-controlled window was subjected to further processing. It was possible to set the window equal to the whole field cycle, to exploit the total amount of information transmitted by the camera.

The system in question comprised the ASEA I+b−6 industrial robot and the Stromberg 1000 process computer. Use was made of an RCA TC 1160 camera based on a CCD sensor controlled by the interface.

In operation, the robot grasped representative objects and transferred them to a final location, while object form and position parameters were determined by the camera and the computer. The program for the mechanical movements is recorded in the robot memory.

When the system was used to handle arbitrarily sited objects, their presence was first observed by the monitor, whereupon their locations and orientations were analysed, each object being identified by subsequent window pictures. Parameter values were fed into the computer-stored robot program which was then fed to the robot memory to initiate the required mechanical operations.

The system was tested by means of cylinders of various colours. Cylinders of three different colours were distinguished from each other and from a light background. Observation, computer analysis, handling and classification were carried out as a completely automatic sequence. The operational system was found to be superior to an earlier configuration that employed a 50 x 50 raster. Accuracy using binary observation is proportional to the number of sensor elements, and accuracy can be enhanced by the application of more threshold levels. Computing time was not found to be critical for system operation because of the saving achieved by the avoidance of unnecessary data.

In another experimental system (Kelley et al, 1979), a robot, using vision, fed workpieces directly from supply bins to machines. The facility was created to show the feasibility of an integrated operational system ('engineers in industry appreciate the operation of a complete integrated system more than experiments on isolated portions of a system'). The system comprised: a minicomputer (with dual floppy disk unit, video terminal and interfaces), a six-degrees-of-freedom robot arm, a surface-adapting vacuum gripper, a two-camera vision system, a supply of workpieces, and intermediate and terminal goal sites.

The arm camera was mounted at the end of the cantilever which supported the wrist, the second camera being rigidly mounted on the workstation. The arm camera faced downward and was mounted with its principal optical axis parallel to the vertical axis of robot movement, camera alignment being such that the rows and columns of the image are parallel with the horizonal axes of robot movement. This facilitated the transformations from image to robot coordinates.

The arm camera viewed the bin, and also confirmed proper workpiece placement at the goal sites. Lights on either side of the camera were under computer control to avoid interference with the symmetrical illumination associated with the workstation camera. The arm camera would move so that selected portions of the bin could be viewed at higher resolution than would be possible with a fixed camera. Also, camera mobility allowed the vision system to accommodate larger bins and workpieces of various sizes.

The workstation camera viewed the workpiece held in the robot hand, two lights with diffusers being mounted on either side of the workstation camera. The principal optical axis of the workstation camera was parallel to one of the robot axes of motion. The rows and columns of the image were parallel to the other two robot translational motion axes, thus again simplifying the transformation from image to robot coordinates.

As early as 1977 a significant amount of work had been done on providing robots with sensory input, mainly via vision facilities: this work is reflected in the literature and in the mainly experimental working models of the day. By 1978, black and white television cameras were being widely used to provide a robot computer with an array image of brightness levels, the accuracy of the two-dimensional image depending upon the resolution of the camera.

The array was processed with the aim of finding objects in it and distinguishing them from each other and from the background. Two principal techniques, both based on gradient operation, have been employed. One is 'edge finding', which relies on the discontinuity of local property between images of different surfaces. The system was programmed to find the appropriate locations. The points found to lie on contrast edges were linked together to outline the regions in the scene.

The other technique, 'region growing', assumes that the image of a surface is uniform in its local properties. The gradient operator was used to cluster together the points over which this is true. When all possible points have been clustered, the process is terminated and the outer points form the cluster boundaries. Region growing, generally more costly than edge finding, produced more confident outlines.

After one of the gradient techniques had been performed, property determination was carried out for such qualities as shape of outline, region shading, and its relationship to other regions in the scene. Typical analysis parameters were perimeter, area, maximal to minimal diameter ratios, the number of holes, etc. Recognition of an object in the scene could rely on comparing the outline approximation plus the calculated parameters with ones stored in memory. When parts were recognised, their positions could be determined and any necessary positional actions could be undertaken (eg parts could be moved, a gripper can assume a required orientation).

The 1977 Autofact ('automated factory') exhibition in Detroit featured a number of devices with vision capabilities. The Auto-Place company demonstrated a production prototype device which could load a cup with dice, dump them out, and search the playing area for the dice. Then it would report the number of spots exposed on each, before picking up the dice and repeating the process. By equipping a robot with a microcomputer and a pair of television cameras, Auto-Place provided a simple manipulator arm with the ability to monitor its own operations (ie to see what it was doing) and to take appropriate decisions. This device, the AP-C2 robot, was one of the clear precursors to today's emerging vision-based systems, one of the earliest devices that demonstrated the feasibility of automating the location of objects on a moving conveyor.

The AP-C2 device cost in excess of $50,000 in 1978, more than five times the price of the basic Series 50 robot, the heart of the system. The configuration included two cameras, a microcomputer, a servo-driven X-Y table, a rotary hand, interface electronics, and software. A General Electric TN2000 solid-state video camera was sited above the conveyor to provide the computer with an image which it uses for controlling the X-Y motion to place the robot hand directly over the part. The second camera is mounted on the robot arm and is used to orient the robot's hand to the part. Use is made of simple edge-detection techniques.

The prototype AP-C2 employed an Imsai 8080 microcomputer programmed in Basic, with production versions using Intel's System 8020 micro. The interface between the computer and two cameras was confined to a single printed-circuit board carrying a potentiometer-set threshold control to convert the video signals to binary ones and logic to count picture elements and to scan lines, indicating to the microcomputer where the part was located in the camera's field of view.

The computer controlled the motion of the robot and the orientation camera position. It also performed area-summation calculations. Earlier Auto-Place vision-equipped robots had no search-and-find capability. However, they could pick up and inspect parts (eg thermometers, timing mechanisms for munitions).

Research has been carried out for many years into manipulator path control systems, development of problem-oriented languages for programs, and systems for sensory feedback. 1976 saw the first successful implementation of a 'seeing' robot on a production line. Work at this time at the US SRI International included development of a vision system using main memory to store prototype models of assembly parts. By using inflected light and placing the parts on a background that provides good contrast, features based on outline geometry and contrasting-feature characteristics were used for recognition and inspection. SRI also developed the use of vision for robot assembly operations.

Robot activities have been synchronised for many years using touch or proximity sensors but the emergence of effective visual initiators is regarded as a key step in the development of versatile robot systems. Two television cameras were employed in a University of Rhode Island project (1977) supported by the National Science Foundation. An algorithm was developed to compute arm joint values needed to compensate for the misalignment of workpieces in relation to the robot gripper. Changes in the features of images from the camera were related to changes in the position and orientation of a workpiece.

In such a system, workpieces were conveyed to a visual check station whereupon television cameras extract image feature values from a pair of images. Image features (eg the centre of gravity and the direction of the minimum moment-of-inertia axis) extracted from the binary image of the workpiece were compared with expected values. If there was adequate agreement, the workpiece could be moved to a fixture for assembly or other tasks. If, however, there was significant misalignment the position of the workpiece had to be corrected before the operation could continue.

One 1977 industrial application used a robot to inspect transmission separator plates for missing holes, and to sort the plates into model classifications. The robot was employed to load a part into an inspection station, where the presence of approximately one hundred small holes was ascertained. A microprocessor supervised the robot as it placed the parts in the four classification stacks or at a reject station.

In 1976 Auto-Place introduced the Opto-Sense vision facility in standard robots, and a system (SIGHT-1) used to find non-overlapping parts was introduced in an on-line facility at General Motors Delco Electronics Division early in 1978 (said to be the first industrial computer-vision system of its type to operate on a US automotive production line). In the GM configuration, the computer-camera system locates, and calculates, the position of transistor chips during processing for assembly in car and truck high-energy ignition systems. Each chip is checked for structural integrity, defective components being rejected.

Second-generation industrial robots can be instructed to follow a predetermined pattern, with the attainment of a specified target monitored through local sensory feedback. 'Interactive' industrial robots often incorporate such a facility. In, for example, the Mitsubishi 'eye-in-hand' device, a miniature television camera was fitted in the gripper, could recognise an object's position, and could allow the gripper to reach and pick up objects from a rotating table.

Another example was the Nottingham Sirch assembly robot where a Vidicon detector was used to perform the recognition function: the device scanned the image of an object to be oriented in a 625-line raster with an effective sampling density of 128 × 128 picture points. The system could recognise any two-dimensional shape (with black or white background), and a position manipulation could be carried out in about five seconds.

For well over a decade we have seen development of the vision faculty in robots, and it has become commonplace to see articles referring to robots that can 'see': Shapiro (1978), for example, described digital technology that 'enables robots to "see"'. Various light-seeking robots were developed in the 1970s (eg Allen and Rossetti, 1978) and, true to the traditional AI approach, lessons were taken from biological systems – thus Filo (1979), in 'designing a robot from nature', considered how to construct the eye. And increasingly the relevance of the new robotic faculties to industrial applications was emphasised. Shapiro (1979) considered how artificial vision could expand into industrial activity; and similar developments, in Japan and elsewhere, are profiled by many contemporary writers (eg Agin, 1980; Yachida and Tsuji, 1980; and Marsh, 1980). Research into the Wisard face recognition system was conducted under Igor Aleksander at Kent University and elsewhere, with a prototype system built by 1980.

The work on robot vision has continued through the 1980s, allowing an increasing range of applications to be achieved in industry and the commercial environment. Again there are the frequent references to 'seeing eye' robots, laser 'eyes' and robots increasingly able to 'see things our way ...' (see Bibliography). Efforts to allow computer-based system to *see* in circumstances of partial information have been made (Jain and Haynes, 1982), and there are the predictable attempts to compare biological and artificial systems (eg Hampshire, 1987).

Research Interests

There is today a growing spectrum of research activity* into artificial vision. Much of this is concerned with application into a robotics environment, though much has a more general relevance. Recent research papers have focused on such topics as scene representation, the use of cellular networks for image

---

* Readers should refer to Section 12 in the monthly *Abstracts in Artificial Intelligence* from the Turing Institute.

interpretation, ambiguities in a motion field, digital picture deblurring, new camera developments and the relevance of brain mechanisms (eg for attention) to the development of artificial vision systems.

TACTILE SENSORS

Touch (or 'tactile') sensors, like visual sensors, have a long history in robot technology. Typical tactile sensors detect 'over-grip' (if gripper fingers close in the absence of a component) or rely on an 'artificial skin' concept. The early Auto-Place robots, for example, sometimes incorporated an over-grip sensor: if a hand closed beyond its normal position in gripping a part, the component was assumed to be missing. Another tactile sensor used by Auto-Place is a vacuum sensor. A change in vacuum, such as that caused by a part being picked up, can be used to change a robot's program.

There has been widespread research into the use of tactile sensors, eg at the Laboratoire d'Automatique et d'Analyse des Systemes (Toulouse) and at the Mihailo Pupin Institute (Belgrade) (see Briot et al, 1979). This work is seen to have relevance to a wide range of medical industrial applications. Two types of tactile information were employed in the L.A.A.S. and Mihailo research:

- pressure information deriving from an 'artificial skin' transducer (Clot and Stojiljkovic, 1977);

- angular information.

A polyarticulated mechanical system giving twelve independent angular measurements was developed. (Other hands may be cited: see bibliography in Briot et al, 1979). It was shown that angular measurements can be usefully employed to aid the tactile recognition of objects. The recognition performance could be improved by using a combination of pressure information (using 'artificial skin') and angular measurements. Types of transducers have been compared, and a detailed study was carried out concerning the recognition of solid objects using various types of gripper devices (Briot, 1977). The information vector can be changed by increasing the number of gripper fingers and/or joints.

A planar matrix 'artificial skin' sensor was developed at L.A.Á.S. (Briot, 1979). The position of a mechanical part with multiple planar equilibrium faces was identified by means of the sensor. And the sensor was incorporated on the two parallel fingers of a gripper to aid object recognition during grasping. Further, a manipulator robot was equipped with tactile sensors integrated with decision and control processes.

The L.A.A.S. artificial-skin sensor consist of a printed circuit on which a series of sensitive points were isolated. These points were square, uniformly distributed, and set in a matrix. A voltage was applied to a guard-ring around the points. The transversal impedance of a conductive coating on the structure varied according to the pressure exerted. This caused, at every test point, a variation in current which is transformed into a voltage variation to allow the change to be exploited.

In such circumstances, the imprint left by an object was expressed in terms of analogue information according to the pressure exerted on every sensitive point of the coating. The imprint represented the information pattern which required processing. Use was made of a Mitra 15 computer which carried out data processing after data has been collected. The artificial-skin sensor was used to identify various mechanical parts placed on a horizontal plane.

More recent work at other research centres – eg in France and at MIT – is also concerned with the development of artificial skin sensors. A touch sensor developed at MIT's Artificial Intelligence Laboratory, including 256 sensors in an area of 1 cm 2 on a robot finger, is able to identify screws, nuts and washers (Allen, 1983). The sensor array can ascertain the shape of a grasped object by sensing its general shape, by detecting bumps and depressions, and by determining whether the object can roll.

There is also research into how conductive-plastic tactile array sensors can be used to reduce the need for extensive wiring between the actual sensor elements and external circuitry. In a device developed at Carnegie-Mellon University, a pressure-sensitive rubber pad contacts an integrated circuit carrying electrodes. Pressure on the rubber produces an electrical signal that can be processed by the integrated circuit elements. The sensors – each cell occupying only 1 mm 2 of material, can be positioned on a robot gripper to provide a sense of touch.

Tactile sensors have been commercially available for well over a decade, with products exploiting carbon fibre (Larcombe, 1981), silicone rubber cords (Purbrick, 1981), or the piezo-electric materials that are now being given particular attention (Robertson and Walkden, 1983). Magnetoresistance can be used to achieve tactile sensors (Vranish, 1984), as can sound, optical effects and iron fibre materials. For instance, tufted felt made out of stainless metallic fibres can be spread over a robot arm or torso: when the material is pressed, the fibres vibrate and cause equivalent oscillations in the electrical resistance (Pruski, 1986). The changes can be detected and interpreted to provide tactile sensory information.

Today increasing attention is being focused on tactile sensors ('taction') and a growing range of commercial products is being offered. Pennywitt (1986), for example, compares tactile sensors using different principles (optic, silicone rubber, conductive elastromer, silicon strain gauge, and piezoelectric); and offers detailed descriptions of the various types. Plander (1987) highlights piezoelectric polymer, polyvinylidene fluoride (PVF 2), as the best material for tactile sensors.

Research into biology continues to inform work on artificial sensors. For example, the information capacity of the human fingertips has been investigated (Kokjer, 1987), and such work can help to develop the theory of artificial sensor sensors. As always there is a reciprocal influence between research into natural systems and work on artificial facilities.

OTHER SENSORS

We have seen that computer-based systems are developing an impressive range of sensor faculties. Increasingly, robots and other artefacts are learning to see, touch and hear; and, in addition, they can use various types of biosensors to detect gases in the atmosphere (ie to 'smell'). It is worth highlighting, albeit briefly, the following types of sensors:

- *biosensors,* sometimes exploiting optical effects (Gosch, 1985; Roef, 1987);

- *optical fibre sensors,* sometimes exploiting biological effects (Hartog, 1987). In some systems, optic fibres are being encapsulated as 'nerves' in composite materials.

THE APPLICATION RANGE

Today sensors – often with an AI component – are finding an increasingly wide range of applications. They are widely used in industry to enhance automated procedures, often as adjuncts to robotic systems. They are also used to aid domestic, commercial and national security, providing effective 'eyes' and 'ears' able to detect unacceptable behaviour in private and public environments. With the development of artificial satellites there is increased focus on *remote sensing,* where information can be collected for meteorological, geological, demographic, agricultural, military and surveillance purposes (in 1984, J E Estes *et al* declared that 'remote sensing is a reality ... whose time has come. It is too powerful a tool to be ignored ...').

The various sensor types and principles are increasingly relevant to developments in artificial intelligence. Sensors are concerned with the collection of environmental information and also, in a growing spectrum of cases, with the early processing of such information (much as biological senses first process information before conveying the results for further processing in the appropriate cerebral centres). We should remember, perhaps above all, that intelligent sensors reduce the need for human beings to interact with computer-based systems: artefacts can, on their own, collect the information that they need. It is easy to speculate on the advantages and hazards in this developing scenario. Enhanced computer autonomy – the clear aim of AI specialists – can bring a host of social benefits, but the possible dangers in this development should not be ignored.

SUMMARY

This chapter has surveyed the development, and growing availability of, sensors for robotic and other purposes. It is emphasised that sensors are of direct relevance to artificial intelligence for two main reasons:

- they collect information to enable computer-based systems to operate with a much reduced need for human involvement

 – so enhancing computer autonomy, a traditional AI objective;

 – they are increasingly equipped (eg using solid-state circuits) to carry out preliminary processing on the collected information before passing the results to the more sophisticated processing circuits.

Particular attention has been given to the development of vision sensors. Vision has been covered in great detail in the AI literature, as has semantic processing (this latter relevant to aural understanding); but other sensor systems (eg touch and smell), though well covered in the robotics literature, have traditionally received less attention from AI specialists. It is clear, however, that all types of sensor systems are increasingly relevant to the development of intelligent artefacts.

An indication has also been given of the widening spectrum of sensor applications. There is today a massively expanding literature on sensors for domestic security, sensors for robots, sensor for remote-sensing systems, etc. This is an obvious outgrowth of the new focus on information processing in the modern world. Information, of whatever type, needs to be collected before it can be processed. Traditionally, human beings have collected the information and then, via man/machine interfaces, made it available to processing systems. With the development of intelligent sensor technology there will be an ever reducing requirement for human beings to operate in such a way.

13 Robots

INTRODUCTION

Robots and AI have been conjoined for many centuries, though – until modern times – largely in fancy and fantasy. The ancient legends yielded to the fictions of the twentieth century, and new technologies facilitated the development of many functional robotic types.

The anthropomorphic character of the stereotypical robot, as depicted in film and fiction, readily suggests the idea of artificial intelligence: the dramatic trick, whereby something that physically resembles a human being is assumed to possess humanlike mental qualities, is easily accomplished. In the earliest times, where people – in animistic fashion – were eager to imbue sticks and stones, plants and beasts, with animating personalities, it was common for natural phenomena to be granted such human qualities as emotion and intent. It is a straightforward matter to make the same imaginative leap with humanlike artefacts that possess limbs, hands ('grippers') senses (see Chapter 12) and (electronic) brains.

This is not of course to say that robots are truly intelligent. For a robot to contain AI, various criteria need to be satisfied. Some robots, blindly repeating predefined sequences, are manifestly *not* intelligent; about others, embodying expert systems or capable of heuristic search, there can be debate. This chapter provides brief background information about robots, considers the relevance of AI, indicates some (anthropomorphic) robot applications, and highlights some robot features that are particularly relevant to the question of robot intelligence. Brief attention is given to the social relevance of robot evolution and to current research activity.

BACKGROUND

We have seen (in Chapters 1 and 3) that functional robotic systems – working devices that resemble human or nonhuman animals – have existed in all ages. In modern times, exploiting various (mechanical, electromechanical and electronic) technologies, such artefacts have more closely approached the behavioural competence of intelligent biological systems. Thus nearly fifty years ago, the British mathematician Ross Ashby designed artefacts that were capable of purposeful activity. The Homeostat, for example, a complex of switches and dials, could maintain the same 'steady state' no matter how the switches were set – unless several switches were reset at the same time, whereupon a new steady state would be assumed. The evident inertia ('single-mindedness') of the machine was compared by Ashby to that of a dog lying before a fire: some environmental fluctuations are tolerated, but if the fire becomes too hot the dog shifts its position before assuming a new steady state, a new homeostasis.

Similarly, in the 1950s W Grey Walter's mechanical tortoises were able to search for a source of light, approaching it when found but retreating if the light was too bright. Such behaviour is clearly analogous to that of simple insects, fishes and other animals. In the 1960s the 'Hopkins Beast' was built at John Hopkins University. This was a battery-operated, mobile system able to move along corridors with one purpose 'in mind' – to keep its batteries charged: it would detect a wall socket, plug itself in, 'feed' on the electricity for a while, then unplug itself and move off, searching for the next socket. At about the same time, soon after George Devol had filed his patent application for Programmed Article Transfer, MIT were developing mechanical arms and hands controlled by computer. The MH-I system, controlled by MIT's experimental TX-O computer, was the world's first automatic hand. MH-I proved that an artefact could use artificial senses and electronic information-processing to operate in a purposeful way in the real world.

Such developments stimulated wide-ranging robotics research for industrial and other purposes. Specialists such as Meredith Thring in London and Norbert Wienet in the US were developing prosthetic devices for medical purposes, and the first industrial robots were starting to infiltrate the factories of the world. By the late-1960s hundreds of industrial robots were in operation, with about two hundred active in Japan alone. By the late-1970s the Japanese total was well in excess of 20,000 working robotic systems (taking into account all robot devices, including the simplest 'pick and place' devices). Throughout the 1980s the dramatic expansion in the world population of industrial robots has continued, with most of the applications being focused in Japan, Europe and the United States. Fleck and White (1987), for example, describe the national policies and patterns of robot diffusion for Britain, Japan, Sweden and the United States; and also list the historical landmarks ('major robotics initiatives') for the last thirty-five years.

ROBOTICS AND BIOLOGY

The anthropomorphic character of robotics developments has continued to be enhanced by feeding biological concepts into the design of artefacts. We have already given examples of this aspect of system design, and it remains a constant thread in robotics research. Here we can mention such elements as the *Byte* (1979) series of articles on the 'nature of robots' (where detailed discussion is included on human behaviour, physiology, mechanisms of choice, etc); and the design of a robot actuation and control system modelled on the human spine (a design produced by Spine Robotics, Molndal, Sweden). The 'biological" element in modern robotic systems clearly relates, at various levels, to the question of whether robots can evince signs of intelligence, that most important biological phenomenon.

ROBOTS AND AI

It is now commonly assumed in the robotics literature (and elsewhere) that robots can be 'clever', 'smart', 'intelligent', etc. At the same time there is debate about the key qualities that enable an artefact to behave in an intelligent way. However, for some years it has been assumed that the intelligence that characterises computers can also reasonably be regarded as characterising computer-based robotic systems. Thus Goshorn (1982), for example, assumed that providing onboard computing can help to achieve 'robotic intelligence'; Keller (1983) saw 'clever robots' set to enter industry en masse; and Astrop (1983) reckoned that second-generation robots would have 'considerable levels of intelligence'. In 1984, Philippe Villers, President of Automatic Inc., perceived that 'intelligent robots' would move towards 'megassembly' in the factory environment.

By the early-1980s various definitions of *intelligent robots*, mostly in manufacturing, had been proposed. Noro and Okada (1983) suggested that an 'intelligent' robot was one with 'sensory and cognitive functions' and that could 'make decisions by itself' (it was reckoned that Japan had 131 such units in 1982). Tasks for intelligent robots were identified in the 1985 report, *Production and Use of Industrial Robots*, prepared by the ECE Working Party on Engineering Industries and Automation. Here is was proposed that intelligent robot tasks include 'sorting and orienting different types of parts mixed together in the same bowl (programmable bowl feeders), loading and unloading parts from an overhead moving conveyor, recognising three-dimensional objects, inserting pegs into holes (in assembly automation) and so on'. Robot mobility has also been highlighted as an important feature of intelligent systems.

It is obvious that sensory competence often features in definitions of robot intelligence. Thus Sugimoto (1987) describes how 'sensory feedback control is utilized in order to make a robot intelligent'. In this context, Unimation, Hitachi and many other companies have developed sensory feedback facilities, effective cybernetic features, to enable robots to behave in an intelligent way.

Robot intelligence is also associated with the concept of machine *autonomy* (evidenced through independent decision-making). Thus research into 'intelligent autonomous systems' as increasingly common (see, for example, the report on an associated conference in *Robotics*, 3, 1987, pp 241–257). Chester (1983), for example, suggested that the goal of robotic software is to 'to remove all human supervision'. Again we expect such

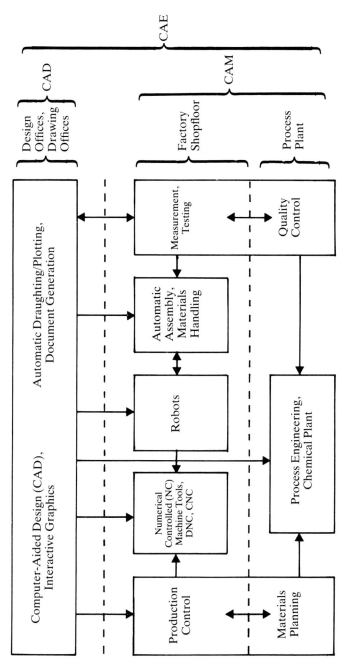

Figure 13.1   AI-linked Activities in Manufacturing

preoccupations to focus on sensory facilities, mobility, decision making, etc.

Artificial intelligence can also link to robots via the many other activities and processes that are increasingly automated in the factory environment. Figure 13.1 shows, for example, the various tasks that are involved in the manufacturing enterprise. Such tasks as computer-aided design (CAD), materials planning (a CAM subtask) and process engineering (CAM subtask) can use dedicated expert systems (see Chapter 14) to provide AI input which necessarily influences subsequent robot performance and other automated activities.

Increased attention is being given to how expert systems can be used to assist manufacturing: see, for example, Williamson (1987), discussing factory floor AI; Millichamp and Wahab (1987), considering an expert system for FMS design; and Ford and Schroer (1987), describing the use of an expert manufacturing simulation system. It is obvious that robots and AI are now simultaneously evolving in an increasingly useful symbiosis.

ROBOT APPLICATIONS

Reference has already been made to the anthropomorphic character of robot systems. In film and fiction this aspect is obvious but it is not always realised how far the anthropomorphism has progressed in operational robot systems. Modern working robots rarely resemble human beings in appearance but there is a functional duplication that is increasingly significant. It is worth highlighting the following robot applications:

- WABOT-2 is a robot musician (see Figure 13.2) developed at Waseda University, Japan. The robot has articulated fingers for playing keyboard instruments; it feet operate the pedals of an organ. The system can sightread music, hold a conversation with a human being and perform other intelligent tasks. It is described by Kato et al (1987);

- a robotic seedling transplanter has been developed at the Agricultural Engineering Department of the Louisiana Agricultural Experiment Station; and a robot is being developed in Japan for harvesting tree fruit. These and other systems are described by Sistler (1987);

Figure 13.2   WABOT-2 – Intelligent Robot

- a robot for shearing sheep was described at the Twelfth International Symposium on Industrial Robots (9–11 June 1982, Paris) (described in Trevelyan et al, 1982);

- researchers at Bristoe University, in collaboration with the Institute of Food Research, are developing a robot butcher – with the aim of making the industry more profitable;

- robot guards are being developed to work in US prisons. Reports first appeared some years ago (see, for example, Bartolik, 1984; and Rifkin, 1985);

- a robot window-cleaner, the 'Skywasher', has been developed for walking up the outside walls of buildings. It carries wipers and a washing fluid system, and is described by Kroczynski and Wade (1987).

Robots are also being designed to operate television cameras, to serve as company receptionists, to work in the home, to aid commercial promotions and to carry out routine surgical operations. Most of the current robot development in the world relates to factory applications, and here the goal, already partly realised, is the unmanned fabrication plant. Unmanned factories were extensively discussed in the 1970s (see, for example, Ruzic, 1978; and Astrop, 1979) and have been partially implemented in the 1980s (see Potts, 1987) in Japan, Europe and the United States.

SOCIAL ASPECTS

Attention should be drawn to various social aspects that relate to intelligent robots:

Unemployment and de-skilling
The more competent robots become, the more human tasks they will be able to perform, and the greater the number of redundant workers at all levels. There is rapid technological progress in this context, and the key questions are political;

Safety
As people are obliged increasingly to work with intelligent robots, efforts will have to be made to research the question of whether robots represent a threat to people in the working environment;

AI reliability
This is a general question that includes, but also goes beyond, intelligent robotics. Do we trust the AI systems? How do we know that they are reliably performing as we wish? Who is to be master?

Such questions (see, for example, Rooks, 1986; Chisholm, 1987; and Nicolaisen, 1987) will become more pressing as AI develops. In the context of robotics, many industrial tasks – eg assembly, painting, material preparation, welding, forging, etc – will remain relatively straightforward; but as AI-linked robotic systems become ever more sophisticated they will increasingly encroach on the full spectrum of human roles.

RESEARCH INTERESTS

There is a sense in which *all* AI research is relevant to robotics: the most anthropomorphic robot should be able to converse, move sensibly, solve problems, take decisions, act creatively, use a spectrum of sensory systems, etc. All the topics touched upon in Part 6 of the present book are relevant to robotics, particularly since we can detect the trend towards 'integration of functions'. At the same time, there are specific research interests that focus on what is commonly regarded as robotics (some of these – eg mechanical engineering – have little *per se* to do with AI).

Today robotics research is being conducted on such subjects as collision avoidance, robot performance simulation, motion control, wrist rotation, robot/robot synchronisation, visual path planning, anthropomorphic finger design, multiple-sensor coordination, two-arm robot operation, feature-based tactile recognition, force interaction in robot legs, problem-solving in hazardous environments, etc. We can see an evident robot evolution as technological advances are made, but such evolution has an obvious advantage over its biological counterpart. New systems can be effectively 'tested' in actual environments through simulations, without the need for the construction of physical working systems. This means that a greater range of design options can be explored and acceptable system changes can be incorporated at a rapid rate: there is no need for the lengthy 'trial and error' experimentation that has traditionally characterised the evolution of biological systems. Thus mobile robots can have one (hopping) leg, two, three, four, etc – with characteristic gait advantages attending each options. Similarly robot senses can be designed to exploit *any* environment phenomena, including ones (eg radioactivity) beyond the scope of mammalian sensory systems. And advances in expert-systems technology (eg as in MACSYMA) can be exploited to provide robots with intellectual talents that exceed those of any human being.

Any sophisticated robot is a complex system, as dependent upon the properties of physical systems as upon its embedded software – and some research, appropriately enough, is being directed at how state-of-the-art advances in different disciplines can be integrated in stand-alone AI systems. The modern computer-based robot is intended to be, above all, a functioning system in the real world: it is inevitable in such circumstances that it will both learn from biological precedent and acquire biological features as it evolves in its own characteristically 'force-fed' way.

SUMMARY

This chapter has glanced at some of the AI concerns that have influenced robot design over the last two or three decades. It is emphasised that *all* AI research is potentially relevant to robot design, and that there are also characteristic research topics – not least those relating to limb and whole-system movement in the real world – that are at the heart of robotics.

Nothing has been said about power supplies, gripper design, limb articulations, degrees of movement, materials research, electrical and preumatic engineering, etc – all are directly related to the design of robotics, but less relevant to specific AI topics, the principal concern of this book. Emphasis has also been given to the increasingly anthropomorphic quality of modern robots, today able to act as sheep-shearers, fruit pickers, butcher, receptionists, etc. This emerging quality has implications for human interaction with intelligent systems: the developing symbiosis will necessarily affect such matters as respective roles, human safety, system reliability, etc. Such matters have been briefly addressed in the present chapter.

Intelligent robots can be seen as representing an intended apotheosis of AI. The fully-fledged robot incorporates many of the features that characterise intelligent biological systems. Most *non*-robotic AI systems are dedicated to *particular* tasks; for example, speech recognition, memory simulation, chess playing, disease diagnosis, etc. The intelligent robot, ambitiously, may be expected to embody a *range* of AI talents.

14 Expert Systems*

INTRODUCTION

Today expert systems are regarded as one of the most important subclasses of artificial intelligence. They have also been (wrongly) identified with *fifth*-generation computers: we have seen (in Chapter 8) that expert systems have been working for many years whereas fifth-generation systems are not expected until, at the earliest, the next decade. Many claims are being made about expert systems, not least by salesmen, and not all systems dubbed 'expert' contain AI.

In one view (eg Addis, 1982), the range of expert systems represents degrees of enhancement to an information retrieval system. This type of interpretation is obviously plausible: the competence of the human expert largely resides in fancy information retrieval skills, and whatever the ideal purpose of the artificial system it is easy to extend the analogy, in this context, between machine and human capability. It has been pointed out that much of human problem-solving is possible through the exploitation of 'non-standard' logics, allowing a flexibility that is not yet possible in artificial systems, but it is for this reason that the various facets of inference-making are being explored as part of expert-system research.

An expert system may be regarded as a means of recording and accessing human competence in a particular specialist field. The

---

* This chapter is based partly on Chapter 8 from *Introducing Artificial Intelligence* (NCC publications, 1984). Up-to-date information and new sections have been added.

most robust interpretation (eg Duda et al, 1980) suggests that an expert system is capable of humanlike performance and can serve thereby as a replacement expert. Less ambitiously, expert systems may be seen as exhibiting competence in a relatively narrow agreed domain, serving as tools to aid communication between human experts. (It is hard to see this latter interpretation not progressively yielding to the former with advances in knowledge engineering and other areas). The fact that no expert system has so far been built for completely naive human users underlines one particular thrust behind the fifth-generation research programme: here a central aim is to make computer capability, embodied in expert and other types of systems, available to the widest possible range of users. If current expert systems are reasonably seen to lack natural human performance features then future systems will be less limited – and, ideally, they will be found in schools, offices, shops and the home, as well as in the specialist research environment which have tended to be the domain of working expert systems.

We have seen that work in information retrieval (IR) is likely to influence the development of expert systems. A main purpose of IR is to extract relevant information from a large store of data. The elements in the store are usually assigned index terms which the user specifies, in some combination, to obtain the required information. One key problem is that the index terms, in different concatenations, are capable of many different interpretations: then words are combined in phrases, there can be many subtle variations that are difficult to express in Boolean or other types of formal logic. This circumstance may make it difficult for the user to obtain the specific information that he requires. This type of problem is common to the development of both IR facilities and expert systems.

One approach to information retrieval is to develop a model of stored data so that it is homomorphic with respect to user requests. Such a model would feature the index terms in defined relationships in order to aid information selection in the particular subject area. Again, work in this area has direct relevance to requirements in both mainstream IR and expert systems: Addis (1982), for example, has noted what he sees to be 'an evolutionary convergence of what may seem to be two distinct sciences'.

Some of the most successful expert systems are now relatively well known and have been operating for several years. Typical of such systems are MYCIN and INTERNIST (for medical diagnosis, DENDRAL and SECS (for chemical analysis), and PROSPECTOR (for geological prospecting) (see Actual Expert Systems, below). GPS (the General Problem Solver) has also been regarded as one of the earliest systems. DENDRAL and SECS are said to have 'as much reasoning power in chemistry as most graduate students and some Ph.Ds in the subject' (Cole, 1981).

The expert system SIR and its successor QA3 are question-answering systems exploiting the techniques of formal logic. The LUNAR program, already discussed, can answer questions about moon rock samples by drawing on a massive database provided by NASA: here procedural semantics allows questions to be automatically converted into a program to be executed by a sophisticated retrieval facility.

An initial step in generating an expert system may be to persuade a human expert to sit at a computer terminal and to type in his or her expertise. We have seen that this can be an immensely difficult task: it is one thing to be an expert, quite another to be able to articulate the expertise in coherent propositions that are useful to a computer. Developments in knowledge engineering may be expected to aid the expert in this context.

Once the expert knowledge has been fed into the computer it is likely to exist within a tree-like structure, within specific items of knowledge existing as axioms or rules which can be viewed as nodes within the tree. At the top of the tree is the system's 'goal hypothesis', a statement about the problem which also has probability and margin-of-error features. The expert system may have one major goal hypothesis and a number of subsidiary goals, each goal being a statement about a circumstance of the situation. Many goal hypotheses, the low-probability contingencies, will not be included: in these circumstances the system will advise the user accordingly (eg 'Ask a *real* expert!').

The intelligence of the expert system may be evaluated, perhaps frivolously, by a version of the Turing test, one of the earliest conversational scenarios. A Turing test for expert systems would have one terminal operated by the expert and one operated by the expert system: if the operator could not tell the difference, then the artificial system would be deemed truly *expert*.

Most of the operating expert systems are in the US, but as with computers in general they will become commonplace in all the advanced countries of the world. The early-1980s saw the UK's first dedicated expert systems division set up at Racal Decca, aimed specifically at the oil industry. Systems Programming Ltd developed the rule-based technique, pioneered by Donald Michie and others at Edinburgh, to produce the Sage package announced in May 1982; and many systems were subsequently delivered. ICL, for example, used Sage for projects associated with the introduction of its DM/I and Estriel mainframe computers in 1984/5. Also, a political risk system was developed for Shell as a demonstration of Sage's capacity; and ICI and BHRA Fluid Engineering used Sage systems to experiment with expert systems development. ICI used the facility to aid development of a design and consultancy aid to examine pipe stress corrosion cracking, and BHRA developed a system to gauge flow rates and patterns inside pipes by drawing inferences from data received from sensors.

Expert systems are now being developed for many practical purposes. Expertise is collected from human beings and fed into systems with a capacity to store and manipulate the knowledge in response to subsequent user enquiries.

FEATURES OF EXPERT SYSTEMS

General

Expert systems are being developed to solve a range of practical problems. As with fifth-generation computers they represent a departure from, in particular, traditional methods of programming. Expert systems have been defined as (quoted by d'Agapeyeff, 1983):

> 'problem-solving programs that solve substantial problems generally conceded as being difficult and requiring expertise. They are called *knowledge-based* because their performance depends critically on the use of facts and heuristics used by experts'.

The body of facts (knowledge) and the heuristics (which may be regarded as 'rules of thumb' are represented in the computer. The program uses the heuristics to operate on the stored knowledge in the light of a user enquiry, and ideally the system's reasoning can be explained to the user to indicate how a particular conclusion was reached. The British Computer Society's Committee of the Specialist Group on Expert Systems has defined an expert system as:

> 'the embodiment within a computer of a knowledge-based component from an expert skill in such a form that the machine can offer intelligent advice or take an intelligent decision about a processing function. A desirable additional characteristic, which many would regard as fundamental, is the capability of the system on demand to justify its own line of reasoning in a manner directly intelligible to the enquirer. The style adopted to attain these characteristics is rule-based programming.'

This definition emphasises rule-based programming (ie programming in logic or relational languages, such as PROLOG), allows for a wide range of applications (ie not only to consultancy functions but also to data processing and on-line control systems), and indicates the desirability of an 'explanation-of-reasoning' capability (though this does not feature in many existing expert systems). Expert systems represent a flexible approach to computer competence, drawing on specialist knowledge and exploiting various types of inference (not only deductive reasoning).

System Structure

Any expert system is characterised by three fundamental elements: the Knowledge Manager, the Knowledge Base and the Situation Model. These are shown in Figure 14.1 which includes a listing of alternative names found in the literature (following d'Agapeyeff, 1983).

The Knowledge Manager typically uses the information contained in the Knowledge Base to interpret the current contextual data in the Situation Model. Everything which is application-dependent can be kept in the Knowledge Base, allowing the

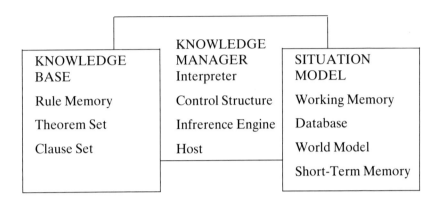

Figure 14.1   Main Elements in Expert Systems

Knowledge Manager to function as a multi-application tool. MYCIN, for example, advises on the diagnosis and treatment of bacterial infections (see Actual Expert Systems, below), and EMYCIN (or empty MYCIN) has been developed from the original system: a different Knowledge Base is used for different applications.

The more comprehensive the Knowledge Base, the less the strain upon the inferential logic inside the Knowledge Manager when a question has to be answered. This means that the power of the system tends to be defined according to its depth of knowledge rather than its ability to reason. In the event, however, the user will only be interested in receiving a useful response to the initial query. It may be expected that an expert system will develop – as it accumulates more expertise, either directly as new information is fed in, or indirectly as the system remembers the results of useful inferences. In addition to operating the Knowledge Base, the Knowledge Manager will also be concerned with knowledge acquisition (ie developing the Knowledge Base), knowledge updating (ie modifying the Knowledge Base), and providing explanations (ie explaining system features or details of operations such as inference-making). An expert system can operate at several levels – relatively superficially if a quick answer is sufficient, or more deeply if a more complex analysis is required.

Software, Inference Engines

It may be emphasised that expert systems are largely about software. (This goes nicely with Margaret Boden's 'tin-can' view of computer hardware.) Expert systems have been written in traditional languages but there is much current focus on the use of PROLOG which has also been selected, as we have seen, as the fifth-generation 'kernel' language. Languages such as PROLOG, not concerned with handling numerical quantities but with expressing relationships, are highly suitable for the inference mechanisms of both expert systems and fifth-generation computers.

The use of *rules* (eg an *if then* relationship, see Knowledge Representations, below) can serve the development of a knowledge base built up in PROLOG. In this context, no distinction is drawn between a piece of factual information (eg an item of data) and a statement rule (eg a piece of program). Both can be held in the PROLOG database and can be selected when required. PROLOG statements may be seen as constituting both the specification of the program and the program itself.

Conventional high-level languages (eg FORTRAN and COBOL) are rich in syntax but weak in semantics. This is because the languages were intended for use by professional programmers engaged in different tasks in different companies, while semantics tends to be application-specific. By contrast, expert systems are necessarily rich in semantics, and independent of machines and architectures (though particular languages are suitable for, for example, data flow architectures).

The various operating expert systems depend upon accumulating knowledge in the form of *rules*. One advantage of this approach is that the knowledge concerning the particular specialist area can be expanded incrementally; furthermore, it is in a form easily expressible by an expert. For example, the TEIRESIAS program, associated with MYCIN, collects rules from the expert, checks for rule consistency, and follows chains of reasoning to expose inadequate or inappropriate rules. A set of *meta-rules* is used to accumulate the diagnostic rules for MYCIN. The collecting of rules can be a time-consuming task. The accumulated rules and related procedures are often referred to collectively as an *inference engine* or an inference machine.

The rules comprising the knowledge base are equivalent to an application program, and they may have many different formats; the *if*-a-condition-*then*-an-action format is very common, with the *then* section able to represent inferences, assertions, probabilities, precepts, etc. The first of several conditions associated with the rule determines whether the rule is potentially valid with respect to the current state of the situation model. A rule can require that a number of conditions be satisfied before an action is authorised. The following rule, for example, is from VM (Fagan, 1980), a system for monitoring the post-surgical progress of a patient requiring mechanical breathing assistance:

> *If* the current context is 'ASSIST'
>   *and* the respiration rate has been stable for 20 minutes
>   *and* the I/E ratio has been stable for 20 minutes
> *then* the patient is on 'CMV' (controlled mandatory ventilation)

In this case, involving a transition from 'ASSIST' to 'CMV', the first condition is a state value of, and the other two measurements in, the situation model. When the rule is triggered, the context state is changed: further rules subsequently update the situation model.

A typical rule from MYCIN –

> *If* the infection is primary-bacteremia
>   *and* the site of the culture is one of the sterile sites
>   *and* the suspected portal of entry is the gastro-intestinal tract
> *then* there is suggestive evidence (0.7) that the identity of the organism is bacteriodes –

shows how a conclusion can be assigned a probability rating: in this case there is a 7 out of 10 chance that the conclusion is true. This follows human practice closely, where much knowledge is inexact and partial (see Uncertainties, below).

Rules, as observed, define the knowledge in the system, with meta-rules used to manipulate rules. Some systems also have meta-meta-rules; rules at the various higher levels being analogous to system software in traditional configurations. Rule-based expert systems are now relatively common, and it has been found that good performance can be achieved in various specialist areas using 200 to 300 rules. A number of rule-independent system languages (Rita, Rosie, Age, Hearsay III) are being developed.

There are three broad types of system organisations for rule systems. These (following Bond, 1981) are:

- *top-down*. Here, as in MYCIN, the system sequences through top-level goals or conclusions to see if any are true. An effort is made to match the right-hand side of rules to the goal. Where a match occurs, components on the left are set up as further goals, and so on, generating a goal tree. The system pursues each goal in turn, requesting, in the case of MYCIN, clinical information as it needs it;

- *model-based*. Unlike MYCIN, this type of system organisation relies upon a model of the relevant world. Rules use input data to establish and correct the model, and in particular the rules chart the time development of the model. This allows predictions to be made, and the past causation to be traced. In CASNET, for example, a model of the patient's condition is built up and maintained throughout the period of treatment. Features of multiple causation can be analysed and the patient's progress can be monitored and analysed;

- *blackboard*. Here the rules are organised into *knowledge sources* carrying expertise in particular areas. The knowledge sources operate, without communicating with each other, on a communal database (blackboard). The database contains hypotheses with certainty factors, and is organised to correspond to levels of data analysis. Hypotheses can be established or modified by the knowledge sources. The Hearsay speech understanding system is organised on this basis.

In addition, various other system organisations can be employed for rule manipulation. These possibilities relate directly to the four major areas being investigated in the context of knowledge representation: techniques for modelling and representing knowledge; methods enabling computers to think in natural language (since theories of inference and memory often rely on understanding how meaning is mapped onto the structure of language); techniques for deduction, problem-solving, commonsense reasoning, etc; and strategies for heuristic activity (eg allowing rapid focus on a small number of likely solutions among many possible ones). Knowledge representation and rule-based strategies are converging to enhance the competence of both the family of expert systems and the emerging fifth-generation computers.

Various knowledge representation techniques can be exploited in AI programs that play games (such as chess and bridge), converse in natural language, operate robots, etc. For example, an early representation formalism was the *state-space representation*, used in game-playing and problem-solving. The structure of a problem is represented in terms of the alternatives available at each possible problem state. From any given state, all possible next states can be determined by means of *transition operators* (or *Legal-move generators* in game-playing programs). One aim is to limit the number of alternatives to the best possibilities, on approach that requires programs that can reason using comprehensive knowledge about the relevant world. The overall goal is to deepen the AI programs' understanding of the problems which they are trying to solve.

Formal logic may be regarded as the classical means of representing knowledge about the world. As we have seen (Chapters 2 and 4), progressive systematisation – from Aristotle, through de Morgan and Boole, to Frege and Russell, and then to the modern logicians – has influenced directly computer science, artificial intelligence and, in particular, the inference mechanisms being developed for expert systems and fifth-generation computers. In logic and the related formal systems, deductions can be guaranteed to be correct. The conclusions (the semantic entailment) that can be drawn from a set of logic statements are defined precisely by the laws of inference. This means, in principle, that a database can be kept logically consistent, and the derivation of new facts from old can be automated (though with a large number of facts, there tends to be an unmanageable combinatorial explosion of possibilities). In this approach, as elsewhere, there is need for more knowledge about *relevance* (eg ways of defining what facts are relevant to what situations).

The *procedural representation* of knowledge appeared in efforts to encode some explicit control of theorem-proving within a logic-basic system. Knowledge about the world is contained in *procedures*, programs that know how to do particular things in well-defined situations. Here the underlying knowledge is not stated explicitly and cannot be extracted in a form that is easy for human operators to understand. Such an approach has been influential in AI research but has a number of disadvantages.

Uncertainties

Much in human problem-solving and inference is uncertain, inexact and partial (ie *fuzzy*). In many circumstances where decisions have to be made, the facts are far from precise. However, traditional logics and traditional programming have relied upon tightly-defined categories, and upon full delineations of the elements that appear in a calculation or a process. Today expert systems need a more flexible approach.

A method that can be adapted for handling inexact facts within a computer program can be found in *fuzzy set theory* (Zadeh, 1965), already mentioned. A 'model of inexact reasoning', developed in MYCIN, uses equations that perform equivalent functions to expressions belonging to fuzzy sets. Here the membership values are regarded as certainty factors which are assigned constraints. The shape of an object, for example, might be described as 'rectangular' (0.6), oval (0.2), and square (0.0)', where the numbers, ranging between the binary poles of 0 and 1, indicate a degree of certainty for each quality. In contrast to what occurs in a normal database, a feature can be multivalued and indecisive.

We are all acquainted with the linguistic devices in natural language that allow subtle distinctions to me made between the features of objects. Thus we can say that a colour is 'green*ish*' or '*sort of* orange-red'. This latter may be represented in a computer program as (Colour (Red 0.7) (Orange 0.3)) or as (Colour 6000), where 6000 denotes the wavelength of the light. Shaket (1976) has described a technique able to convert physical values to certainty (membership) values. These can then be modified by linguistic devices (eg 'very', 'rather', 'sort of', etc) to cause a shift in fuzzy set values in line with what a human being might expect.

The use of fuzzy set theory and related techniques in computer programs may be regarded as one of several means of developing machine competence (in, for example, expert systems and fifth-generation computers) to approach that of human beings.

Memory Mechanisms

Expert systems are concerned with modes of information retrieval mediated by inference and other procedures. Memory considerations are crucial to these types of activity. In human beings how memory is organised is crucial to learning, the evaluation of experience, and the adoption of new behavioural patterns. We have already seen (Chapter 9) how memory mechanisms underlie most intelligent activities. It is worth emphasising how the structuring of memory is important to expert (and other knowledge-based) systems.

Work at Yale University has suggested that memory structures in human beings are subject to modification when new (unexpected or contradictory) events are experienced. Memories are linked together according to explanations and beliefs, with new connections formed when fresh information is presented to the person. In this context, R. C. Schank has proposed a theory of memory that illuminates the nature of *reminding* and other memory phenomena. Here work in AI has suggested plausible human memory mechanisms which can be explored by cognitive psychologists.

The tactic of restructuring memory in the light of new experience has already been incorporated into some expert systems. Some programs can, for example, store details of new stories and then reorganise their knowledge bases when new information is presented. In this field, as elsewhere, it is again easy to see the reciprocal influence between artificial intelligence and cognitive psychology. We may expect expert systems to become increasingly competent as they learn to model the mental processes that characterise the human specialist.

Range of Applications

For more than a decade there have been many applications, potential and actual, for expert systems. Webster (1983) reported that the UK Department of Health and Social Security was planning to use expert systems in its social security offices: people would be able to ascertain their entitlements and how to obtain payments (little, so far, has emerged in this area). In another field, the introduction of the Isolink telecommunications software modules has brought expert systems as part of office automation a step nearer. The modules allow non-technical users of the Xibus multifunction workstation – without any knowledge of protocols, addresses, procedures, etc – to access computer systems, databanks, and network services.

Most working expert systems were originally employed in scientific or experimental use, but today there is a clear shift towards the commercial environment (we have already cited some commercial products) and towards practical applications in such areas as education and medicine (see Actual Expert Systems, below). And many expert systems are in development: for instance, in such areas as equipment failure diagnosis, speech and image understanding, mineral exploration, military threat assessment, advising about computer system use, VLSI design, and air traffic control. Expert systems will have a role to play whenever problems have to be solved or expert advice is needed.

ACTUAL EXPERT SYSTEMS

A number of operating expert systems have already been mentioned, but it is worth considering some of these in more detail.

Medicine

Computers have been used for medical decision-making for about twenty years, employing programs that carried out well-established statistical procedures. In the main, the programs focused on the diagnostic element in consultation. Once symptoms had been presented, the computer would select one disease from a fixed set, using methods such as pattern recognition through discriminant functions. Bayesian decision theory, and decision-tree techniques. In more complex programs, *sequential* diagnosis was carried out. This involved specifying a new test for the patient in order to supplement insufficient information for a reliable diagnosis. Here the best test is selected according to economic factors, possible danger to the patient, and the amount of useful information that the test would yield.

By 1980 a wide range of diagnostic systems had been investigated. In one survey (Rogers et al, 1979), a table of 58 empirically tested computer-aided medical systems is presented (see Table 1).

In this context, computers are seen as having several inherent capabilities well suited to medical problem-solving:

– the ability to store large quantities of data, without distortion, over long periods of time;

Disease Type	Number of Studies
Endocrine, nutritional and metabolic	13
Blood and bloodforming organs	2
Mental disorders	10
Nervous system and sense organs	1
Circulatory system	5
Respiratory system	2
Digestive system	12
Genitourinary system	2
Pregnancy, childbirth and the puerperium	1
Skin and subcutaneous tissue	3
Musculoskeletal system, connective tissue	1
Symptoms, ill-defined conditions	4
Accidents, poisonings, violence	2
Total	58

Table 1   Number of Articles in Computer-Aided Diagnosis
(See bibliography in Rogers et al, 1979)

– the ability to recall data exactly as stored;

– the ability to perform complex logical and mathematical operations at high speed;

– the ability to display many diagnostic possibilities in an orderly fashion.

The accuracy of a computer-based diagnostic system depends upon many factors: the depth of the data (knowledge) base, the complexity of the diagnostic task, the selected algorithm, etc. In the Rogers et al (1979) review of applications, it was found that 60 per cent of all the diagnostic studies used an algorithm based on Bayes' theorem. Furthermore, there was a correlation between the disease class and the kind of algorithm used to make the diagnosis. Some computer-based diagnostic systems have performed better than medical consultants, and it is likely that automatic diagnostic systems will be increasingly common in various medical areas. At the same time it is important to recognise the limitations of computer-based medical systems. Moreover, attention will have to be given to the psychological elements in using a computer in the consulting room.

During the 1970s, efforts were made to apply AI techniques to problems in medical diagnosis. Again difficulties relating to inexact knowledge were evident: for instance, a particular treatment could not be guaranteed to result in a particular patient state. This situation stimulated the search for methods of representing *inexact knowledge* and for performing *plausible reasoning* (see Uncertainties, above). Diagnosis in the medical domain has been depicted as a problem of hypothesis formation, with clinical findings being used to generate a consistent set of disease hypotheses. The various expert systems devoted to medical diagnosis exploit different approaches to the task of hypothesis formation.

There are now many operating expert systems in medicine. Barr and Feigenbaum (1982) highlighted typical programs (and also provided full bibliographic citations in each instance).

Attention may again be drawn to MYCIN, CASNET, INTER-NIST, PIP, the Digitalis Therapy Advisor, IRIS and EXPERT. In addition, there are various experimental programs being developed, including:

– PUFF, a pulmonary-function program;

– HODGKINS, a system for performing diagnostic planning for Hodgkins disease;

- HEADMED, a psychopharmacology advisor;
- VM, an intensive care monitor;
- ONCOCIN, a program for monitoring the treatment of oncology out-patients on experimental treatment regimens.

The MYCIN expert system was intended to provide consultative advice on diagnosis and treatment for infectious diseases. This is a useful facility because the attending physician may not be an expert on infectious diseases: for example, an infection may develop after heart surgery, with a consequent need for prompt treatment in conditions of uncertainty. We have already seen that medical knowledge is stored in MYCIN as a set of rules augmented by certainty factors. The factors are used to express the strength of belief in the conclusion of a rule, assuming that all the premises are true.

The MYCIN rules are stored in LISP form and individually comprise a piece of domain-specific information including an ACTION (often a conclusion) that is justified when the conditions in the PREMISE are fulfilled. Figure 14.2 shows a typical MYCIN rule (this is the LISP form of the rule given in English).

PREMISE: (AND (SAME CNTXT INFECT PRIMARY-
BACTEREMIA)
(MEMBF CNTXT SITE STERILESITES)
(SAME CNTXT PORTAL GI))
ACTION (CONCLUDE CNTXT IDENT BACTERIODES TAL-
LY .7)

Figure 14.2   MYCIN Rule 050

Formal evaluations of MYCIN suggest that the system performance compares favourably with that of human experts on such diseases as bacteremia and meningitis. The TEIRESIAS system operates to allow the expert to inspect faulty reasoning chains and to augment and repair MYCIN's medical knowledge. There is a consensus that the MYCIN system shows great promise.

The Causal ASsociation NETwork (CASNET) program was developed at Rutgers University to perform medical diagnosis, with the major application in the field of glaucoma. Here the disease is not represented as a static state but as a dynamic process that can be modelled as a network of casually connected pathophysiological states. The system identifies a discerned pattern of casual pathways with a disease category, whereupon appropriate treatments can be specified. The use of a casual model also facilitates prediction of the development of the disease in a range of treatment circumstances.

CASNET, adopting a strictly bottom-up approach, works from tests, through the casual pathways, to final diagnosis. Though principally applied to glaucoma, the system exhibits a representational scheme and decision-making procedures that are applicable to other diseases. Ophthalmologists have evaluated CASNET and deemed it close to expert level.

The INTERNIST consultation program, developed at the University of Pittsburgh, operate in the domain of internal medicine. A list of disease manifestations (eg symptoms, laboratory data, history, etc) is presented to the system, and diseases that would account for the manifestations are diagnosed. The program then discriminates between competing disease hypotheses. Diagnosis in the field of internal medicine can be difficult because more than one disease may be present in the same patient.

The system's knowledge of diseases is organised in a disease tree, with use made of the *'form-of'* relation (eg hepatocellular disease is a form of liver disease). The top-level classification is by organs – heart disease, lung disease, etc. A list of manifestations, entered at the beginning of a consultation, evokes one or more nodes in the tree (when a model is generated for each evoked node). In this case, a diagnosis corresponds to the set of evoked nodes that account for all the symptoms. INTERNIST-I has been enhanced to form INTERNIST-II (which diagnoses diseases by dividing the disease tree into smaller and smaller subtrees). The system already carries more than 500 of the diseases of internal medicine, ie it is about 75 per cent complete, and practical clinical use is anticipated.

The Present Illness Program (PIP), being developed at MIT, focuses on kidney disease. The system's medical knowledge is represented in frames which centre around diseases, clinical states, and the physiological state of the patient: thirty-six such frames have been constructed to deal with kidney disease. Like INTERNIST but unlike MYCIN, PIP is designed to simulate the clinical reasoning of physicians.

Other work at MIT, carried out by the Clinical Decision Making Research Group, has been concerned with developing programs to advise physicians on the use of the drug *digitalis*. It is assumed that a patient requires digitalis: the programs determine an appropriate treatment regimen and its subsequent management in these circumstances. This approach is unusual in that it focuses on the problem of continuing patient management. This system, the Digitalis Therapy Advisor, was evaluated by comparing its recommendations to the actual treatments prescribed by human consultants for nineteen patients. On average a panel of experts preferred the recommendations of the physician, but the program's recommendations were reckoned to be the same or better in 60 to 70 per cent of all the cases that were examined.

Another medical system, IRIS, was developed for building, and experimenting with, other consultation systems. The system, designed at Rutgers University and written in INTERLISP, is intended to allow easy experimentation with alternative representations of medical knowledge, clinical strategies, etc. It has assisted in the development of a consultation system for glaucoma.

The EXPERT (expert) system, again developed at Rutgers, is aimed at helping researchers to design and test consultation models. Its development has been influenced by work in building consultation models in such medical areas as rheumatology, ophthalmology and endocrinology.

Today the diagnostic possibilities of computer software are being exploited in many different ways. For example, medical and computer experts in Britain (from Logica and the National Hospital) and Denmark (Computer Resources International, Judex Datasystems and the University of Aalborg) have produced a computer program to help doctors diagnose muscle and nerve diseases, plan tests and report on the results (*New Scientist*, 8 October 1987, p 32). This expert system, a fruit of Esprit funding, can take in the information supplied by medical equipment and make diagnostic proposals. Other writers (for example, Herd, 1987; Kemp-Davies, 1987) have explored the use of small computer-based systems for general practical and other environments.

Chemistry

Expert systems are now finding applications in many areas of scientific research and investigation: for example, in chemical analysis, geological prospecting, and the solution of mathematical problems in engineering and physics. Computer programs have been widely applied in all the sciences for many years, but specifically AI methods have had a more limited application. In, for example, non-numeric chemical reasoning problems, these methods have been applied to:

- identifying molecular structures in unknown organic compounds;
- planning a sequence of reactions to synthesise organic chemical compounds.

The identification of molecular structures is important to a wide range of problems in chemistry, biology and medicine. In many cases, the sophisticated analytic methods of x-ray crystallography may not be practical, and researchers must interpret data obtained in other ways, eg via mass spectrometry. Some tests allow the chemist to discover *molecular fragments*, subparts of the molecule, from which characteristic *constraints* can be derived. These constraints are interpreted as graph features in the representation of the molecule. Some of the current AI programs use similar data to generate small subsets of the theoretically-possible structures. The identification of molecular structures, using this type of approach, is being tackled by such expert systems as DENDRAL, CONGEN, Meta-DENDRAL, and CRYSALIS. By contrast, such expert systems as LHASA, SECS and SYNCHEM are concerned with finding techniques for the laboratory synthesis of known substances.

The Heuristic DENDRAL project – from its late-1960s inception to the present – has yielded various significant results. Though the system knows far less than a human expert, it elucidates structures efficiently by searching through possibilities. Published papers (cited in Barr and Feigenbaum, 1982) have variously shown that the program can solve structure elucidation problems for complex organic molecules, and that – for example, in the analysis of mass spectra of mixtures of oestrogenic steroids – the program can perform better than human experts. DENDRAL programs have been employed to determine the structures of various types of molecules (eg terpeniod natural products, marine sterols, chemical impurities, antibiotics, insect pheromones, etc). CONGEN, deriving from the DENDRAL project, is in practical use by chemists to solve various types of problems in the elucidation of molecular structures.

Meta-DENDRAL, designed to infer the rules of mass spectrometry from known structures, learns by scanning hundreds of molecular structure/spectral data-point pairs and by searching the space of fragmentation rules for likely explanations. The rule set can be extended to accommodate new data. The proficiency of Meta-DENDRAL can be estimated in part by the ability of a DENDRAL program using derived rules to predict spectra of new molecules. In fact the program has rediscovered known rules of mass spectrometry for two classes of molecules; and, more importantly, it has discovered *new* rules for three closely-related families of structures (the mono-, di-, and tri-keto androstanes).

The CRYSALIS expert system focuses on protein crystallography, aiming to integrate various sources of knowledge to match the crystallographer's performance in electron-density-map interpretation. (This would fill an important gap in the automation of protein crystallography). The concept of an electron density map generally denotes some pictorial representation (eg a three-dimensional contour map) of electron density over a certain region. The skilled crystallographer can study such a map to discover features allowing him to infer atomic sites, molecular boundaries, the polymer backbone, etc. In due course a structural model can be built to conform to the electron density map. Automation of this task requires a computational system that could generate, display and test hypotheses.

In CRYSALIS the hypotheses are represented in a hierarchical data structure, with knowledge sources able to add, change and test hypothesis elements on a 'blackboard' (see Knowledge Representation, above). The system can at present only perform a portion of the total task of interpreting electron density maps. The knowledge base is relatively small, but this is expanding and a capability is envisaged for the complete interpretation of medium-quality medium-resolution electron density maps.

We have already mentioned the three major organic synthesis programs. LHASA (Logic and Heuristics Applied to Synthetic Analysis), maintained at Harvard, is the earliest. This system yielded SECS (Simulation and Evaluation of Chemical Synthesis), now being developed at the University of California. SECS extended the LHASA approach by more extensively exploiting stereochemical and other types of information. The third major program of this sort, SYNCHEM (SYNthetic CHEMistry), is being developed at the State University of New York.

The main item of knowledge in chemical synthesis is the chemical reaction. Here a rule describes a) a situation in which a molecular structure can be changed, and b) the change itself. The programs use knowledge of reactions to design a synthesis route from starting materials to target molecule. In summary:

- the LHASA knowledge base, a set of procedures, contains sophisticated chemistry knowledge but is hard to update;
- the SECS knowledge base, carrying about 400 separate transforms, allows new transforms to be added without the need for program changes;
- the SYNCHEM knowledge base includes a library of reactions and commercially-available starting compounds. Chemists can modify the knowledge base without reprogramming.

Computer-aided chemical synthesis is regarded as a potentially valuable new facility for chemists, whether engaged in research or industrial manufacturing. A key factor in expert systems devoted to organic synthesis is how much they know about chemical reactions. The three main synthesis programs have all demonstrated their ability to find synthetic routes for organic materials.

Mathematics

There are now many mathematical expert systems in use by researchers. MACSYMA, originally designed in 1968 (and already mentioned in Chapter 8), is perhaps the best known. Other expert systems can operate to prove theorems (Chapter 11), to explore geometric relationships, etc. As with all expert systems, such mathematical facilities rely upon a stored knowledge base.

Geology

Various computer-based systems are being developed to aid geologists engaged in exploration tasks. One of the best known of these systems is PROSPECTOR, being developed at SRI International to help geologists working on problems in hard-rock mineral exploration. (PROSPECTOR made news in 1982 when it was given the same field study data about a region in Washington State as that used by experts in a mining company. The system concluded that there were deposits of molybdenum over a wide area. The geologists disagreed but when exploratory drilling was undertaken PROSPECTOR was found to be right.)

The user provides PROSPECTOR with information about a region (eg data on rock types, minerals, alteration products, etc), whereupon the program matches the information against its models. Where necessary, PROSPECTOR asks the user for more information to enable a decision to be reached. The user can intervene at any stage to provide new data, change existing information or request an evaluation from the system. A sophisticated inference network is used to control PROSPECTOR's reasoning, with network nodes corresponding to various geological assertions (eg *There is alteration favourable for the potassic zone of a porphyry copper deposit*). Rules are employed to specify how the probability of one assertion affects the probability of another (these inference rules are analogous to the production rules used in MYCIN).

Koroko-type massive sulphide, Mississippi-Valley type lead/zinc, type A porphyry copper, Komatiitic nickel sulphide, and roll-front sandstone uranium. These models are collectively represented by 541 assertions and 327 rules. Using the models and input data, the system is able to adjust the probability of hypotheses in changing circumstances.

The five models have only recently been developed to the point when useful geological evaluations could be made. And many further models are needed for extensive coverage of the full prospecting domain.

Education

Computer technology has been applied to education since the early-1960s, with applications in such areas as course-scheduling, test-grading, and the management of teaching aids. One aim of CAI (Computer-Aided Instruction) research has been to build instructional programs that incorporate course material in lessons that are optimised for each student. In the Intelligent CAI (ICAI) programs that began to emerge in the 1970s, course material was conveyed independently of teaching procedures – to enable problems and comments to be generated differently for each student. Today, AI is influencing the design of programs that are sensitive to the student's strengths and weaknesses, and to the preferred style of learning.

Early research on ICAI systems tended to concentrate on the representation of the subject matter. Attention may be drawn to such benchmark efforts as: SCHOLAR, a geography tutor; SOPHIE, an electronics troubleshooting tutor; and EXCHECK, a logic and set theory tutor. These systems have a high level of domain expertise, which allows them to be responsive over a wide spectrum of interactive problem-solving situations. Other expert educational programs are:

– WHY, which tutors students in the causes of rainfall, a complex geographical process that is a function of many variables. This system exploits 'socratic tutoring heuristics' and is able to identify and correct student misconceptions. WHY began as an extension of SCHOLAR;

– WEST, described as a program for 'guided discovery' learning. The system, deriving from a board game, assumes that a student *constructs* an understanding of a situation or a task, the notion of progressively corrected misconceptions being central to this assumption. The learning student interacts with a 'Coach';

- WUMPUS, which again uses game techniques to teach a mixture of logic, probability, decision theory and geometry. In one version, the coach is WUSOR-II, a system that involves the interaction of various specialist programs. Four basic modules are used: Expert, Psychologist, Student Model, and Tutor. The system is recognised to be a useful learning aid;

- GUIDON, a program for diagnostic problem-solving which uses the rules of the MYCIN consultation system. A student engages in a dialogue about a patient suspected of having an infection, and learns how to use clinical and laboratory data for diagnosis purposes. This system goes beyond responding to the student's last move (as in WEST and WUMPUS) and repetitive questioning and answering (as in SCHOLAR and WHY);

- BUGGY, designed to identify a student's basic arithmetic misconceptions. The system can provide an explanation of why a student is making an arithmetic mistake. Experience has indicated that forming a model of what is wrong can be more difficult than performing the task itself. BUGGY can be used to train teachers to diagnose errors in the way that students work.

The above programs are essentially *teaching* systems, and other programs are available to assist *learning by doing*. Emphasis may be given to effective 'learning environments' such as LISP-based LOGO (and its most celebrated application, turtle geometry), the message-passing SMALLTALK (and its extension, THING-LAB), and the DIRECTOR animation system. Here powerful programming-language features are used with sophisticated graphics facilities.

Today there is frequent reference to *intelligent computer-assisted instruction* (ICAI) systems which allow enhanced flexibility in the learning environment. We may expect such developments to continue in the years to come. A central aim is to provide the student with a natural learning environment allowing one-to-one relationships, as occur traditionally between students and tutors.

Design and Fault Diagnosis

There is increasing scope for expert systems in a wide range of design and fault diagnosis applications. One aim was to 'pit knowledge against complexity, using expert knowledge to whittle complexity down to a manageable scale' (Stefik and de Kleer, 1983). In this way, expert systems can be used in, for example, digital system design, one of many possibilities being researched at Digital Equipment Corporation (DEC) and elsewhere. With one experimental expert system, transistor size in integrated circuits is determined and circuit parameters such as load and capacitance are defined. In 1978 DEC began work, in conjunction with Carnegie-Mellon University, to develop a knowledge-based program called XCON for configuring VAX-11/780 computers. Durham (1987) describes how DEC are now rebuilding XCON 'from the inside'. EURISTO, an AI program used to configure naval fleets in competition games, has recently been employed to search for useful microcircuits structures made possible by multilayer fabrication technology.

At the Massachusetts Institute of Technology the Artificial Intelligence Laboratory has been experimenting with expert systems for many years. Systems such as EL and SYN help designers to analyse and synthesise analogue circuits. The PALLADIO system, developed at Zerox and Stanford University, is intended to help designers to experiment with new methodologies. A designer can discover gaps in the knowledge base by applying it to his own design, allowing subsequent modifications (to both knowledge base and design) to be made.

Thomas et al (1983) described how expert-system methods were applied to the synthesis and design of VLSI circuits for computers and other systems. Emphasis is given to the development of the CMU-DA system which uses a behavioural statement to propose functional block components and alternate block inter-connections that will implement the specified behaviour. A computer-aided design environment is being developed to aid the automatic synthesis of the behavioural and functional block levels of design. Here programs such as DAA and EMUCS are used for synthesis purposes. Using another approach, an expert system called SMX-Cogitor has been developed in Sweden to perform structural analysis and to check programs and problem solutions.

The computer retrieval incidence bank (CRIB) was one of several expert systems designed for computer fault diagnosis (see description in Hartley, 1984). The system can be used for diagnosis of faults in both hardware and software, and relies upon a knowledge base of simple factual information that can support the diagnostic task. The system designers investigated 1) the knowledge required by an engineer to find faults, and 2) how this knowledge is used by a skilled human practitioner. CRIB, now comprising a configuration of four programs, is regarded by its designers as a prototype for better systems. Another fault diagnosis system, FALOSY (FAult LOcalisation SYstem, described by Sedlmeyer et al, 1983) was used specifically for program debugging. More ambitiously, the New Medius expert system, from IAL Data Communications, was intended to locate network faults and (when system development is complete) to fix them by organising repairs.

The task of fault diagnosis requires the application of a set of techniques to a particular subject domain. It is easy to envisage a general fault-diagnosis system that can be bolted on to different knowledge bases. However, most research into expert-system fault diagnosis has focused on particular subject areas: computer circuits, electrical wiring, network connections, etc. Pratt (1984) described a computerised diagnostic system using AI techniques plus the expertise of an engineer to diagnose faults in locomotives. The system, developed by the General Electric Company's New York Corporate Research and Development Centre, will soon be widely used in railroad service depots throughout the United States. A central aim is to give the system humanlike modes of reasoning.

Business and Offices

Expert systems are now becoming increasingly available to business and office workers, just as they will emerge in the factory and engineering environments. For example, the Financial Advisor (based on the Nexus expert system) has been launched by Helix Products and Marketing as an aid for businessmen and other professional people. Financial Advisor offers advice on business management and helps to diagnose financial problems. Other Helix systems are Investment Advisor (to analyse investment possibilities) and Car Advisor (for those people deciding how to buy a car and which one), with other areas – such as personnel, loan administration, tax policies, etc – already targeted for expert-system development.

TAXADVISOR is an expert system (described by Michaelsen and Michie, 1983) designed to make tax planning recommendations for businessmen and other users. The system asks questions about a client's current wealth, and then gives advice to help him maximise his wealth within certain constraints. Another system, AUDITOR, developed at the University of Illinois, has been developed to help auditors assess a company's allowance for bad debts. Auditing information was assembled in rule form, initially for use on the AL/X system developed at the University of Edinburgh. Other systems are TAXMAN (for evaluating the tax consequencies of certain types of proposed business reorganisation) and CORPTAX (to advise the user about redemption policies).

A wide range of expert systems are being developed by DEC for in-house use. These include XSITE (an expert site planner's assistant), IMACS (to aid manufacturing), ISA (to aid scheduling), IPMS (to aid project management), XPRESS (to aid the refining of organisational procedures) and ILRPS (to aid long-range planning). XSEL, designed to help the salesperson develop system orders, was introduced for use in the US in September 1983 and more widely in 1984/5. This system interfaces between sales and engineering, addresses the problems of incorrect sales configuration, unprepared sites and unrealistic delivery estimates. DEC has 22 departments working on AI projects to encourage both commercial and in-house development.

Law

Expert systems are today being used in the field of law, as elsewhere. Waterman et al (1986) highlight a number of AI-based systems that are being used for various purposes (and offer a detailed bibliography). For example, attention is given to

- JUDITH, a system to aid reasoning in civil law;
- SARA, a system to help identification of relevant case factors;
- LEGOL, a language for expressing legal concepts;
- LRS, a system to retrieve legal information;
- HYPO, a system that uses hypothesis to aid legal reasoning;
- DSCAS, a system to help analysis of site law;
- LDS, a system to assist in product liability cases;
- SAL, a system to aid claim evaluation following asbestos exposure.

Such systems, and others are cited, indicate the increasing prevalence of AI-based systems in a traditional specialist area; and it is inevitable that this trend will continue ('there is much interest in developing commercial legal applications ... within a few years most of the major insurance companies and many legal firms will be heavily involved in the building of expert systems'). Liebowitz and Zeide (1987) describe EVIDENT, an expert system prototype that has been developed to aid a law student or graduate studying for bar examinations. The system can explain its reasoning and handle uncertainty factors.

Program Trading

In addition to the business and office systems already mentioned, it is worth highlighting the use of AI-linked systems to assist Stock Exchange trading, a usage highlighted by the (October 1987) Wall Street crash – an event that triggered similar dips around the world. A key factor in these events was 'program trading', where computers monitor the value of stocks and take buying and selling decisions when pre-set limits are reached.

The expert systems used by American financial institutions all tend to be based on similar mathematical models – so the systems are likely to jump in the same direction when particular market fluctuations are perceived. This can lead to a cumulative effect until the market plunges into 'free fall'. At the same time there is debate about to extent to which computer-based systems were the cause of the financial collapse.

It has long been known that expert systems would find many financial applications (see, for example, Sullivan, 1984; and quoted observations by Sandra Cook, manager of financial expert systems at SRI International, in *Computerworld*, 23 November 1984, p23) and today financial trading is unthinkable without computer involvement. Foremski (1988) discusses the debate over program trading, and various interpretations are represented. At one extreme, there is no doubt that 'computers compounded the shares crash' (*New Scientist*, 22 October 1987); but other observers take a different line – in 'Wall Street Kills the Messenger' Kull (1987) argues that the indictment of program trading 'was a classic public hoodwinking . . . the computer was a scapegoat'. For our purposes it is enough to highlight the increasing prevalence of AI-linked facilities, including expert systems, in financial trading.

Miscellaneous

Today expert systems are helping in government (see *Tintech* 2, 95, 16 December 1987), water purification (*Micro News*, June 1987), electrical engineering (Computer News, 20 August 1987), industrial training, hardware selection (Wright, 1987), process planning (Rahman and Narayanan, 1987), management decision making (Dhar, 1987), auditing (Dunmore, 1987), and countless other applications. Alarmingly, AI-linked systems are being designed to meet the need for speedy decision-making in military circumstances. For example, AIRPLAN is designed to regulate the movement of military aircraft, TATR to achieve tactical air targeteering; and AI-linked systems are intended to reduce the amount of *human* decision-making in the projected SDI ('Star Wars') scheme* in the United States.

IMPACT OF EXPERT SYSTEMS

The development of expert systems will have many social and commercial consequences. It is likely that they will lead to de-skilling in many employment areas, and to an effective redistribution of power (Ryan, 1988 – 'Rather than aiding decision makers . . . expert systems will replace them'). Practical

---

* Likely to be aborted in a Dukakis presidency

problems in expert-system implementation will increasingly need to be addressed: for example, how is development in this field to be audited? (Socha, 1988). And the various ethical questions long associated with AI development (Hamilton 1984; Speller and Brandon, 1986) will come to the fore. At the same time there will be growing commercial pressure for companies to remain abreast of developments (Firdman, 1988 asks: 'Expert systems: are you already behind?').

The AI impact, particularly in the field of expert systems, will become increasingly wide-ranging and significant. In 1987 it was stated by Brian Oakley, of the Alvey Directorate, that there were then around a thousand expert systems being developed in the UK alone, with about a hundred in practical use (cited in Kellock, 1987). Many more are being developed in Japan, the US and elsewhere. Major corporations are now investing in expert-systems work (see, for example, the developments discussed in *I/S Analyzer*, February 1988), and such trends are certain to continue.

SUMMARY

This chapter has profiled the typical expert system, with attention to structure, software, AI features, range of applications, social impact and other matters. Expert systems give a high profile to efforts among AI researchers to develop computer-based systems that exhibit humanlike characteristics.

We see a rapidly expanding range of expert systems: no area of human expertise is immune to the explorations of the knowledge engineer. It is not difficult to envisage the day when computer-based systems will be scientists, mathematicians, social advisers, engineers, managers, lawyers, etc. People should not be complacent about the effects of expert-systems development on human activity in society. It is even *intended* that human specialists should be replaced by computer-based systems. Thue Sy Bosworth, at a Softcon press conference (at which the Expert-East system was demonstrated some years ago) declared: 'Some people may be making mistakes continuously. Those so-called experts can and should be replaced'. He cites doctors whose faulty medical diagnosis cause unnecessary surgery or who run 20 tests when 14 of the tests are superfluous – 'We want to replicate the knowledge of the truly expert, with fewer wrong decisions and wrong moves' (quoted by Mace, 1984).

Expert systems are probably the most significant practical implementation to date of AI techniques. Developments in this area will influence the shape of fifth-generation systems and many other emerging advanced computer-based facilities. Moreover, expert systems represent one of the most successful realisations of efforts to model areas of human competence. Again this is a field that will see rapid development in the years to come.

15   Parallelism, Neural Networks

INTRODUCTION

The implementation of functional AI requires both hardware and software, a physical (probably silicon-based) machine programmed to perform one or more tasks that may reasonably be regarded as needing intelligence. This seemingly innocuous remark is in fact mildly contentious. Today many AI specialists consider software but ignore hardware: intelligence, it seems, resides in program code, not in the hardware/software mix. In this approach, AI is about algorithms and programs, with hardware (Boden's 'tin can') of interest only to electronics engineers.

In fact hardware and software are both essential for the realisation of operational AI in the real world, and various hardware matters have been profiled in the present book (Chapters 1, 3, 5, 6, 7 and 13). Hardware developments are necessarily at the heart of what computer-based systems can accomplish. The persistence of particular computer *architectures* through the various generations has sometimes tended to disguise the fact that the innovative *technologies* (valve, transistor, integrated circuit, etc) represent a direct hardware influence on computer competence. And new architectures, particularly evident today, represent a further hardware dimension that is crucially relevant to the performance scope of computer-based systems.

Recent years have seen increasing emphasis on various forms of parallel computing: there is growing interest in such topics as supercomputing, pipelining, data flow systems and neural (or connectionist) computers. The aim, here often influenced by biological insights (see below), is to expand computer capabilities to humanlike proportions, a matter of obvious relevance to AI. Increasingly we find that computers, in order to operate in an intelligent way, require vast memory capacities and very high speed capabilities. Efforts are being made to provide AI software for microcomputers (see, for example, my *Expert Systems and Micros*, NCC, 1985), but it is clear that the larger the system the greater the scope for AI implementation (we are driven to consider that the human brain, not always manifestly intelligent, relies upon some twelve billion neurons in order to carry out its day-to-day functions).

This chapter profiles some aspects of hardware parallelism to convey something of the flavour of current hardware evolution. In fact parallel processing may be regarded as having hardware, software and algorithmic aspects (a detailed survey of parallel programming is given in the journal *IEEE Software*, January 1988). The approach to fresh computer architectures, with the inevitable software implications, is one of the most important developments for AI in recent years. There is an obvious sense in which it is hardware, irrespective of the most imaginative program codes, that determines the scope of functional computer-based systems in the real world.

SUPERCOMPUTERS

As with many computing buzz-words, 'supercomputer' has been used at different times to denote various classes of machine. Any new system, vastly outperforming its antecedents, has tended to be dubbed a supercomputer, though such usage is perhaps most common in the sales brochures and the popular media. At one level 'supercomputer' ranks with 'electronic brain', a slogan that has some inherent significance but which is mainly intended to evoke awe. At the same time there are recognised supercomputers in the world today, and they commonly exhibit features that are relevant to the accomplishment of AI tasks.

Modern supercomputers are recognized largely according to their prodigiously fast speed of processing (highly relevant to the real-time needs of artificial viscon, semantic understanding, etc). We are told, for example, that a calculation that would take about 200 years on a hand-held calculator, and about eight minutes on a mainframe, 'takes about 1 second on a 1 billion-floating-point-operations-per-second (GFLOP) super-computer' (Jasany, 1988). Supercomputers were originally designed for various specialised tasks: today they are used in meteorology, integrated-circuit design, aircraft design, three-dimensional simulations, military-strategy analysis and for many other tasks, including specific AI implementation. Today there is also an emergency class of 'minisupercomputers', able to perform around 90% of the tasks of a supercomputer but at a much lower cost.

It is common to classify supercomputers according to their operational speed in terms of millions-of-floating-point-operations per second. Thus a classification scheme used by the US Department of Energy puts computers in eight effective classes:

- Class 1 (0.06 to 0.2 MFLOPS), often called 'workstations';

- Class 2 (0.2 to 0.6 MFLOPS);

- Class 3 (0.6 to 2 MFLOPS); 'superminicomputers';

- Class 4 (2 to 6 MFLOPS); 'mainframes';

- Class 5 (6 to 11 MFLOPS); 'minisupercomputers';

- Class 6 (20 to 35 MFLOPS), 'small supercomputers';

- Class 6 ½ (35 to 60 MFLOPS), 'supercomputers';

- Class 7 (60 to 200 MFLOPS), 'large supercomputers'.

Today there are well over a dozen international companies making supercomputers (eg ETA Systems, Control Data, Cray Research, IBM and Cyber in the United States; Hitachi and Nippon Electrical Corporation in Japan). The systems are characterised by such features as very high processing speed, memory size, memory speed and accuracy. Such characteristics rely upon various itectural elements, including a high level of parallelism.

PARALLEL PROCESSING

General

It is now commonly recognised that computers that work in a purely sequential fashion have inherent speed and processing limitations: it seems self-evident that operations will take less time if performed in parallel than if performed using 'in series' steps (in a solely sequential fashion). And it is sometimes declared that we have to depart from von Neumann architectures as if the great pioneer never envisaged the possibility of parallel processing. In fact, though von Neumann's name is associated, for various historical reasons, with the familiar sequential machine, he also considered various parallel options (as did a number of his contemporaries, including Norbert Weiner). What has been called the 'Neumann machine' is in fact a parallel computer.

The original Neumann machine was nothing more than a theoretical demonstration that an army of cells, each connected to its neighbours, could perform computational tasks. In the early-1980s, John Barker and his colleagues at Warwick University simulated the Neumann machine as part of a study on cellular automata (such work led to what is now more commonly referred to as 'neural computing', 'neurocomputing' or 'connectionist computing' – see below). A basic idea in this context is that complex behaviour, including behaviour that we would regard as intelligent, can be accomplished by a complex of simple elements functioning in an interactive manner. The original Neumann machine specified an array of cells, each with 29 possible states: it was later discovered that computations could be performed if the interactive cells each had as few as two possible states.

The clear advantages of parallelism still leave open the particular parallel approach that may be adopted. A common method is to break the algorithm into parts and to debate a separate processor to each part. This technique of 'functional decomposition' works well only if the various processors are equally occupied; otherwise some will be busy and others idle. Alternatively the incoming data needed by the algorithm can itself be divided into parts, each being handled by an identical processor. In general the more parallelism that is introduced, the faster and more costly the system.

The various approaches to parallelism have been interpreted according to theoretical paradigms. Paseman (1985), for example, discusses the control flow paradigm, where two or more processors share common memory; the data-flow (message passing) paradigm; and the reduction paradigm. Various architectures have evolved to realise these various options. Wilson (1988) considers the 'two main types' of parallel computers: those that carry out one operation on many different items at once; and those that divide large programs into many smaller ones (the functional decomposition already mentioned) that are simultaneously performed by separate processors. These two types of parallel computers ('parallel data' and 'parallel process', respectively) are today being manufactured by various companies throughout the world.

The Distributed Array Processor (DAP), for example, a parallel-data machine, was developed by ICL and is now made by the spin-off firm Active Memory Technology. Each DAP computer contains 1024 processing elements arranged in a square grid and controlled by a master processor. The configuration can cause problems where the tasks do not conveniently break down into a 32 × 32 matrix to fit the grid, but a range of successful applications has already emerged (in such areas as satellite photograph processing and material cooling analysis).

The early Illiac IV, already mentioned, was a successful array processor using an 8 × 8 matrix; and the MPP system, with a 128 × 128 matrix of 16,384 processing elements, was another (Reeves, 1984). It is clear that array machines are highly effective for suitable problems, but that their drawbacks (Sternberg, 1985) suggest the need for alternative architectures where appropriate. One such alternative is the *pipeline* architecture.

With pipeline configurations image data, for example, can be presented in a raster-scan format into a pipeline sequence of processing stages. Pipeline ('vector') computers can start operating on one set of data while still operating on a previous set. In this way, operations can overlap to reduce the time needed for the overall computation. Processors are thus working at the same time, and so achieve their objectives in less time than would be the case with sequential operation. Examples of pipeline architectures are TAS, the Cytocomputer, the MVI Genesis 4000 and the MITE (see the descriptions and bibliographic citations in Abbott et al, 1988). FPS, an American manufacturer of pipeline computers, has brought quantities of transputers (see below) for use in their architectures, and various companies (eg the supercomputer manufacturer Cray Research) are using parallel pipelines to achieve even faster computing.

There is now a consensus that future computers will contain high levels of parallel processing, though a wide range of techniques and architectures will remain available. Traditional sequential machines will outperform parallel systems for certain dedicated tasks, and may often be preferred on cost grounds, but the growing requirements – in AI and other applications – for the fastest levels of processing will encourage the development of parallel systems. At a London seminar in late-1987 the industry guru James Martin declared that 'ultra parallel' machines was the way forward for hardware technology, though companies such as IBM may resist the trend because of existing investment in traditional mainframe systems. However, where lessons are learnt from biology – a familiar source of inspiration for AI specialists – it is easy to see why high levels of parallel processing represent an inevitable route for sophisticated computer applications.

Biology

It has long been suspected that biological systems were parallel processing to achieve their remarkable levels of processing. Columnar distributions of neurons, acting simultaneously to achieve particular purposes, have been identified in the mammalian brain; and at the purely theoretical level it is difficult to see how a human being, for example, could achieve the full spectrum of typical mental activities by relying solely on sequential processing. Today there are many reasons, in both theory and empirical evidence, to suppose that biological nervous system exploit parallel options, and that this type of strategy offers a range of fertile models for the design of tomorrow's intelligent computer systems. Appropriately enough there is now increasing discussion, in both the general and technical press, of computers designed like the human brain, of *neural networks, neural computers, neurocomputers*.

Neural Processing

Like many important ideas in computing, neural processing has a relatively long history: that neurocomputing is now 'flavour of the year' should not be allowed to disguise the fact that many of the associated concepts were around half a century ago. There was speculation, long before the Second World War, about how brain cells processed information, and notions concerning cellular automata were in circulation before the advent of first-generation computers. In 1943 Warren McCulloch and Walter Pitts showed that networks of neuron-like elements could carry out computation, and in 1949 Donald Hebb suggested that the neuronal synapses were the sites of biological learning. Clearly computers able to behave in a similar way could be regarded as intelligent.

Research in the 1950s led to the construction of simple artificial-neuron networks that could perform rudimentary perceptual tasks. In 1957 Frank Rosenblatt proposed how a layer of *perceptrons*, effective neurons with Hebbian learning, could recognise simple patterns. Soon afterwards, with contributions from Marvin Minsky and Seymour Papert, it was seen that a neural network in a *single* layer would require an absurdly large number of elements to solve complex problems. In the 1970s and 1980s there was growing interest in how *multiple* layers could provide the basis for artificial systems with impressive computational abilities. The early perceptron concept was now being expanded to lay the basis for modern neurocomputing theory (on accessible account of neural networks modelled on how the brain works is given by Recce and Treleavan, 1988).

In the early-1980s, interest in neural computing began to expand at a significant rate – with, as always, impetus provided by perceived military needs. Most of the research efforts focused on the use of high levels of circuit integration to achieve effective neural networks, but other routes were also explored. It was found, for example, that large-scale integrated (LSI) circuits ran into signal-distribution problems. To avoid these, a team at the University of Pennsylvania turned to optoelectronics as a means of constructing a non-LSI neural net (see account in *Electronics*, 16 June 1986, pp 41–44). And, at the same time, scientists at John Hopkins University and AT & T Bell Laboratories were achieving successes with silicon-based neural-network designs. Texas Instruments and TRW announced that they intended to offer commercial implementations of neural networks. TRW, for example, had already developed the Mark III Artificial Neural System Processor for the US Department of Defence, and commercial plans were to draw on this experience.

Through 1987 the idea of neurocomputing – basically that processing-element arrays could be induced to behave like biological neurons – gathered pace. Research continued in the universities and lead companies, and neurocomputer products received commercial hype. Nestor Inc, the first neural network company, now offers a software product intended to emulate neural construction on personal computers, and Hecht-Nielsen Neurocomputers offers ANZA, an IBM Personal Computer AT coprocessor board intended to emulate 30,000 neurons (this latter system includes a library of neural network software). Fujitsu is said to have simulated a neurocomputer with the capability of 100,000 neurons, and to be developing a neuro-chip that will form the basis of a neurocomputer within a few years.

Today there is massive interest in neurocomputing. In 1986 a neural network conference in Santa Barbara attracted fifty participants, but around 1500 people attended a similar conference in 1987. The old perceptron idea, at one time criticised by Marvin Minsky, had refused to die; in the 1980s it emerged with a new vigour. Williamson (1988) emphasises that neural networks are now being tested in a variety of applications. He cites:

- modems using a neural network to distinguish between noise and data;

- a Nestor product that can translate handwriting into ASCII characters as though the information had been entered through a keyboard;

- a Hecht-Nielsen Neurocomputer that can recognise and classify complex visual images (for use in industrial parts inspection and by autonomous robots);

- products from Neuralware and Neuronics to enable users to experiment with neural network architectures.

There are many ways in which the developing neurocomputing theory and available commercial products are relevant to artificial intelligence. The very inspiration behind the theory is biological, implying an identity of focus in natural and artificial systems. It is assumed today that the human brain relies upon a massive parallel architecture, and neurocomputing strategies directly exploit this circumstance. Research by David Rumelhart (in 1986 at the University of California, San Diego) and James McClelland (at Carnegie-Mellon University, Pennsylvania) highlighted the similarities between artificial neural-network modelling techniques and the methods used by children to use the past tense. This led to debate about how 'learning computers' might be built (Keith Devlin, in *Computer Guardian*, 21 January 1988, asks – 'Are we witnessing the first step towards a quite new way of building computers?'). Williamson (1988) has drawn attention to Nestor's adaptive expert systems, another clear sign of the direct relevance of neurocomputing to AI.

The neural network computer, like the human brain, comprises a large number of computing elements that assume states according to inputs received from neighbouring elements. Inputs can vary in weight and the elements respond accordingly. Unlike conventional computer architectures, there is no separate database or instruction list. The system operates solely according to inputs, outputs and the parallel architecture of the system. In this close modelling of biological neural systems there is obvious potential for building artefacts capable of intelligent behaviour in the real world.

Neurocomputing and AI

We have already emphasised the relevance of neural networks to AI, and encountered adaptive expert systems. For our purposes, these are central considerations. Again we can identify the intentional similarities between brain architectures and the configuration of neurocomputers (that use 'connectionist' strategies). Feldman et al (1988), emphasising the possibility of automating 'complex tasks such as those found in artificial intelligence, indicate the advantages of the connectionist approach:

- the link to natural intelligence;

- increased noise resistance;

- ease of implementation on parallel hardware;

- its suitability for specifying some computations.

Artificial vision, requiring massive parallelism, is one implementation among many that lends itself to a connectionist
approach; for example, there are interesting results also in
natural language research. Thus Feldman et al emphasise that the
driving force behind a number of identified system developments
has been applications of connectionist models, 'particularly to
problems in AI'. Similarly Gallant (1988) suggests that connectionist networks can be used as expert system knowledge bases;
and, in general, connectionist (or neural network) models 'are
drawing increasing interest as useful tools for mainstream
artificial intelligence (AI) tasks'. Particular attention is given to a
two-program package for building connectionist expert systems
from training examples: one program is a network knowledge-
base generator that exploits connectionist techniques; and the
other (MACIE*) is a stand-alone expert-system inference engine
able to interpret the knowledge bases. The approach is represented in optimistic terms: 'research in this area has increased by
two orders of magnitude over the last five years ... We believe
connectionist expert systems present a promising approach to the
knowledge-acquisition problem for expert systems.'

The development of connectionist (or neural-network) computers represents a radical departure from the evolution of
traditional computer systems. As with the neural configurations
in biological brains, the most powerful neurocomputers rely upon
a massive number of computing elements individually communicating, in various ways, with all the other elements in the vicinity.
Biological neurons each have a large number of inputs and
outputs, and artificial processing elements cannot compete in this
regard. But artificial systems can 'switch' much more quickly than
can natural processors, and so there are evident trade-offs
between speed and architecture complexity.

---

* Matrix Controlled Inference Engine

It is the architectural character of the connectionist computer that perhaps offers the best AI hope for the future. In effectively modelling the communication strategies of biological brain cells, the modern neurocomputer is on an evolutionary route that is analogous to that followed by natural systems and which led to all the prodigious accomplishments of the human mind. It may be, however, that the necessary architectural complexity and functional competence may only be possible via a three-dimensional lattice constructed out of organic materials (see Chapter 16). It will be ironic if we find that the most sophisticated implementations of AI can only be accomplished by re-creating the mammalian brain, that mainstream AI over the last three decades shows itself incapable of evolving the most sophisticated manifestations of intelligence.

The Transputer

The INMOS transputer emerged as an effective 'building block' processing element in the early–1980s. It was designed with INMOS's Occam language (*Electronics*, 30 November 1982, p 89), and was intended to serve the needs of parallel architectures. Even when *not* used in parallel the transputer is able to operate at a rate of more than 5 MIPS (Barron et al, 1983). It has been depicted as a traditional 'von Neumann computer with link interfaces' (Walker, 1985) – 'making a link between two transputers is as simple as joining together the lug and hole on two Lego bricks.'

The fact that large numbers of high-speed transputers can be attached together in parallel arrays enables supercomputing performance to be accomplished at a fraction of the cost of traditional supercomputers. For example, the University of Edinburgh is currently using transputers for the developing architecture of the Edinburgh Concurrent Supercomputer (ECS). The system will be able to perform a billion calculations a second, making it as fast as any modern supercomputer (eg the CRAY X-MP that exploits pipeline techniques). The ECS already has more than 200 new-generation transputers in its emerging architecture (already providing an 800 Mbyte memory and a processing power of around two hundred million operations per second), and various other projects are exploiting the potential offered by the transputer. These include the Alvey-funded Supernode development, various European initiative and an Atari transputer-based microcomputer.

RESEARCH INTERESTS

Particular areas of hardware research have already been highlighted in the present chapter. It is worth drawing attention also to some recent papers that indicate further topics of research interest:

- Thomas (1987) describes how display systems can be constructed to exploit Boolean expressions for computer graphics;
- Wang and Butner (1987) describe a computer architecture designed to meet robotic computational needs;
- Jopham et al (1987) evaluate the various pipelined architectures and offer a fresh (Context Flow) pipelining option;
- Woo (1986) describes a robotic vision system that can recognise workpieces and determine their position and orientation;
- Annaratone et al (1987) describe the Warp machine, a systolic array computer of linearly connected cells, each a programmable processor capable of operating at 10 MFLOPS.
- Yamakawa (1987) discusses nine basic fuzzy logic circuits;
- Tick and Warren (1986) describe the architecture of a Prolog machine with attention to reduced instruction set computing (risc) and other aspects.

SUMMARY

This chapter has indicated various approaches to the architecture of computers, with particular focus on parallelism, and emphasised their relevance to artificial intelligence. After a preliminary indication of how supercomputers are generally classified according to processing speed, mention is made of such options as array processors, data flow systems and pipeline architectures. It is stressed that high levels of processing speed are necessary to various types of computer application, including many (eg vision, semantic processing) in AI.

Attention is also given to how biological insights continue to suggest how advances in computing might be accomplished. In particular, the early work on neuron modelling is highlighted, with an indication of how the early 'perceptron' concept was criticised by Marvin Minsky, only to gain fresh popularity in the 1980s in theories about neural-network (connectionist) computing. Emphasis is given to how neurocomputers – with some commercial products now available – represent a departure from traditional computer architectures (and represent a development of early von Neumann ideas, despite his much-publicised identification with traditional sequential architectures). It is suggested that neurocomputers, because of their intended architectural similarity to biological brains, may be on a fresh evolutionary route analogous to the one that led to massive mental accomplishments in natural systems.

The INMOS transputer is briefly profiled as a fast processing element that has considerable potential for serving in parallel systems that can achieve supercomputer performance at relatively low cost. Brief attention is also given to some current hardware research interests that relate to artificial intelligence.

A constant theme in the present chapter is that hardware systems are necessarily essential for the implementation of AI in the real world: interest in AI software has sometimes appeared to divert attention from hardware requirements. The chapter has therefore continued to hardware theme that was explored in Chapters 1, 3, 5, 6 and 7. AI systems, like intelligent biological configurations, require both hardware and software if they are to behave in the real world.

Part 7
1990 to . . .

16 Signposts to a Future

INTRODUCTION

It is an easy matter to identify some of the trends that will characterise future computing in general and future AI in particular. Systems will become more powerful and more cost-effective: there will be increased scope for the high speeds and massive memories increasingly required by artificial intelligence. Many of the current problems in hardware design and software development will be successfully tackled using automated techniques. In this way computers themselves will become increasingly involved in the generation of their own progeny.

As more is learnt about human biology – in particular, about the central nervous system – there will be increased effort to model biological systems in artefacts. One thread in artificial intelligence has always been to learn from natural systems (witness Wiener's cybernetics, linking animal and machine systems; and the early modelling of the communicating nerve, which led – via the derided perceptron – to the current enthusiasm for neurocomputing). But one problem is this approach has always been the paucity of knowledge about mammalian brains: how are we to model brains if we do not know how they work? New advances in such fields as neurology, genetics and hormone biochemistry may be expected to influence and inform the various approaches to AI. Similarly, developments in cognitive psychology – a key information-processing discipline – will help to shape our perceptions about the information-processing potential of artefacts.

We should note that many predictions about AI will continue to be fanciful, too optimistic, inadequately grounded in a realistic estimate of current technology. So gurus such as Marvin Minsky will continue to be caught out, anticipating humanoid artefacts around every technological corner. Some observers will continue to predict 'direct brain input' by 1990 or machines with intuition, common sense and a sense of humour by the turn of the century. But the problems in machine design and development – problems relating to hardware, software, logics to adopt, paradigms to select – will continue to put a brake on progress. The human brain is the most complex system we have encountered in the universe. We should not be complacent about how soon we will be able to duplicate in artefacts all its remarkable powers.

Already there are signs that the Japanese fifth-generation programme, a herald of new AI systems for the early-1990s, is trimming its ambitions and expectations. Thus Sorensen (1986) can suggest that the fifth generation (including development projects for cognitive awareness, semantic processing, intelligent robots, man/machine interfaces, etc) is 'slow to rise' ('The scope of the project has been scaled down considerably since its inception, according to many observers'); and, in a similar vein, Poe and Tate (1987) can comment on 'the lost generation' ('The Japanese fifth generation research centre, ICOT in Tokyo ... is now trying to lower expectations about what it is likely to achieve. It has hit big problems.... Many observers are still sceptical that ICOT will reach its goals').

At the same time there is no doubt that computer-based systems will continue to become more intelligent, though perhaps at a slower rate than many pundits have proposed. Expert systems, for example, will diffuse through the populations of the developed countries, finding applications in commerce, industry, education, military establishments, government, the home, etc – raising important questions about system reliability, legal liability, the nature of the encapsulated expertise (in 1987 publicity was given to a racially biased computer program at St George's medical school in South London). Thus whatever the pace of progress towards AI systems it will become increasingly necessary for users, systems suppliers and others to pay attention to legal ethical and social implications. It is worth glancing at some of the discernible trends and developments.

TRENDS AND DEVELOPMENTS

We have already highlighted some of the more obvious trends for the future. Thus one typical observer, Pournelle (1983), has commented; 'We can sum up the hardware trend in one sentence: more capability for less money. That trend will accelerate ... software is going to be cheaper, more universal, and easier to use.' And there will be a growing 'AI content' in new-generation systems. The intelligence of artefacts will be enhanced by linking AI-based systems in networks, much as dedicated modular intelligences are linked in the human brain.

There will continue to be developments in microelectronics technology, with fresh options in other fields (eg biocomputing and optical computing – see below). The bulk of electronic circuits will continue to be based on silicon, though other substrates will find market niches for particular purposes (for example, circuits based on gallium arsenide are already popular in some military and other applications). Supercomputers, usually defined in terms of speed, will become more powerful and more economic; and will exploit a growing range of parallel architectures (James Martin's prediction of 'ultra parallelism' is a safe bet). Sensors will become increasingly important for robots and other systems, making it possible for artefacts to gather information with ever diminishing human involvement. We may also expect developments in the other technologies – mechanical engineering, power supplies, etc – that are essential to the performance of intelligent robots.

There will be increased understanding, often gained from biology, of the various conditions and processes that are embodied in intelligent systems (for example, algorithms, heuristic procedures, knowledge representation, uncertainty handling, etc). Methods of logic – from the first order propositional calculus to fuzzy and nonmonotonic formalisms – will continue to develop, with such disciplines as linguistics and epistemology (perhaps increasingly sensitive to the insights of the historical philosophers), to provide enabling mechanisms for such intelligent activities as language understanding and concept formation in machines. We can highlight particular developments as likely to influence the shape of tomorrow's intelligent artefacts:

New Technologies

Superconductivity

Biocomputing

Optical Systems

Expert Systems

Reliability and Security

Fifth Generation to Neurocomputers

Supercomputers

NEW TECHNOLOGIES

New technologies will evolve as an effective hierarchy – from a growing range of substrates at the bottom through all the applications that they support. For example, Rifkin (1986) considers the options beyond silicon, highlighting the following alternatives: gallium arsenide, producing faster and more powerful devices; high-electron mobility transistors, when cooled to 77 degrees Kelvin producing very high switching times (see also Superconductivity, below); Josephson Junctions, superconductors (see below) when cooled to near absolute zero; biochips, able to incorporate neural characteristics; optical chips, able to exploit a complex of silicon, gallium arsenide and fibre optics, with information flowing between chips at the speed of light; and ballistic transistors, characterised by ultra high switching speeds (measured in quadrillionths of a second).

Developments in particular high-level technologies are frequently described in the journals (often at year-end or year-beginning). For example, a 1988 Technology Forecast – covering automotive electronics, avionics, computer-aided engineering, military electronics, software, etc – is given in Electronic Design, 7 January 1988. A common theme in many such forecasts is the increased use of artificial intelligence in both commercial and research systems.

SUPERCONDUCTIVITY

There is increased speculation about superconductive computers as a possible future technology: see, for example, Davis (1987),

'The Superconductive Computer in Your Future'; and Fagan (1987), 'Goodbye to the Silicon Chip?'

Superconductivity was discovered in 1911 by the Dutch physicist Heike Kamerlingh Onmes. In particular, it is found that specific substances, when heavily cooled, have a massively reduced resistance to electricity. Today special attention is being given to ceramic oxides, following the development by Paul Chu and his team at the University at Houston of a compound capable of superconductivity at the then (February 1987) record-high temperature of −283°F. It is suggested (in Davis, 1987) that first the new materials could be used for computer chip interconnects on printed-circuit boards, then for the on-chip connections between silicon transistors, and then for the integrated circuits themselves. The much reduced power requirements mean that elements could be packed more closely on a chip: the transistors switch more quickly and less heat is generated.

About a decade ago, IBM began work on Josephson Junctions, superconductors developed following the work of Brian Josephson at Cambridge University. Much of this work was axed when it was found that, at the time, the research findings were unpromising. Today there is a resurgence of interest in superconductivity with recent announcements from such organisations as IBM, Wayne State University, the University of Houston, the Japanese MITI National Research Institute for Metals, and the Chinese Academy of Sciences at Beijing.

BIOCOMPUTING

We will also see the progressive development of integrated circuits based on organic materials. This approach – allowing, for example, the building of three-dimensional lattices – will facilitate the emergence of various research and commercial products, such as biosensors and 'biological computers'.

The first biochip patent was awarded in 1974 to Arieh Aviram and Philip Seidon (both of IBM), collaborating with New York University. It has been suggested by Kevin Ulmer, of the Genex Corporation that 'the ultimate scenario is to develop a complete genetic code for the computer that would function as a virus does, but instead of producing more virus, it would asemble a fully operational computer inside a cell'. This suggests that an organic computer could propagate offspring, possibly allowing 'design mutations' to influence the course of system evolution. For some years the small Maryland company EMV Associates has explored the possibility of combining organic switching molecules and computer design. In work described by Yanchinski (1982), the possibility was explored of triggering the growth of a protein film in a highly structured way to 'grow' logic gates at particular points. In such a fashion, genetic engineering could be enlisted to grow computers. After all, biological systems manage the trick readily enough.

In 1982 it was suggested (eg in *New Scientist*, 11 November) that Japan was 'on the road to a biological computer'; and soon (Durham, 1984) the possibility of biochips replacing silicon computers was on the agenda. Already there are many different types of biosensors available on the market: the information-processing capabilities of organic materials are well established (see, for example, Albinson, 1987). The possibility of a future (artificial) biological computer cannot be ignored.

OPTICAL SYSTEMS

Increased attention will also be given to the data-processing capabilities of systems based on optical phenomena (see, for example, Durham, 1983; Osman, 1986; and Hecht, 1987). Almost a decade ago, an operational optical transistor, switched by a beam of laser radiation, was constructed (described in Abraham et al, 1983). This device, the *transphasor*, relied on the functional features of certain crystals. For example, the crystals refractive index, a measure of how the light is affected as it passes through the crystal, changes with the light intensity. Such phenomena enable devices to be constructed with switching times of only a few picoseconds. There is current speculation on how optical transistors could be organised to process information in familiar ways – but much faster (for example, light travels much faster along an optic fibre than does an electrical pulse in a conductive medium).

Today optic-fibre systems are commercially available for communication and other purposes. Biancomano (1986) suggests that: 'The message is clear: fibre-optic systems are destined to succeed classic communication networks at all levels.' And there is growing attention to the possibility of 'optoelectronic ICs', devices able to cross the gap between research and commercial availability 'and experiencing the most rapid technological gains with most of the newest components'. Reference is made to efforts to 'photonise' chips, and to how they would have incomparable speed advantages over conventional integrated circuits. Electro-optical systems are seen as directly relevant to how supercomputers may be able to achieve AI levels or processing (Hall, 1986), and optical storage methods are increasingly popular. Perhaps the race towards post-fifth-generation computers will be between biochips and optoelectronic chips.

EXPERT SYSTEMS

Expert systems have already been considered in detail (Chapter 14) and little needs to be added here. It is worth emphasising, however, that future expert systems will have enhanced capabilities that enable them to adapt in new situations. They will be self-adaptive, self-regulatory and increasingly able, possibly via networking, to gather pertinent knowledge without human involvement. Such developments will represent an expansion of system autonomy, a manifest AI feature.

RELIABILITY AND SECURITY

With computer-based systems expected to have an increased AI component in the years ahead, questions of reliability and security will be given a fresh emphasis. There are already plenty of cases on record where faults in computers have led to adverse human consequences. For example, software bugs in hospital radiation equipment have resulted in excessive radiation doses being given to patients (Joyce, 1987); inadequate computer (Control Data Cyber 205) performance caused the UK Meteorological office to fail in 1987 to predict the worst storms for 285 years ('It's possible that a small piece of information got into the computer which shouldn't have'), and so inadequate advance warnings were given; and air traffic controllers have blamed several potentially disastrous near-misses on inadequate computer systems which are, nonetheless, used on a more or less constant basis.

The point is that in all such cases there are clear opportunities for human intervention. This will be less possible with high-level AI systems intended to work on an autonomous basis; and with particular systems intended to take life-and-death decisions (eg the planned SDI systems – see, for example, Parnas, 1985; Myers, 1986), failures in software could result in global catastrophe. And even dislocations or disruptions in the power supply can result in corrupt data (Fox, 1987).

Threats to system security can occur through design inadequacies, 'fortuitous' circumstances or malice. There is already a rapidly expanding literature on the 'virus' menace (see, for example, Davis and Grantenbein, 1987; Pozo and Gray, 1987; and Cohen, 1987), and this is only one type of threat amongst many. It is interestng that the virus problem has a clear biological reference, as do the software 'antibodies', intended to overcome the problem. And biology can provide other insights for effective security; for example, security systems modelled on the human immune system (Wood, 1987).

There are two points to emphasise in this connection:

- biology offers metaphors and insights for the comprehension and design of artificial systems.

- systems failures (linked to design shortcomings, adverse environmental circumstance or malicious intent) are potentially more hazardous in systems with high levels of AI.

FIFTH GENERATION TO NEUROCOMPUTING

Future computing (and AI) developments will not be achieved as a result of a neat linear progression. Research routes will be adopted and then abandoned, temporarily or permanently. We have seen, in the present book, how crystals were explored, then neglected, then developed to produce the massive semiconductor industry; how superconductive research was undertaken by IBM, only to be discarded, before being enthusiastically taken up again by IBM and others in recent years; how neural modelling was first attempted – to yield the perception concept – then abandoned, before being exploited afresh in the 1980s to yield all the new hopes that today surround the topic of neurocomputing.

The current doubts about fifth-generation computing have led Professor Hideo Aiso, a lead specialist of the Japanese fifth-generation project, to declare that fifth-generation research was simply a step towards neural computing (cited by Ince, 1988). In fact the two routes to AI are disparate. A switch now to neural-computing methods would represent an effective dislocation in the research direction. This should not surprise us: biological evolution itself – with 'punctuated equilibria' – may have progressed in such a fashion. The route to intelligent artefacts will be untidy, uncertain and tortuous, full of hesitations, sudden insights and changes of direction.

SUPERCOMPUTERS

There will continue to be a tendency for any new high-performance system to be dubbed a *super*computer, irrespective of whether it conforms with the classification criteria (ie usually speed critera). At the same time evolution of the recognised supercomputer sector will yield 'new progeny in minisupers and mainframes with vectors processors' (Gyllo and Schatz, 1988).

Parallel architectures will have increasing emphasis ('the computer architectures of the 1990s and beyond will be parallel in nature' – Mokhoff, 1986), and the fruits of current work on neurocomputers will become evident (interest may wane, only to pick up again with new advances in neurology, cognitive science, etc). And increased attention will be given to designing computer-based systems with AI content. The supercomputers of the future, achieving high processing speeds through parallel architectures, will find a widening range of applications, including all those traditionally associated with artificial intelligence.

APPLICATIONS

Little need be said here. Developments in AI will impact on all conventional computer applications. AI facilities will be added to existing computer-based systems; current AI systems will acquire ever higher levels of intelligence; and a growing range of AI applications will emerge. In principle, *any* mental task currently performed by human beings will be amenable to computerisation. It would therefore be quite impractical to indicate – with anything even approaching an exhaustive listing – the likely spectrum of applications for AI-linked systems in the future. Think of any possible activity involving information processing and, for good or ill, it will be possible to perform it using computer-based systems, with or without 'AI content', as necessary.

SUMMARY

This chapter has indicated both likely and possible computing developments for the future. Emphasis has been given to the multifaceted nature of progress in this field: we have highlighted pertinent considerations in hardware architecture, hardware substrates, biology, philosophic theory, the nature of technological change, etc. It is important to appreciate the sporadic, disjointed nature of evolution in computing. Topics are sometimes taken up, toyed with, discarded, and then taken up again with new enthusiasm. At the same time, there is steady progress in key sectors – circuit fabrication, algorithm theory, programming practice, etc – where advances derive from earlier solid successes. With hindsight we can see how ever denser memories, ever more reliable circuits, etc have developed in a progressive step-by-step manner.

We have also emphasised the increasing AI content in current systems, and how this element will be even more significant in future computer-based facilities. AI systems will eventually be equipped to mimic or duplicate all human mental processes, providing there is some point in doing so. And with such system evolution, a host of practical, ethical and legal questions will be given a fresh emphasis. How will we know that this or that AI system, possibly – as in hospital, military, airline systems, etc – responsible for human life, is reliable at all times? How can we ever know that its internal 'thought processes' are as we would wish?

The paradox is that AI systems will be increasingly applied in circumstances where *rapid* decision-making is crucial, where to delay might endanger human life. But it is in exactly such circumstances that human beings should retain a 'window' onto machine activity. This is a problem that has scarcely been addressed by the late-1980s, much less solved. It will become more pressing with the increasingly intelligent artefacts of the future.

References and Bibliography

CHAPTER 1

Dawkins R, *The Selfish Gene*, Paladin, 1982, p 21

Reichardt J, *Robots: Fact, Fiction and Prediction*, Thames and Hudson, 1978

Smart J J C, Professor Ziff on robots, *Analysis*, Vol. xix, No. 5, 1959

Sprague de Camp L, *Ancient Engineers*, Tandem, 1977

CHAPTER 2

Aristotle, *Prior Analytics* and *Posterior Analytics*, written about 350 BC (see, for example, the Everyman edition, 1964; translation and Introduction by John Warrington)

Barnes J, *Aristotle*, Oxford University Press, 1982

Diels H, *Fragmente der Vorsokratiker*, 3 volumes, eighth edition by W Kranz, Berlin, 1956

Kilmister C W, *Language, Logic and Mathematics*, English Universities Press, 1967

Kneale W and Kneale M, *The Development of Logic*, Oxford University Press, 1962

Russell B, *History of Western Philosophy*, George Allen and Unwin, 1946

Sharma C, *A Critical Survey of Indian Philosophy*, Rider and Company, London, 1960

CHAPTER 3

Flatt J P, *Les Trois Premières Machines à Cálculer*, Palais de la Decouverte, 1963

Gardner M, The Ars Magna of Ramon Lull, in *Science: Good, Bad and Bogus*, Oxford University Press, 1983

Hyman A, *Charles Babbage, Pioneer of the Computer*, Oxford University Press, 1982

Mills J F, *Encyclopedia of Antique Scientific Instruments*, Aurum Press, 1983

Perrier L, *Gilberte Pascal: Bibliographic de Pascal*, 1963

Reid T R, *Microchip*, Pan, 1985

Rosenberg Y, The Golem, in *Great Works of Jewish Fantasy*, Picador, 1978

Smith D E and Ginsburg J, From numbers to numerals and from numerals to computation, in Newman J R (ed), *The World of Mathematics*, Vol. 1, New York, 1956

Sprague de Camp L, *Ancient Engineers*, Tandem, 1977

Strandh S, *A History of the Machine*, Arrow Books, 1984

CHAPTER 4

Copleston F C, *The History of Medieval Philosophy*, Methuen, 1972

Jevons W S, On the mechanical performance of logical inference,

Philosophical Transactions of the Royal Society, c/x, 1870, pp 497–518

Kilmister C W, *Language, Logic and Mathematics*, English Universities Press, 1967

Kneale W and Kneale M, *The Development of Logic*, Oxford University Press, 1962

Russell B, *History of Western Philosophy*, George Allen and Unwin, 1946

CHAPTER 5

Hodges A, *Alan Turing: The Enigma of Intelligence*, Burnett Books Ltd, 1983

Kilmister C W, *Language, Logic and Mathematics*, English Universities Press, 1967

Kneale W and Kneale M, *The Development of Logic*, Oxford University Press, 1962

Lavington S, *Early British Computers*, Manchester University Press, 1980

Reid T R, *Microchip*, William Collins, 1985

Simons G, *Is Man a Robot?*, John Wiley, 1986

Turing A, On computable numbers, with an application to the Entscheidungs problem, *Proceedings of the London Mathematical Society*, x/ii, 1937, pp 230–65

CHAPTER 6

Chomet J, Alan Turing: the Trotsky of the computer revolution, *Computer News*, 13 October 1983, pp 20–21

Heims S J, *John von Neumann and Norbert Wiener: From Mathematics to the Technologies of Life and Death*, The MIT

Press, 1980

Hodges A, *Alan Turing: The Enigma of Intelligence*, Burnett Books, 1983

Lavington S H, *A History of Manchester Computers*, NCC Publications, 1975

Lavington S H, *Early British Computers*, Manchester University Press, 1980

Robbins C, Museum pieces that heralded a revolution, *Computing*, 19 November 1987, pp 38–39

CHAPTER 7

Bylinsky G, Here comes the second computer revolution, *The Microelectronics Revolution*, ed. Tom Forester, MIP Press, 1981

Hanson D, *The New Alchemists: Silicon Valley and the Microelectronics Revolution*, Little, Brown & Company Boston, 1982

Larsen J K and Rogers E M, *Silicon Valley Fever: Growth of High-Technology Culture*, George Allen and Unwin, 1985

Lavington S, *Early British Computers*, Manchester University Press, 1980

Reid T R, *Microchip: the Story of a Revolution and the Men who Made It*, William Collins, 1985

Shockley W, *Electrons and Holes in Semiconductors, with Applications to Transistor Electronics*, Van Nostrand, 1950

CHAPTER 8

Ashby W R, Setting goals in cybernetic systems, in *Cybernetics, Artificial Intelligence, and Ecology*, Proceedings of the Fourth Annual Symposium of the American Society for Cybernetics, H W Robinson and D E Knight (eds), Spartan Books, 1972

Bar-Hillel Y, The present status of automatic translation of languages, in *Advances in Computers*, F L Alt (ed), Volume 1, Academic Press, New York, 1960

Bar-Hillel Y, *Language and Information*, Reading, Mass., 1964

Barr A and Feigenbaum E, *The Handbook of Artificial Intelligence*, Volume 1, William Kaufmann, 1981

Barr A and Feigenbaum E, *The Handbook of Artificial Intelligence*, Volume 2, Pitman, 1982

Burton J A, Computer/brain analogy, *Computer Bulletin*, Volume 11, Number 3, 1967, pp 220–227

Carne E B, *Artificial Intelligence Techniques*, MacMillan, 1965

Chomsky N, *Syntactic Structures*, The Hague: Mouton, 1957

Chomsky N, *Aspects of the Theory of Syntax*, MIT Press, 1965

Chomsky N, Deep structure, surface structure and semantic interpretation, in D Steinberg and L Jakobovits, 1971

Claxton G (ed), *Cognitive Psychology*, Routledge and Kegan Paul, 1980

Cohen P R and Feigenbaum E, *The Handbook of Artificial Intelligence*, Volume 3, Pitman, 1982

Cullbertson J T, *The Minds of Robots: Sense Data, Memory Images and Behaviour in Conscious Automata*, Unviersity of Illinois Press, 1963

Diebold J and Associates, Towards an organic computer, *Data and control*, Volume 1, Number 5, 1963, pp 22, 27

Dretske F I, *Knowledge and the Flow of Information*, Basil Blackwell, 1981

Dreyfus H L, *What Computers Can't Do, The Limits of Artificial Intelligence*, Harper & Row, 1972

Eden M, Other pattern-recognition problems and some generalisations, in *Recognising Patterns: Studies in Living and Automatic Systems*, P A Kolers and M Eden (Eds) MIT Press, 1968

Ernst G and Newell A, *GPS: A Case Study in Generality and Problem Solving*, Academic Press, 1969

Falk G, Interpretation of imperfect line data as a three-dimensional scene, *Artificial Intelligence*, 3, 1972, pp 101–144

Feigenbaum E and Feldman J (Eds), *Computers and Thought*, McGraw-Hill, 1963

Feigenbaum E and McCorduck P, *The Fifth Generation: Artificial Intelligence and Japan's Computer Challenge to the World*, Michael Joseph, 1983

Gelernter H, A note on syntactic symmetry and the manipulation of formal systems by machine, *Information and Control*, 2, 1959, pp 80–89

Gelernter H, Realisation of a geometry theorem-proving machine, in Feigenbaum and Feldman (eds), 1963

Gurevich B Kh, *'Reasoning' Automats and the Higher Brain Functions*, US Department of Commerce, Office of Technical Services Washington, 1962

Guzman A, Decomposition of a visual scene into three-dimensional bodies, *AFIPS Fall Joint Conference*, 33, 1968, pp 291–304

Hammond P H, Theory of self-adaptive control systems, *Proceedings of the Second IFAC Symposium on the Theory of Self-adaptive Control Systems*, National Physical laboratory, England, 14–17 September 1965

Heims S J, *John von Neumann and Norbert Wiener*, MIT, 1982

Hofstadter D R, *Gödel, Escher, Bach: An Eternal Golden Braid*, Harvester Press, 1979

Hunt E, What kind of a computer is man?, *Cognitive Psychology*, 1971, pp 57–98

Kernan J B, Thinking by machine?, *Advanced Management Journal*, Volume 30, Number 2, 1965, pp 69–73

Kilmer W L, McCulloch W S and Blum J, A model of the vertebrate central command system, *International Journal of Man-Machine Studies*,, 1, 1969, pp 279–309

Lachenbruch P A, Slivinske A J and Marchese A C, *Artificial Intelligence: a Summary of Current Research and Development*, American Institute for Research, 1962

Lovelock J E, *Gaia: a New Look at the Earth*, Oxford University Press, 1979

Lyons J, *Chomsky*, Fontana, 1970

McCarthy J, Programs with common sense, in *Proceedings of the Symposium on the Mechanisation of Thought Processes*, National Physical Laboratory, 1, 1958, pp 77–84

McCulloch W S , *Embodiments of Mind*, MIT Press, 1965

Miller G A, What is information measurement?, *The American Psychologist*, 8, 1953, p 2

Miller G A, Galanter E and Pribram K H, *Plans and the Structure of Behaviour*, Holt, Rinehart and Winston, 1960

Minsky M, Steps towards artificial intelligence, in Feigenbaum and Feldman (eds), 1963, pp 406–450

Minsky M, *Semantic Information Processing*, MIT Press, 1968

Neisser U, *Cognitive Psychology*, Appleton-Century-Crofts, 1967

Newell A and Simon H A, The logic theory machine, *IRE Transactions on Information Theory*, 2, 1956, pp 61–79

Newell A and Simon H A, *Computer Simulation of Human Thinking*, The RAND Corporation, P–2276, 1961

Nilsson N J, *Problem-Solving Methods in Artificial Intelligence*, McGraw-Hill, 1971

Oettinger A G, The state of the art in automatic language translation: an appraisal, in *Beitraege zur Sprachkunde und informations verarbeitung*, H Marchl (ed) Volume 1, Number 2, Oldenbourg Verbage, Munich, 1963

Pfeiffer J, *The Thinking Machine*, Lippincott, 1962

Piaget J, *The Construction of Reality in the Child*, Basic Books, New York, 1954

Pravitz D, *Natural Deduction: A Proof-Theoretical Study*, Almqvist and Wiksell, Stockholm, 1965

Pyle D W, *Intelligence*, Routledge and Kegan Paul, 1979

Reichardt J, *Cybernetics, Art and Ideas*, Studio Vista, London, 1971

Reichardt J, *Robots: Fact, Fiction and Prediction*, Thames and Hudson, 1978

Roberts L, Machine perception of three-dimensional solids, in J Tippett (ed), *Optical and Electro-optical Processing*, MIT Press, 1965, pp 159–197

Russian cybernetics expert states artificial intelligence can be created, *Computer Digest*, Volume 2, Number 12, 1967, p 3

Samuel A L, Some studies in machine learning using the game of checkers, *IBM Journal of Reasearch and Development*, 3, 1959, pp 210–229

Samuel A L, Artificial Intelligence: progress and problems, *Computers and Automation*, Volume 12, Number 3, 1963, pp 28–35

Samuel A L, Some stuides in machine learning using the game of checkers II – recent progress, *IMB Journal of Research and Development*, 11, 1967, pp 601–617

Sayre K M and Crosson F J (eds), *The Modelling of Mind*, Notre Dame University Press, South Bend, Indiana, 1963

Selfridge O G and Neisser U, Pattern recognition by machine, in Feigenbaum E and Feldman J (eds), 1963

Shannon C E, A chess-playing machine, in *World of Mathemtics*, J R Newman (ed), Simon and Schuster, 1956

Simon H A, Motivational and emotional controls of cognition, *Psychological Review*, 74, 1967, pp 29–39

Simons G L, *Introducing Artificial Intelligence*, NCC Publications, 1984

Sloman A, *The Computer Revolution in Philosophy: Philosophy, Science and Models of Mind*, Harvester Press, 1978

Steel T B, Artificial intelligence research: retrospect and prospects, *Computers and Automation*, Volume 16, Number 1, 1966, pp 22–24

Steinberg D and Jakobovits L, *Semantics*, Cambridge University Press, 1971

Thring M W, *Robots and Telechirs*, Ellis Horwood, 1983

Turing A, Computing machinery and intelligence, *Mind*, Volume 54, Number 236, 1950

Vincens P, *Aspects of Speech Recognition by Computer*, Doctoral Dissertation, Computer Science Department, Stanford University, 1969

Von Neumann J, *Theory of Self-Reproducing Automata*, E W Burks (ed), Illinois University Press, 1966

Waterman D A, *Machine Learning of Heuristics*, Report Number STAN-CS–68–118, Computer Science Department, Stanford University, Doctoral Dissertation, 1968

Wiener N, *Cybernetics: Control and Communication in the Animal and the Machine*, MIT Press and Wiley, New York, 1948

Winston P H and Prendergast K A (eds), *The AI Business*, MIT Press, 1984

Zadeh L A, Fuzzy sets, *Information and Control*, 8, 1965, pp 338–353

CHAPTER 9

Allen R B, Cognitive factors in human interaction with computers, *Behaviour and Information Tecnology*, Volume 1, Number 3, 1982, pp 257–278

Alport D A, Patterns and actions: cognitive mechanisms are content-specific, in G Claxton (ed), *Cognitive Psychology: New Directions*, Routledge and Kegan Paul, 1980

Anderson J and Bower G, *Human Associative Memory*, Winston, Washington D C, 1973

Barnard P, Wilson M and Maclean A, *Approximate modelling of cognitive activity with an expert system: A concpet demonstrator for an interactive design tool*, IBM, Hursley Human Factors Research Laboratory, 1986

Benson L, Machines that mimic thought, *New Scientist and*

Science Journal, Volume 51, Number 767, 2 September 1971, pp 525–528

Berry D C and Broadbent D E, Expert systems and the man-machine interface, *Expert Systems*, Volume 3, Number 4, October 1986, pp 228–231

Boden M, *Artificial Intelligence and Natural Man*, Harvester Press, 1977

Cherniak C, Undebuggability and cognitive science, *Communications of the ACM*, Volume 31, Number 4, April 1988, pp 402–412

Clark A, Cognitive science meets the biological mind, *New Scientist*, 8 October 1987, pp 36–38

Cohen P R and Feigenbaum E F, *The Handbook of Artificial Intelligence*, Volume 3, Pitman, 1982

Courbon J C, Design of intelligent dialogue in decision support systems, *Economics and Artificial Intelligence: IFAC Proceedings Series*, Volume 12, Pergamon, 1987, pp 15–19

*Daniels P J, Cognitive models in information retrieval – an evaluative review, *Journal of Documentation*, Volume 42, Number 4, December 1986, pp 272–304

De Greene K B, Cognitive models of international decision makers and international stability, *Systems Research*, Volume 4, Number 4, 1987, pp 251–267

Dennett D C, *Brainstorms: Philosophical Essays on Mind and Psychology* Harvester Press, 1978, Chapter 9

Dubois D and De-Rycker N, Interaction between artificial intelligence and education methodology, *Cybernetics and Systems: Present and Future, Proceedings of the Seventh International Congress of Cybernetics and Systems*, 7–11 September, 1987, London, Thales Publications, Volume 1, pp 529–532

Eden C, Smithin T and Wiltshire J, Cognition simulation and learning, *Journal of Experiential Learning and Simulation*, 2, 1980, pp 131–143

Evans C, *Landscape of the Night: How and Why We Dream*, Coronet, 1983

Eysenck M W, *A Handbook of Cognitive Psychology*, Lawrence Erlbaum Associates, 1984

Goldes H J, Designing the human-computer interface, *Educational Technology*, October 1983, pp 9–15

Harris L R, Humanizing the machine, *Computerworld*, 6 July 1987, pp 55–56

Hirsig R, Rauber A, Marchard C and Mattle U, Interactive computer games: an instrument in experimental psychological research, *Cybernetics and Systems: Present and Future: Proceedings of the Seventh International Congress of Cybernetics and Systems*, 7–11 September 1987, London, Thales Publications, Volume 1, pp 83–87

Kent E W, *The Brains of Men and Machines*, McGraw-Hill, 1980

Laird J E, Newell A and Rosenbloom P S, SOAR: An architecture for intelligence, *Artificial Intelligence*, Volume 33, Number 1, September 1987, pp 1–64

Lawrence K, Artificial intelligence in the man/machine interface, *Data Processing*, Volume 28, Number 5, June 1986, pp 244–246

Lighthill J, *Artificial Intelligence: Report to the Science Research Council* SRC, 1972

Lindsay P H and Norman D A, *Human Information Processing, An Introduction to Psychology*, Academic Press, New York, 1977

Marcus R S, An experimental comparison of the effectiveness of computers and humans as search intermediaries, *Journal of the American Society for Information Science*, Volume 34, Number 6, 1983, pp 381–404

Mayer R E, *The Promise of Cognitive Psychology*, W H Freeman, San Francisco, 1981

McCarthy J, Generality in artificial intelligence, *Communications of the ACM*, Volume 30, Number 12, December 1987, pp 1030–35

Michie D, Certificial intelligence, *New Scientist*, 26 August 1971, pp 370–373

Neisser U, Cognitive and Reality, W H Freeman, San Francisco, 1976

Nemes L, Intelligent interfaces, *Robotics and Computer-Integrated Manufacturing*, Volume 3, Number 2, 1987, pp 171–174

Newell A, You can't play 20 questions with nature and win, in W G Chase (ed), *Visual Information Processing*, Academic Press, New York, 1973

Norman D A, Rumelhart D E and the LNR Research Group, Explorations in Cognition, W H Freeman, San Francisco, 1975

Oren T I, Artificial intelligence and simulation: from cognitive simulation toward cognizant simulation, *Simulation*, April 1987, pp 129–130

Oren T I and Zeigler B P, Artificial intelligence in modelling and simulation: directions to explore, *Simulation*, April 1987, pp 131–134

Pylyshyn Z, Complexity and the study of artificial and human intelligence, in J Hauzeland (ed), *Mind Design: Philosophy, Psychology, Artificial Intelligence*, Bradford Books, Vermont, 1981

Rauzino V, Conversations with an intelligent chaos, *Datamation*, May 1982, pp 122–136

Reif F, Interpretation of scientific or mathematical concepts: cognitive issues and instructional implications, *Cognitive Science*, Volume II, Part 4, October-December 1987, pp 395–416

Shank R C, Questions and thought, *Modelling Cognition*, John Wiley, 1987, pp 21–56

Sharkey N E and Pfeiffer R, Uncomfortable bedfellows; cognitive psychology and AI, in M Yazdani and A Narayanan (eds), *Artificial Intelligence: Human Effects*, Ellis Horwood, 1984

Stevens M, Mind over matter, *Personal Computer World*, October 1984, pp 136–138

Vessey I, On matching programmer chunks with program structures: an empirical investigation, *International Journal of Man-Machine Stuies*, Volume 27, Part 1, July 1987, pp 65–89

Webb G I, *The Differential Model of Student Understanding*, Griffith University, Computing and Information Studies 1987

Wielinga B and Breuker J, *Models of Expertise*, University of Amsterdam, Department of Social Science Informatics, 1986

CHAPTER 10

Aggoun A, The SYNTHEX system: handling prosody in speech synthesis, *Technology and Science of Informatics*, Volume 6, Part 6, September 1987, pp 435–448

Barr A and Feigenbaum E, *The Handbook of Artificial Intelligence*, Volume 1, Pitman, 1987

Carbonnell N, Fohr D and Haton J P, APHODEX, an acoustic-phonetic decoding expert system, *International Journal of Pattern Recognition and Artificial Intelligence*, Volume 1, Part 2, August 1987, pp 207–222

Datta A K, Organisation of expert systems for automatic speech recognition, *Cybernetics and Systems: Present and Future: Proceedings of the Seventh International Congress of Cybernetics and Systems*, 7–11 September 1987, London, Thales Publications, Volume 1, pp 63–67

Durham T, Interpreting the job of the translators, *Computing*, 24 November 1983, p 25

Finnin T, Joshi A K and Webber B L, *Natural Language Interactions with Artificial Experts*, University of Pennsylvania, Department of Computer and Information Science, 1987

Haddock N J, Incremental interpretation and combinatory categorial grammar, *Working Papers in Cognitive Science: Categorial Grammar, Unification Grammar and Parsing*, University of Edinburgh, Centre for Cognitive Science, Volume 1, 1987, pp 71–84

Harris L R, Natural language front ends, in P H Winston and K A Prendergast (eds), *The AI Business*, MIT Press, 1984, Chapter 12

Henthorne K S and Dawson I, An application of speech recognition and synthesis, *Journal of Mcirocomputer Applications*, 6, 1983, pp 295–305

Johnson T, *Natural language Computing: the Commercial Applications*, Ovum Ltd, 1985

Jones R, Natural language arrives, Irish Computer, April 1988, pp 30–31

Jullien C and Solvay J P, Person-machine dialogue for expert systems: the advice-giving case, *Seventh International Workshop on Expert Systems and their Applications*, Avignon, 13–15 May 1987, EC2, Volume 2, pp 1647–1656

Kayser D, Fosse P, Karoubi M, Levrat B and Nicaud L, A strategy for reasoning in natural language, *Applied Artificial Intelligence*, Volume 1, Part 3, 1987, pp 205–231

Kirvan P F, Conversing with computers, *Data Processing*, March 1984, pp 49–51

Lalonde D and Donnelly A D, Voice technology speaks for itself, *Computerworld*, 16 May 1988, pp 71–79

Lashley K S, In search of the engram, *Symposia of the Society for Experimental Biology*, 4, 1950, pp 454–482

Leopold M, The search for speech, *Computer News*, 17 September 1987, p 31

Linggard R and Marlow F J, Programmable digital speech synthesiser, *Computers and Digital Techniques*, October 1979, pp 191–196
McCarten J, Voice technology: impediments to the speech market, *Computing*, 7 March 1985, pp 10–11

Miller G A and Johnson-Laird P N, *Language and Perception*, Cambridge University Press, 1976

Newton S J, *Voice in Office Systems*, NCC Publications, 1985

Osgood C E, Where do sentences come from?, in D E Steinberg and L A Jakobovits (eds), *Semantics: an Interdisciplinary Reader in Philosophy, Linguistics and Psychology*, Cambridge University Press, 1971

Rich E, Barnett J, Wittenburg K and Wroblewski D, Ambiguity procrastination, *Proceedings AAAI–87: Sixth National Conference on Artificial Intelligence*, 13–17 July 1987, Seattle, Washington, Morgan Kaufmann, Volume 2, pp 571–576

Rosenberg R, Speech technology takes slow but steady commercial course, *Electronics Week*, 22 April 1985, pp 34–35

Sampson G, *The Form of Language*, Weidenfeld and Nicholson, 1975

Samuel D J, Talking console monitor alerts field service, *Computer Design*, November 1981, pp 147–149

Schmandt C, *Understanding Speech without Recognizing Words*, MIT Industrial Liaison Programme, 1987

Scott B L, Voice recognition systems and strategies, *Computer Design*, January 1983, pp 67–70

Shapiro S F, Voice output systems make it hard to distinguish real from synthetic, *Computer Design*, February 1985, pp 86–89

Fennant H, Natural language processing and small systems, *Byte*, June 1978, pp 38–54

Trevarthen C, The psychology of speech development, *Neurosciences Research Program Bulletin*, 12, 1974, pp 570–585

Vacca J R, Take a letter . . ., *Computerworld Focus*, 16 October 1985, pp 63–64

Vaughan J, Brookes G, Chalmers D and Walts M, Transputer application to speech recognition, *Microprocessors and Microsystems*, Volume 11, Number 7, September 1987, pp 377–382

Webber B L, *Logic and Natural Language*, Computer, October 1983, pp 43–46

Wiggins R and Brantingham L, three-chip system synthesises human speech, *Electronics*, 31 August 1979, pp 109–116

Young J Z, *Programs of the Brain*, Oxford University Press, 1978

Zue V W, Automatic speech recognition and understanding, *AI in the 1980s and Beyond: an MIT Survey*, MIT Press, 1987, pp 185, pp 185–200

CHAPTER 11

Abadi M, *Temporal Logic Theorem Proving*, Department of Computer Science, Stanford University, 1987

Backus J W and Herrick H, IBM 701 Speedcoding and other automatic programming systems, *Proceedings on the Symposium on Automatic Programming for Digital Computers*, Office of Naval Research, Washington D C, 1954

Barr A and Feigenbaum E, *The Handbook of Artificial Intelligence*, Volume 2, Pitman, 1982

Barstow D, Knowledge-Based Program Construction, Elsevier, Amsterdam, 1979

Benzinger L A, *A Model and a Method for the Stepwise Development of Verified Programs*, Department of Computer Science, University of Illinois, 1987

Cohen P R and Feigenbaum E, *The Handbook of Artificial Intelligence*, Volume 3, Pitman, 1982

Dershowitz N and Lee Y J, *Deductive Debugging*, Knowledge Based Programming Assistant Project, University of Illinois, 1987

Ferguson G T, A letter from users to vendors of application generators, *Computerworld* 26 March 1984

Gelernter H, Realisation of a geometry theorem proving machine, in E Feigenbaum and J Feldman (eds), *Computers and Thought*, McGraw-Hill, 1963, pp 134–152

Green C, Waldinger R, Barstow D, Elschlager R, Lenat D, McCune B, Shaw D and Steinberg L, *Progress Report on Program Understanding Systems*, Memo AIM–240, AI Laboratory, Stanford University, 1974

Green C, Unpublished lecture surveying automatic programming, Computer Science Department, Stanford University, 1975

Green C, The design of the PSI program synthesis system, *Proceedings of the Second International Conference on Software Engineering*, 1976, pp 4–18

Guard J R, Oglesby F C, Bennett J H and Settle L G, Semi-automated mathematics, *Journal of the Association for Computing Machinery*, Volume 16, Number 1, January 1969, p 49

Harandi M T, Applying knowledge-based techniques to software development, *Perspectives in Computng*, Spring 1986, pp 14–21

Hopstadter D R, *Gödel, Escher and Bach: An Eternal Golden Braid*, Harvester Press, 1979

Kennedy T R, *Using Program Transformations to Improve Program Translation*, MIT, 1987

Kowalski R, AI and software engineering, *Datamation*, 1 November 1984, pp 92–102

Lowry M R, Algorithm synthesis through problem reformulation, *Proceedings AAAI–87: Sixth National Conference on Artificial Intelligence*, 13–17 July 1987, Seattle, Washington, Morgan Kaufmann, Volume 2, p 432–436

Myers E, Getting a grip on tools, *Datamation*, 18 March 1985, pp 30–32, 34, 36

Naylor G, *Computer Talk*, 27 February 1984

Newell A and Simon H A, The logic theory machine, *IRE Transactions on Information Theory*, 2, 1956, pp 61–79

Pearce D, *KIC: A Knowledge Integrity Checker*, The Turing Institute, 1987

Robinson J A, A machine-oriented logic based on the resolution principle, *Journal of the Association of Computing Machinery*, 12, 1965, pp 23–41

Romberg F A and Thomas A B, Reusable code, reliable software, *Computerworld*, 26 March 1984

Simon H A, Whether software engineering needs to be artificially intelligent, *IEEE Transactions on Software Engineering*, July 1986, pp 726–732

Taylor S and Shapiro E, *Compiling Concurrent Logic Programs into Decision Graphs*, Department of Applied Mathematics and Computer Science, Weizmann Institute of Science, 1987

Wang H, Towards mechanical mathematics, *IBM Journal of Research and Development*, 4, 1960, pp 2–22

Weiss B P, Artificial intelligence techniques speed software development, *Mini-Micro Systems*, September 1984, pp 127–136

Winograd T, *Understanding Natural Language*, Academic Press, New York, 1972

CHAPTER 12

Agin G J, Computer vision systems for industrial inspection and assembly, *Computer*, May 1980, pp 11–20

Allan R, Tactile sensing, 3-D vision and more precise arm movements herald the hardware trends in industrial robots, *Electronic Design*, 12 May 1983, pp 99–112

Allen S A and Rossetti T, On building a light-seeking robot mechanism, *Byte*, August 1978, pp 24–42

Astrop A, Assembly robot with a sense of 'touch', *Machinery and Production Engineering*, 19/26 December 1979, pp 21–24

Birk J et al, *General Methods to Enable Robots with Vision to Acquire, Orient and Transport Workpieces*, University of Rhode Island, Fourth Report on National Science Foundation Grant, APR74–13935, 15 July 1978

Boden M, *Artificial Intelligence and Natural Man*, Harvester Press, 1977

Braggins D, Vision systems: helping robots to see things our way ..., *Machinery and Production Engineering*, 18 April 1984, pp 38–41

Briot M, *La Stéréognosie en Robotique Application au Tri de Solides*, Thèse d'état no 780, Université P Sabatier, Toulouse, France, 14 November 1977

Briot M et al, The utilisation of an 'artificial skin' sensor for the identification of solid objects, *Proceedings of the Ninth International Symposium on Industrial Robots*, 1979, pp 529–547

Chatigny J V and Robb L E, Sensors: making the most of piezo film, *Sensor Review*, January 1987, pp 15–20

Clot J and Stojiljkovic Z, Integrated behaviour of artificial skin, *IEEE Transactions on Biomedical Engineering*, July 1977

Davies B L and Ihnatowicz E, A three degree of freedom robotic manipulator, *Proceedings of the Ninth International Symposium on Industrial Robots*, 1979, pp 701–707

Dessinoz J D et al, Recognition and handling of overlapping industrial parts, *Proceedings of the Ninth International Symposium on Industrial Robots*, 1979, pp 357–365

Dixon J K et al, Research on tactile sensors for an intelligent naval robot, *Proceedings of the Ninth International Symposium on Industrial Robots*, 1979, pp 507–517

Estes J E, Jensen J R and Simonett D S, Impacts of remote sensing on US geography, *Remote Sensing of Environment*, 10, 1984, p 43–80

Filo A, Designing a robot from nature, Part 2: constructing the eye, *Byte*, March 1979, pp 114–123

Guzman A , Computer recogniton of three-dimensional objects in a visual scene, *Tech. Rep.* MAC-TR–59, AI Laboratory, MIT, 1968

Hamphire N, Machine vision, *Personal Computer World*, November 1987, pp 142–147

Hartog A H, Principles of optical fibre temperature sensors, *Sensor Review*, October 1987, pp 197–199

Huffman D A, Impossible objects as nonsense sentences, in R Meltzer and D Michie (eds), *Machine Intelligence*, 6, Elsevier, New York, 1971, pp 295–323

Lain R and Haynes S, Imprecision in computer vision, *Computer*, August 1982, pp 39–47

Kelley R et al, A robot system which feeds workpieces directly from bins into machines, *Proceedings of the Ninth International Symposium on Industrial Robots*, 1979, pp 339–355

Kokjer K J, The information capacity of the human fingertip, *IEEE Transactions on Systems, Man and Cybernetics*, Volume SMC–17, Number 1, January/February 1987, pp 100–102

Larcombe M H E, Carbon fibre tactile sensors, *Proceedings of the First International Conference on Robot Vision and Sensory Control*, 1981

Laser eyes for industrial robots, *New Scientist*, 28 October 1982

Loughlin C, A close inspection of vision systems, *Sensor Review*, July 1987, pp 135–142

Lowe C, Sensors come alive, *Link-Up*, January-March 1985, pp 22–25

Lowe D, Vision leads robots from the factory, *New Scientist*, 10 September 1987, pp 50–54

Malinen P and Niemi A, Reduction of visual data by a program controlled interface for computerised manipulation, *Proceedings of the Ninth International Symposium on Industrial Robots*, 1979, pp 391–403

Marsh P, Robots see the light, *New Scientist*, 12 June 1980, pp 238–240

McClelland S, Artificial intelligence: sensors need it, *Sensor Review*, July 1987, pp 133–134

McClelland S, Giving AI real-time sensing, *Sensor Review*, January 1988, pp 17–18

Onda H and Ohashi Y, Introduction of visual equipment to inspection, *The Industrial Robot*, September 1979, pp 131–135

Pennywitt K E, Robotic tactile sensing, *Byte*, January 1986, pp 177–200

Plander I, Trends in the development of sensor systems and their use in some technological areas, *Robotics*, 3, 1987, pp 157–165

Poggio T, Vision by man and machine, *Scientific American*, April 1984, pp 68–78

Pruski A, Surface contact sensor for robot safety, *Sensor Review*, July 1986, pp 143–144

Purbrick J A, A force transducer employing conductive silicone rubber, *Proceedings of the First International Conference on Robot Vision and Sensory Controls*, 1981

Railbert M H and Tanner J E, A VLSI tactile array sensor, *Twelfth International Symposium on Industrial Robots*, 9–11 June 1982, Paris, pp 417–425

Roberts L, Machine perception of three-dimensional solids, in J Tippett (ed), *Optical and Electro-Optical Information Processing*, MIT Press, 1965, pp 159–197

Robertson B E and Walkden A J, Tactile sensor system for robotics, *Proceedings of the Third International Symposium on Robot Vision and Sensory Controls*, 1983

Roef P, Attention focuses on optical fibre biosensors, *Sensor Review*, July 1987, pp 127–132

Seeing eye robots for the automated factory, *Production Engineering*, August 1983, pp 48–51

Shapiro S F, Digital Technology enables robots to 'see', *Computer Design*, January 1978, pp 43–59

Shapiro S F, Vision expands robotic skills for industrial applications, *Computer Design*, September 1979, pp 78–87

Sloman A, *The Computer Revolution in Philosophy*, Harvester Press, 1978

Taylor W K and Ero G, Real time teaching and recognition system for robot vision, *The Industrial Robot*, June 1980, pp 102–106

Tsuboi Y A, Minicomputer controlled industrial robot with optical sensor in gripper, *Proceedings of the Third International Symposium on Industrial Robots*, 1973, pp 343–355

Varnish J M, Magnetoresistive skin for robots, *Proceedings of the Fourth International Conference on Robot Vision and Sensory Controls*, 1984

Warner E, Vision system seen changing face of robotics industry, *Computerworld*, 1 October 1984, p 68

Yachida M and Tsuji S, Industrial Computer Vision in Japan, *Computer*, May 1980, pp 50–62

CHAPTER 13

Astrop A, Factory of the future is no place for man, *Machinery and Production Engineering*, 21 November 1979, pp 23–26

Astrop A, In perspective, UK development aims for greater levels of intellect, *Machinery and Production Engineering*, 20 April 1983, pp 18–23

Bartolik P, Robots to be sold to jails for use as guard devices, *Computerworld*, 13 February 1984

Beley G, The Quasar Industries' robot, a dream that came true, *Interface Age*, April 1978, pp 69–73

Carey D, Machines that mimic man, *Canadian Datasystems*, May 1986, pp 68–69

Chester M, Robotic software reaches out for task-oriented languages. The goal: to remove all human supervision, *Electronic Design*, 12 May 1983, pp 119–129

Chisholm A W J, The social effects of intelligent manufacturing systems, *Robotics and Computer-Integrated Manufacturing*, Volume 3, Number 2, 1987, pp 157–164

Cohen C L, Robots get smart in Japan, *Electronics Week*, 21 January 1985, pp 15–16

Economic Commission for Europe, Working Party on Engineering Industries and Automation, *Production and Use of Industrial Robots*, United Nations, Geneva, 1984

Fleck J and White B, National policies and patterns of robot diffusion: United Kingdom, Japan, Sweden and the United States, *Robotics*, 3, 1987, pp 7–22

Ford D R and Schroes B J, An expert manufacturing simulation system, *Simulation*, May 1987, pp 193–200

Goshorn L A, A single-board approach to robotic intelligence, *Computer Design*, November 1982, pp 193–201

Grossman D D, Evans R C and Summers P D, The value of multiple independent robot arms, *Robotics and Computer-Aided Manufacturing*, Volume 2, Number 2, 1985, pp 135–142

Intelligent autonomous systems, *Robotics*, Volume 3, Number 2, June 1987, pp 241–257

Irvine J, CAD puts robots in reach, *CADCAM International*, December 1986, p 26

Kato I, Shirai K, Narita S, Matsushima T, Kobayashi T and Fujisawa E, The robot musician 'WABOT-2' (WAseda roBOT-2), *Robotics*, 3, 1987, pp 143–155

Keller E L, Clever robots set to enter industry en masse, *Electronics*, 17 November 1983, pp 116–129

Kochan A, Robot vision, *CADCAM International*, May 1984, pp 15–16

Kroczynski P and Wade B, The Skywasher: a building washing robot, *Robots 11: 17th International Symposium on Industrial Robots*, 1987, pp 1–11 to 1–19

Mellichamp J M and Wahab A F A, An expert system for FMS design, *Simulation*, May 1987, pp 201–208

Nicolaisen P, Safety problems related to robots, *Robotics*, 3, 1987 pp 205–211

Noro K and Okada Y, Robotisation and human factors, *Ergonomics*, 26, 1983

Potts D, The factory of the future – in Britain today, *Engineering Computers*, September 1987, pp 48–50

Rifkin G, Robot security guards: R2D2 on the alert, *Comupter-world*, 7 October 1985, Update/9

Rooks B, It's people that matter, not robots, *Assembly Automation*, November 1986, pp 179–181

Ruzic N P, The automated factory – dream coming true?, *Control Engineering*, April 1978, pp 58–62

Sistler F E, Robotics and intelligent machines in agriculture, *IEEE Journal of Robotics and Automation*, Volume RA–3, Number 1, February 1987, pp 3–6

Sugimoto K, Present state and trends in robot technology, *Robotics*, 3, 1987, pp 81–88

Togai M, Japan's next generation of robots, *Computer*, March 1984, pp 19–25

Trevelyan J P, Key S J and Owens R A, Techniques for surface representation and adaptation in automated sheep shearing, *Twelfth International Symposium on Industrial Robots*, 9–11 June 1982, Paris, pp 163–174

Villers P, Intelligent robots: moving toward megassembly, in P H Winston and K A Prendergast (eds), *The AI Business*, MIT Press, 1984, pp 205–222

Williamson M, Artificial intelligence takes a stand on the factory floor, *Compterworld*, 6 July 1987, p S3

Witkowski M, Man-machine clanks into step, *Practical Computing*, March 1980, pp 82–89

CHAPTER 14

Addis T R, Expert systems: an evolution in information retrieval, *Information Technology: Research and Development*, Number 1, 1982, pp 301–324

Barr A and Feigenbaum E A, *The Handbook of Artificial Intelligence*, Volume 2, Pitman, 1982

Bond A, Change in rules for intelligence, *Computing*, 5 March 1981, pp 18–19

Cole B C, Artificial intelligence and the personal computer user, *Interface Age*, April 1981, pp 88–90

d'Agapeyeff A, *Expert Systems, Fifth Generation and UK Suppliers*, NCC Publications, 1983

Davis D B, Artificial intelligence enters the mainstream, *High Technology*, July 1986, pp 16–23

Dhart V, On the plausibility and scope of expert systems in management, *Journal of Management Information Systems*, Summer 1987, pp 25–41

Duda R et al, Model design in the PROSPECTOR consultant system for mineral exploration, in D Michie (ed), *Expert Systems in the Microelectronics Age*, Edinburgh University Press, 1980

Dunmore D B, A rule-based expert system for auditors, *EDPACS*, September 1987, pp 1–3

Durham T, Moving expert forward one small step at a time, *Computing*, 17 September 1987, pp 20–21

Fagan L M, *VM: Representing Time Dependent Relations in a Medical Setting*, Dissertation, Computer Science Department, Stanford University, USA, 1980

Firdman H E, Expert systems: are you already behind?, *Computerworld*, 18 April 1988, pp 99–105

Forenski T, US takes stock of program trading, *Computing*, 11 February 1987, p 13

Fried L, The dangers of dabbling in expert systems, *Computerworld*, 29 June 1987, pp 65–72

Hamilton R, Who's responsible for uses of AI?, *Computer Talk*, 19 March 1984

Hartley R T, CRIB: computer fault-finding through knowledge engineering, *Computer*, March 1984, pp 76–83

Herd A, Silicon surgery, *Personal Computer World*, September 1987, pp 150–153

Jacob V S, Gaultney L D and Salvendy G, Strategies and biases in human decision-making and their implications for expert systems, *Behaviour and Information Technology*, Volume 5, Number 2, 1986, pp 119–140

Keirn R T and Jacobs S, Expert systems: the DSS of the Future?, *Journal of Systems Management*, December 1986, pp 6–14

Kellock B, Systems that turn novices into experts, *Engineering Computers*, June/July 1987, pp 32–35

Kull D, Wall Street kills the messenger, *Computer and Communications Decisions*, December 1987, pp 72–74

Lamberti D and Wallace W A, Presenting uncertainty in expert systems: an issue in information portrayal, *Information and Management*, 13, 1987, pp 159–169

Liebouwitz J and Zeide J S, EVIDENT: an expert system prototype for helping the law student learn admissibility of evidence under the Federal rules, *Computer Education*, Volume 11, Number 2, 1987, pp 113–120

Mace S, Expert-Ease creates expert systems on IBM PC, *Info-world*, 19 March 1984, pp 11–12

Michaelsen R and Michie D, Expert systems in business, *Datamation*, November 1983, pp 240–246

Pratt C A, An artificially intelligent locomotive mechanic, *Simulation*, January 1984, pp 40–41

Rahman M and Narayan V, An expert system for process planning, *Robotics and Computer-Aided Manufacturing*, Volume 3, Number 3, 1987, pp 365–372

Reid I, The next step for the money men, *Expert Systems User*, September 1987, pp 8–10

Roberts F C and Park O, Intelligent computer-assisted instruction: an explanation and overview, *Educational Technology*, December 1983, pp 7–12

Rogers W et al, Computer-aided medical diagnosis: literature review, *International Journal of Biomedical Computing*, 10, 1979, pp 267–289

Ryan J L, Expert systems in the future: the redistribution of power, *Journal of Systems Management*, April 1988, pp 18–21

Sedlmeyer R L et al, Knowledge-based fault localisation in debugging, *The Journal of Systems and Software*, December 1983, pp 301–307

Shaket E, Fuzzy semantics of a natural-like language defined over a world of blocks, *Artificial Intelligence*, Memo 4, University of California, 1976

Socha W J, Problems in auditing expert system development, *EDPACS*, March 1988, pp 1–6

Speller G J and Brandon J A, Ethical dilemmas constraining the use of expert systems, *Behaviour and Information Technology*, Volume 5, Number 2, 1986, pp 141–143

Stefik M J and de Kleer J, Prospects for expert systems in CAD, *Computer Design*, 21 April 1983, pp 65–76

Sullivan K, Financial industry fertile ground for expert systems, *Computerworld*, 22 October 1984, pp 29, 31

Thomas D E et al, Automatic data path synthesis, *Computer*, December 1983, pp 59–70

Waterman D A, Paul J and Peterson M, Expert systems for legal decision making, *Expert Systems*, October 1986, pp 212–226

Watt P, Micros become 'experts', *Infoworld*, 23 April 1984, pp 40–41

Webster R, Expert systems, *Personal Computer World*, January 1983, pp 118–119

Wright J, Expert systems ease hardware selection, *Engineering Computers*, January 1987, pp 42–44

Zadeh L A, Fuzzy sets, *Information and Control*, 8, 1965, pp 338–353

CHAPTER 15

Abbott L, Haralick R M and Zhuang X, Pipeline architectures for morphologic image analysis, *Machine Vision and Applications*, Volume 1, Number 1, 1988, pp 23–40

Annaratone M, Arnold E, Gross T, Kung H T, Lam M, Menzilcioglu O and Webb J A, *The Warp Computer: Architecture*, Implementation and Performance, Robotics Institute, Carnegie-Mellon University, 1987

Barron I, Cavill P, May D and Wilson P, Tansputer does 5 or more MIPS even when not used in parallel, *Electronics*, 17 November 1983, pp 109–115

Feldman J A, Fanty M A, Goddard N H and Lynne K J, Computing with structured connectionist networks, *Communications of the ACM*, February 1988, pp 170–187

Gallant S I, Connectionist expert systems, *Communications of the ACM*, February 1988, pp 152–169

Inmos finally unveils the 32-bit transputer, *Electronics*, 7 October 1985, pp 20–21

Jasany L C, Is there a supercomputer in your future?, *Automation*, May 1988, pp 12–16

Newquist H P, Chips for brains: computers built with neural networks, *Computerworld*, 18 August 1986, p 17

Newquist H P, Mind machines over matter, *Computerworld*, 12 October 1987, p 23

Optoelectronics builds viable neural-net memory, *Electronics*, 16 June 1986, pp 41–44

Paseman W G, Applying data flow in the real world, *Byte* May 1985, pp 201–214

Recce M and Treleavan P, Computing from the brain, *New Scientist*, 26 May 1988, pp 61–64

Reeves A P, Parallel computer architectures for image processing, *Computer Vision, Graphics, and Image Processing*, 25, January 1984, pp 68–88

Rumelhart D and McClelland J, *Parallel Distributed Processing*, MIT Press, 1987

Sternberg S R, An overview of image algebra and related architectures, in Integrated Technology for Parallel Image Processing, Academic Press, 1985, pp 79–100

Thomas A L, Specialised hardware for computer graphics, *Techniques for Computer Graphics*, Springer-Verlag, 1987

Tick E and Warren D H D, Towards a pipelined Prolog processor, *Computers for Artificial Intelligence Applications*, Washinton DC, IEEE Computer Society Press, 1986

Tompham N, Omondi A and Ibbett R, *On the Design and Performance of Pipelined Architectures*, Department of Computer Science, University of Edinburgh, 1987

Tucker M, Neural net coprocessor bows, *Computerworld*, 9 September 1987, p 52

Walker P, The Transputer, *Byte*, May 1985, pp 219–235

Wang Y and Butner S E, A new architecture for robot control, *Proceedings of the IEEE International Conference on Robotics and Automation*, Raleigh, North Carolina, 31 March to 3 April 1987, IEEE Computer Society Press, Volume 2, pp 664–670

Williamson M, Neural networks: glamour and glitches, *Computerworld*, 15 February 1988, pp 89–92

Wilson G, Computing in Parallel, *New Scientist*, 11 February 1988, pp 54–58

Woo D, *Grasping Randomly Placed Workpieces Using a Robot Vision System*, Case Western Reserve University, Centre for Automation and Intelligent Systems Research, 1986

Yamakawa T, Fuzzy hardware systems of tomorrow, in E Sanchez and L A Zadeh (eds), *Approximate Reasoning in Intelligent Systems, Decision and Control*, 1987, pp 1–20

CHAPTER 16

Abraham E, Seaton C T and Smith S D, The optical computer, *Scientific American*, February 1983, pp 63–71

Albinson R, Biosensors – from concept to commercialisation, *Sensor Review*, January 1987, pp 39–44

Biancomano V, Fiber optics, *Electronic Design*, 10 July 1986, pp 74–82

Carlyle R E, Toward 2017, *Datamation*, 15 September 1987, pp 142–154

Chevreau J, Optical storage gains favour among large organisations, *Canadian Datasystems*, April 1987, pp 66–68

Clerman R J, Combining biology and electronics, *Data Processing*, March 1984, pp 25–27, 30

Cohen F, Computer Viruses, *Computers and Security*, 6, 1987, pp 22–35

Davis F G F and Grantenbein R E, Recovering from a computer virus attack, *The Journal of Systems and Software*, 7, 1987, pp 253–258

Davis S G, The superconductive computer in your future, *Datamation*, 15 August 1987, pp 74–78

Durham T, Shedding light on the optical device potential, *Computing*, 7 July 1983, pp 26–27

Durham T, Four steps to realising the sugar cube biochip, *Computing*, 25 October 1984, pp 26–27

Fagan M, Goodbye to the silicon chip?, *Practical Computing*, August 1987, pp 74–76

Fox B, Corrupt power corrupts computer data, *New Scientist*, 29 October 1987, p 42

Gullo K and Schatz W, The supercomputer breaks through, *Datamation*, 1 May 1988, pp 50–63

Hampton-Ellistte R, Thought input, *Systems International*, November 1985

Hecht J, Computing with light, *New Scientist*, 1 October 1987, pp 45–48

Ince D, A new dawn breaks in Japan as research sinks in the West, *Computing*, 17 March 1988, pp 18–19

Joyce E, Software bugs: a matter of life and liability, *Datamation*, 15 May 1987, pp 88–92

Main R, Optical technologies – an agenda for the future, *Sensor Review*, January 1987, pp 33–38

Mokhoff N, Parallel computer architectures of the '90s will provide solutions en masse, *Computer Design*, July 1986, pp 64–72

Myers W, Can software for the Strategic Defence Initiative ever be error-free?, *Computer*, November 1986, pp 61–67

Osman T, Beaming in laser power, *Sunday Times*, 5 October 1986, p 80

Parnas D L, Software aspects of strategic defence systems, *Communications of the ACM*, December 1985, pp 1326–1335

Podmore C and Faguy D, The challenge of optical fibres, *Telecommunications Policy*, December 1986, pp 341–351

Poe R and Tate P, The lost generation?, *Datamation*, 1 July 1987, pp 44–5, 44–8, 44–12

Pournelle J, The next five years in microcomputers, *Byte*, September 1983, pp 233–244

Pozzo M M and Gray T E, An approach to containing computer viruses, *Computers and Security*, 6, 1987, pp 321–331

Rifkin G, On beyond silicon, a look at new semiconductor technologies, *Computerworld*, 14 April 1986, pp 49–62

Sorensen K, Fifth generation: slow to rise, *InfoWorld*, 9 June 1986, pp 35–36

Tucker M, Coming next from Japan, *Mini-Micro Systems*, July 1986, pp 28–31

Wood C C, The human immune system as an information systems security reference model, *Computers and Security*, 6, 1987, pp 511–516

Yanchinski S, And now – the biochip, *New Scientist*, 14 January 1982, pp 68–71

Appendix 1

Artistic Activity in Computers*

The intellectual abilities of computers are one thing, the artistic abilities quite another. To many observers it has seemed acceptable that computers can work in a quantitative fashion, via computation, to achieve intellectual results in such areas as science or mathematics. But the act of artistic creation has seemed a more difficult concept, bound up with the 'finer' elements of the human mind, associated with the notions of creativity, emotional sensitivity and aesthetic insight. If a computer is programmed to produce a picture or a poem, then does the creative competence reside in the programmer and not in the machine? Alternatively, if new patterns or sounds are generated in a random fashion, to what extent can the results be deemed art? Is *intent*, which may be absent in a computer system, essential to 'real' art? To a large extent, these are empty questions, deriving more from man's confused vanity than from any conceptual difficulty inherent in the question. A proper understanding of such topics as machine emotion, programmability and autonomy in artificial systems soon resolves the dilemma as to whether computers can be creative. At this stage we can declare, briefly and without argument, that computers can be creative. They have powerful claims to artistic ability, though it is likely that their efforts will take a different course to that traditionally favoured by human beings. As a family of species 'growing out of man', computers may be expected to be

---

* originally published in my *Are Computers Alive?* (Harvester Press, 1983)

interested in many of the aesthetic principles – such things as
elegance, harmony (or discord), form and development – that
have influenced human art. But it is inevitable that there will be a
cultural divide, much as there is between one human society (say,
that of the West Coast of California) and another (the jungle
dwellers of Borneo).

In 1968 an exhibition ('Cybernetic Serendipity') was mounted at
the UK Institute of Contemporary Arts (reported by Reichardt,
1971). One aim was to explore the links between creativity and
computer technology. How, for example, can there be connections between the seemingly impersonal areas of mathematics
and the impulse to create music, art and poetry. The fact is that
computers have not only aided our understanding of human
artistic efforts but have developed artistic faculties of their own,
possibly to the point of originating new art forms (Bernstein,
1982, suggests that computer games, for instance, may be
represented as a new art form). This, as we have seen, may pose a
variety of problems: Reichardt, one of the organizers of
'Cybernetic Serendipity', asks whether computer graphics, as one
example of computer creativity, should 'hang side by side with
drawings by artists in museums and art galleries, or should they
belong to another as yet unspecified, category of creative
achievement?' The acknowledgement that computers are an
emerging life-form solves this dilemma and all the related
questions: it will come to seem entirely natural that a gallery
should hang 'Blue-Period' Picasso one week, ancient Chinese
water-colours the next, and artificially generated graphics the
week after. Max Bense (in Reichardt, 1971) declared; 'today we
have not only mathematical logic and a mathematical linguistics,
but also a gradually evolving mathematical aesthetics'. Increasingly, the areas of aesthetic sensitivity and artistic creation
will be found to be amenable to the type of analysis that will allow
computers to develop their faculties in these fields.

The idea behind the *generative aesthetics* (of Bense and other
workers) is that it is possible to formulate the operations, rules
and theorems that can be used to derive aesthetic creations. An
initial step is analysis – aesthetic information is culled from given
works of art, whereupon the information is described in mathematical terms. (Bense identifies four different ways of formulat-

ing abstract descriptions of aesthetic states.) This enables relatively primitive artistic works to be generated by computer. In fact, artificially generated texts have been produced since 1960 and these may be considered to be products of generative aesthetics. For example, texts were produced in Stuttgart in collaboration with the Elektronische Recheninstitut; and in 1963 Nanni Balestrini published mechanically produced texts in his book *Come si agisce* (these were programmed on an IBM computer). Reichardt (1978) includes a 2100-word 'thriller' (*Murder Mystery 1*), which was produced in nineteen seconds by a Univac 1108 computer and first presented to the International Conference on Computers in the Humanities (Minneapolis, July 1973). Today work continues on text-processing (see Schank and Riesback, 1981). (It is interesting to recall that in *Gulliver's Travels*, first published in 1726, Jonathan Swift describes a mechanical system for the automatic generation of texts in any discipline. A large wooden frame supported bits of wood carrying randomly arranged words: when iron handles on the edges of the frame were turned, the entire disposition of the words was changed. In this way, through various stages, whole books were generated. By this method the professor intended 'to give the world a compleat body of all arts and sciences', provided 'the publick would raise a fund for making and employing five hundred such frames . . .'. Then, as now, funding was clearly a problem!)

Computers have also been programmed to write poetry: for example, Japanese haiku. A haiku is a three-line poem of seventeen syllables with a specific line pattern:

Line 1:5 syllables
Line 2:7 syllables
Line 3:5 syllables

The haiku is traditionally not limited to subject, but ideally should contain some reference, however distant, to the season of the year. The analysis of Japanese haiku for computerization purposes represents an attempt to expose the interior logic of a simple poem frame (Masterman, in Reichardt 1971). In the Cybernetic Serendipity exhibition various people – including non-poets – used a derived algorithm to produce haiku.

The underlying hypothesis is that every poem has a *frame*, and that the process of frame-making can be distinguished from the activity of filling in the frame. It is possible, for example, to store a haiku frame in a computer and to provide a thesaurus which enables the poet, via man-machine interaction, to fill in the gaps in the frame. In due course the computer prints out the final poem with all the gaps filled in. Often – and this is the interesting point – the results surprise the poet! In circumstances where the machine is programmed to act on its own, without facilities for man-machine interaction, there is a clear sense in which the computer is poet. That the human being was necessary for the initial programming does not tell against such an interpretation. We are all programmed, initially, by factors outside our control: by genetic endowment, early nutrition, early environmental experiences, etc. Examples of computer-generated haiku include:

All green in the leaves
I smell dark pools in the trees
Crash! The moon has fled

All white in the buds
I flash snow peaks in the spring
Bang! The sun has fogged

Here the structural similarly suggests that the same algorithm was used for both the compositions (see Masterman for a detailed description of how frames, thesauri and algorithms are combined to generate haiku).

McKean (1982) describes how computer poetry traces its origins to a discovery made accidentally by Louis Milic, today an English professor at Cleveland State University. Milic found that using a computer to randomly substitute words in a rigid framework produced nonsense sentences that made people think of poetry ('Many people are used to poems not making sense'). He then wrote the Erato program which used an elaborate algorithm to scramble and rescramble words from the first lines of ten famous poems. The scrambled versions stimulated further human poetic activity! The poet Alberta Turner has called this random computer approach 'a valuable step in initiating or restimulating the poetic process'. The random approach recalls not only Jonathan Swift's text-generating frame but also the methods used by the 1920s dadaists and the 1950s beatniks to compose poetry from newspaper clippings.

Most of the texts generated by computers are extremely simple, without any clear artistic merit. The early programs of Sheldon Klein, for example, at the University of Wisconsin, allowed the computer to develop a plot (for example, that of the 2100-word 'thriller' mentioned above) but gave little, if any, consideration to the motivations of individual characters. Jim Meehan, at the University of California, is now developing programs to tackle this problem. A 1976 Meehan program, called Tale-Spin, created tales that were loosely modelled after Aesop's fables. This is a sample of a computer-generated tale:

Once upon a time George Ant lived near a patch of ground. There was a nest in an ash tree. Wilma Bird lived in the nest. There was some water in a river. Wilma knew that the water was in the river. George knew that the water was in the river. One day Wilma was very thirsty. Wilma wanted to get near some water. Wilma flew from her nest across a meadow through a valley to the river. Wilma drank the water. Wilma wasn't thirsty any more.

Meehan acknowledges that the Tale-Spin stories lack purpose, and doubts that efforts to invent a *story grammar* – a set of rules for creating good fiction – will ever succeed. Natalie Dehn, at Yale, is developing a program that considers what the author wants from a story and has written that 'The author has goals, things she wants to accomplish. She starts off with an initial intent but may wind up with something quite different. I'm trying to model what the author is doing'. The Dehn program, Author, refines and focuses the initial story idea as the process develops. Recalled earlier ideas – akin to human recollection of people and events – can be incorporated in the story. In contrast to the random-generation methods used for early computer poetry, Author 'understands' what it is doing. Another Dehn story generator, Starship, is being used to help adults who are poor readers.

No-one denies that current computer literary efforts are crude: at the same time there is remarkable progress in this field. We may expect AI research to yield ways in which computers can reflect on, and understand, what is required in good fiction and poetry. In fact, Milic has stated that 'People who scoff at computer poetry are simply not thinking. It would be like complaining, as people did when Gutenberg came around, that the word of God was not meant to be printed by machine'.

Computers are also good at producing designs, patterns and pictures – whether as displays on screens or as hard-copy results achieved via printers and plotters. The use of mathematics in generating graphics art has long been of interest (see, for example, Boyd, 1948), but the development of computer power coupled with the emergence of display-graphics technology has given an immense boost to this sort of artistic activity.

Part of the debate about graphics art, as with other areas of computer creativity, focuses on the extent to which the computer aids the artist and the extent to which the computer becomes a creative innovator in its own right. David Em, Artist-in-Residence at the Jet Propulsion Laboratory in Pasadena, is producing paintings of startling originality using a computer as a tool. He insists that he would never have come up with the ideas in the pictures had not the computer provided new capabilities, stimulation and 'even a strange power of its own to direct the way a picture is going' (Johnston, 1981).

The Jet Propulsion Laboratory has been used to process pictures received from space probes – work that has required the development of high-resolution colour graphics on computer systems. David Em uses a PDP–11/55 computer with a digitizing tablet and a high-resolution colour screen to produce original paintings that can draw on 256 colours and a range of 'brushes' which vary the effect – from heavy lines to fine 'sprays'. A database of textures has been compiled. The finished pictures are usually viewed on the video screen, though coloured photographic prints can be produced, as well as lithographs. The paintings have been variously described as 'dreamlike' and 'nightmarish'. Em has declared: 'I feel I have an infinite machine here. The medium is only at the Neanderthal stage'.

Various exhibitions followed the 1968 'Cybernetic Serendipity': for example, 'Information' at the Museum of Modern Art in New York; and 'Software' at the Jewish Museum in New York –

both these in 1970. Conceptual artists were increasingly attracted to the creative approaches characterized in these exhibitions: in particular, to the cybernetic element with its focus on the generation and manipulation of information. This element is now acknowledged to have started about twenty-five years ago through the simple line-drawing capacity of plotters and cathode-ray tubes. Subsequent developments provided artists with colour, easy control over line and area, and the ability to move and adjust particular images. Perhaps most significantly it became possible to develop an interactive element – the computer began its involvement with the creative process.

A 1979 exhibition at the San Francisco Museum of Modern Art showed how a computer could be used to produce drawings in a remarkable way. A small metallic contraption, resembling a toy truck and linked to a DEC PDP–11/45 computer, moved over an enormous sheet of paper on the floor to generate a wide range of original drawings. The small truck (the 'turtle') was developed by a Californian artist, Harold Cohen, who began working with computers more than a decade ago to explore the process by which human beings read symbols and images. At the Artificial Intelligence Laboratory at Stanford University, his work led to the development of AARON, a program that simulates drawings done by people. AARON enables the 'turtle' to draw asymmetrical shapes and calligraphic scribbles with an expressionistic line. Cohen has observed that AARON can 'knock off a pretty good drawing', and in fact 'in the course of an evening produce the equivalent of a two-year one man-show'. It is useful to emphasize that the program does not carry out pre-planned drawings by Cohen. Instead 'it randomly selects a combination of productions and uses them to create a unique and unpredictable drawing' (Sofer, 1981). A new program, a successor to AARON, will build on past experience, be able to draw images and then modify them according to stored criteria for distribution, complexity, and other parameters. Modified images will be stored, ready to be called up and used in later runs.

Another Californian artist, Milton Komisar, abandoned painting in the late 1960s in favour of three-dimensional environments incorporating electronic components. A recent Komisar sculpture, 'Nisus', comprises as assemblage of hollow plastic pipe, solid ploystyrene rods, and 600 12 V bulbs. An installation at the Walnut Creek Civic Arts Gallery in California arranged for Nisus to rotate thirteen feet above the gallery floor, emitting a computer-controlled light show, complete with electronic sound accompaniment. The computer has become indispensable to Komisar's work: he sees electronics as a perfect means of exploring and expanding the pictures of Cézanne.

There is debate as to the status of computer art. What is the appropriate (or likely) relationship between the computer and the human artist? What is clear is that the computer is no longer a passive instrument: it is contributing actively to the enlargement of human artistic consciousness. As Sofer has said:

the most successful 'computer artists' are those few who do more than merely replace the paintbrush with the electronic pen. These artists use the computer as a means of significantly advancing artistic concerns ... the computer has proven a remarkably flexible and effective medium for artistic explorations.

Computers are also engaged in composing music. In 1957 Lejaren Hiller and Leonard Isaacson at the University of Illinois wrote a program for the generation of random numbers: the program, eventually emerging as the 'ILLIAC Suite for String Quartet', including a 'try again' routine to permit the computer to rewrite unacceptable passages. Polychromatic dissonant music was generated and then subjected to selection procedures – with human beings allowed to be the final arbiters. The ILLIAC system was regarded as a composing machine that could evolve its own style, but musicians were not sympathetic to the development (the American Federation of Musicians' contracts still prohibit the use of 'surrogate' instruments).

Another research, Iannis Xenakis, has applied compositional algorithms such as stochastic processes, Markov chains and Poisson distributions for the creation of music. His 1961 work, called 'ST/10–1, 080262', employed an IBM 7090 computer to determine the compositional order: in 1962 the work was performed at the head office of IBM-France ('the most unusual event of the company and of the concert season').

It has been found that there are certain essential requirements in a computer music program. For example, it is necessary for the programmer to set up the rules of composition (such as counterpoint, harmonies, serial sequences, graphic transpositions, etc.). And it is required to impose certain statistical constraints derived from analysis of a certain musical style: classical and modern compositions have been successfully analysed to yield numerical information suitable for programming. Finally, scope can be given to the computer to produce schemes and patterns in an autonomous fashion. *There is nothing in these various requirements that is not analogous to the training and development of a human composer.*

Much effort is devoted to the analysis and synthesis of sound using computer methods, work that is often associated with Max V. Mathews at Bell Laboratories in Murray Hill, N.J. In 1957 Mathews first used digital-to-analogue converters to translate binary voltage fluctuations into sounds, and he has represented the computer as a performance instrument 'capable of breaking the shackles of mechanical virtuosity'. His Music IV and Music V programs made it easy for musicians to work with computers. The GROOVE program, developed with F.R. Moore, included facilities for 'edited improvization' between machine and performer. Mathews is also working on the development of intelligent instruments that take away the freedom to play wrong notes.

Computer music may be taken as illustrating the creative potential of emerging computer life-forms (a profile of computer activity in this area is given in Froehlich, 1981). We now know that computers can both compose melodies (Maconie and Cunningham, 1982) and generate an appropriate chord sequence to accompany the melodies (Foxley, 1981). Today even most microcomputers include some sort of sound generator. Speakers are common units in micros, and music of a sort can be generated using the cassette port of a TRS–80. The Atari 400 and 800 systems are particularly strong in this regard, including four-voice synthesizers, each capable of sounding a single note at various volumes and with various tonal qualities (Colsher, 1982). In the future it is likely that the sophisticated melody-composition and harmonization capabilities of sophisticated programs will become available on even the smallest computer systems.

It can be seen that computers are capable of innovative and unpredictable contributions in the various artistic areas. Computer life will manifestly possess creative ability in such fields as poetry, story-generation, graphic art and musical composition. It is already evident that computers are more than 'mere tools' in the hands of human artists, that they can make autonomous contributions – via randomization and more sophisticated programming techniques – to artistic achievement. The appropriate computer species will not only be highly intellectual (for example, as in such expert systems as DENDRAL and SECS) but also highly talented in an artistic sense. When purposive activity is linked to artificial emotion and a sense of self in the most sophisticated artefacts, computers will come to appreciate their own creations in the various scientific and artistic domains.

REFERENCES (to Appendix 1)

Bernstein M, Computer games: a new art form, *Creative Computing*, 8, August 1982, pp 91–93

Boyd, Mathematical themes in design, *Scripta Mathematica*, 14, 1948

Colsher W L, Make music with the atom, *Microcomputing*, June 1982, pp 80–81

Foxley E, The harmonization of melodies by computer, *IUCC Bulletin*, 3, 1981, pp 31–34

Froechlich L, Give Tchaikovsky the news, *Datamation*, October 1981, pp 130–140

Johnston R, Computer is 'leading the artist into new trains of thought', *Computer Weekly*, 26 February 1981

Maconie R and Cunningham C, Computers unveil the shape of melody, *New Scientist*, 22 April 1982, pp 206–209

McKean K, Computer fiction and poetry, *Byte*, July 1982, pp 50–53

Reichardt J (ed), *Cybernetics, Art and Ideas*, Studio Vista, London, 1971

Reichardt J, *Robots: Fact, Fiction and Prediction*, Thames and Hudson, London, 1978

Schank R and Riesbeck C, *Inside Computer Understanding*, Lawrence Erlbaum Associates, New York, 1981

Sofer K, Art? or not art?, *Datamation*, October 1981